PC LEARNING LABS TEACHES WORD 6.0 FOR WINDOWS

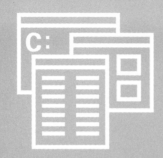

PC LEARNING LABS
TEACHES WORD 6.0
FOR WINDOWS

LOGICAL OPERATIONS

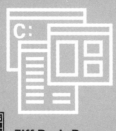

Ziff-Davis Press
Emeryville, California

Writers	Robert Nichols Kulik and Richard P. Scott
Curriculum Development	Logical Operations
Editor	Jan Jue
Technical Reviewer	Heidi Steele
Project Coordinator	A. Knox
Proofreader	A. Knox
Production Coordinator, Logical Operations	Marie Boyers
Cover Illustration	Carrie English
Cover Design	Kenneth Roberts
Book Design	Laura Lamar/MAX, San Francisco
Screen Graphics Editor	Cat Haglund
Technical Illustration	Steph Bradshaw
Word Processing	Howard Blechman
Page Layout	M.D. Barrera and Bruce Lundquist
Indexer	Carol Burbo

Ziff-Davis Press books are produced on a Macintosh computer system with the following applications: FrameMaker®, Microsoft® Word, QuarkXPress®, Adobe Illustrator®, Adobe Photoshop®, Adobe Streamline™, MacLink®*Plus*, Aldus® FreeHand™, Collage Plus™.

Ziff-Davis Press
5903 Christie Avenue
Emeryville, CA 94608
1-800-688-0448

ISBN 1-56276-139-0

Manufactured in the United States of America
10 9 8 7 6

CONTENTS AT A GLANCE

TABLE OF CONTENTS

INTRODUCTION

Welcome to *PC Learning Labs Teaches Word for Windows 6.0*, a hands-on instruction book that will help you attain a high level of Word for Windows fluency in the shortest time possible. And congratulations on choosing Word 6.0 for Windows, a powerful and feature-packed program that will greatly enhance your creation and editing of written documents.

We at PC Learning Labs believe this book to be a unique and welcome addition to the ranks of "how to" computer publications. Our instructional approach stems directly from over a decade of successful teaching in a hands-on classroom environment. Throughout the book, we mix theory with practice by presenting new techniques and then applying them in hands-on activities. These activities use specially prepared, sample Word for Windows files, which are stored on the enclosed Data Disk.

Unlike a class, this book allows you to proceed at your own pace. And we'll be right there to guide you along every step of the way, providing landmarks to help you chart your progress and hold to a steady course.

When you're done working your way through this book, you'll have a solid foundation of skills in:

- Creating, editing, printing, storing, and retrieving text documents.

- Modifying a document's appearance (typestyles and sizes, page layout, and so on)

- Checking of documents for spelling, grammar, style, and wording errors

- Creating, modifying, printing, storing, and retrieving AutoText entries (files that hold frequently used text you can insert in your documents without retyping)

- Creating, modifying, and enhancing of tables

- Creating and modifying multicolumn text

- Inserting, sizing, moving, and modifying graphics (on-screen pictures)

- Creating and generating form letters

- Using templates and styles to simplify the creation of documents

This foundation will enable you to quickly and easily create sophisticated, professional-quality documents.

READ THIS BEFORE YOU PROCEED!

We strongly recommend that you read through the rest of this Introduction before beginning Chapter 1. If, however, you just can't wait to dive in, make sure that you first work through the sections "Creating Your Work Directory" and "Setting Your Defaults to Match Ours," which appear later in this Introduction. You must create a work directory in order to perform the hands-on activities that appear throughout the book.

WHO THIS BOOK IS FOR

This book was written with the beginner in mind. Although experience with word processing and personal computers is certainly helpful, little or none is required. You should know how to turn on your computer and use your keyboard. We explain everything beyond that.

HOW TO USE THIS BOOK

You can use this book book as a learning guide, a review tool, and a quick reference.

AS A LEARNING GUIDE

Each chapter covers one broad topic or set of related topics. Chapters are arranged in order of increasing proficiency; skills you acquire in one chapter are used and elaborated on in later chapters. For this reason, you should work through the chapters in strict sequence.

Each chapter is organized into explanatory topics and step-by-step activities. Topics provide the theory you need to master Word for Windows; activities allow you to apply this theory to practical, hands-on examples.

You get to try out each new skill on a specially prepared sample Word for Windows file stored on the enclosed Data Disk. This saves you typing time and allows you to concentrate on the technique at hand. Through the use of sample files, hands-on activities, illustrations that give you feedback at crucial steps, and supporting background information, this book provides you with the foundation and structure to learn Word 6.0 for Windows quickly and easily.

 ## AS A REVIEW TOOL

Any method of instruction is only as effective as the time and effort you are willing to invest in it. For this reason, we strongly encourage you to spend some time reviewing the book's more challenging topics and activities.

 ## AS A QUICK REFERENCE

General procedures such as opening a document or italicizing selected text are presented as a series of bulleted steps; you can find these bullets (•) easily by skimming through the book. These procedures can serve as a handy reference.

At the end of every chapter, you'll find a quick reference that lists the mouse/keyboard actions needed to perform the techniques introduced in that chapter.

 SPECIAL LEARNING FEATURES

The following features of this book will facilitate your learning:

- Carefully sequenced topics that build on the knowledge you've acquired from previous topics

- Frequent hands-on activities that sharpen your Word for Windows skills

- Numerous illustrations that show how your screen should look at key points during these activities

- The Data Disk, which contains all the files you will need to complete the activities (as explained in the next section)

- Easy-to-spot, bulleted procedures that provide the general, step-by-step instructions you'll need to perform Word for Windows tasks

- A quick reference at the end of each chapter, listing the mouse/keyboard actions needed to perform the techniques introduced in the chapter

 THE DATA DISK

One of the most important learning features of this book is the *Data Disk*, the 3½-inch floppy disk that accompanies the book. This disk contains the sample Word for Windows files you'll retrieve and work on throughout the book. To perform the activities in this book, you will first need to create a work directory on your hard disk (as explained in the upcoming section, "Creating Your Work Directory"). You'll then copy the sample files from the Data Disk to your work directory. This directory will also hold all the Word for Windows files that you will be creating, editing, and saving during the course of this book.

WHAT YOU NEED TO USE THIS BOOK

To run Word 6.0 for Windows and complete this book, you need a computer with a hard disk and at least one floppy-disk drive, a monitor, a keyboard, and a mouse (or compatible tracking device). Although you don't absolutely need a printer, we strongly recommend that you have one.

Windows must be installed on your computer; if it is not, see your Windows reference manuals for instructions. Word for Windows must also be installed; for help see Appendix A.

 ### COMPUTER AND MONITOR

You need an IBM or IBM-compatible personal computer and monitor that are capable of running Microsoft Windows (version 3.1 or higher). A 286-based system is technically sufficient, but both Windows and Word for Windows will run slowly on it; we recommend that you use a 386 or higher (486, and so on) computer.

You need a hard disk with at least 24 megabytes (24 million bytes) of free storage space (if Word 6.0 for Windows is not yet installed) or 1 megabyte of free space (if Word 6.0 for Windows is installed).

Finally, you need an EGA or higher (VGA, SVGA, and so on) graphics card and monitor to display Windows and Word for Windows at their intended screen resolution. (**Note:** The Word for Windows screens shown in this book are taken from a VGA monitor. Depending on your monitor type, your screens may look slightly different.)

 KEYBOARD

IBM-compatible computers come with various styles of keyboards; these keyboards function identically, but have different layouts. Figures I.1, I.2, and I.3 show the three main keyboard styles and their key arrangements.

Word for Windows uses all main areas of the keyboard:

- The *function keys*, which enable you to access Word for Windows' special features. On the PC-, XT-, and AT-style keyboards, there are 10 function keys at the left end of the keyboard; on the 101-key Enhanced Keyboard there are 12 at the top of the keyboard.

- The *typing keys*, which enable you to enter letters, numbers, and punctuation marks. These keys include the Shift, Ctrl, and Alt keys, which you need to access several of Word for Windows' special features. The typing keys are located in the main body of all the keyboards.

- The *numeric keypad*, which enables you either to enter numeric data or to navigate through a document. When *Num Lock* is turned on, you use the numeric keypad to enter numeric data, just as you would on a standard calculator keypad. When Num Lock is turned off, you use the numeric keypad to navigate through a document by using the cursor-movement keys: Up, Down, Left, and Right Arrows; Home, End, PgUp (Page Up), and PgDn (Page Down). To turn Num Lock on/off, simply press the Num Lock key. To enter numeric data when Num Lock is off, use the number keys in the top row of the typing area.

- The *cursor-movement keypad*, which is available only on Enhanced Keyboards, enables you to navigate through a document by using the Home, End, Page Up, and Page Down keys. The cursor-movement keypad works the same when Num Lock is turned on or off. This enables you to use the numeric keypad for

Figure I.1 **IBM PC–style keyboard**

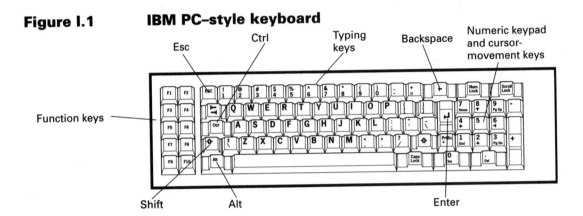

Figure I.2 **XT/AT–style keyboard**

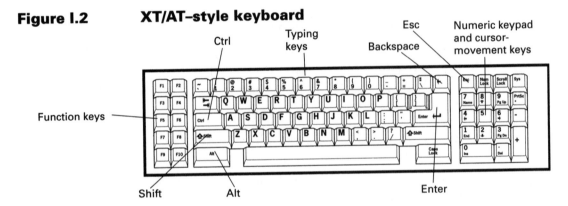

Figure I.3 **The 101-key Enhanced Keyboard**

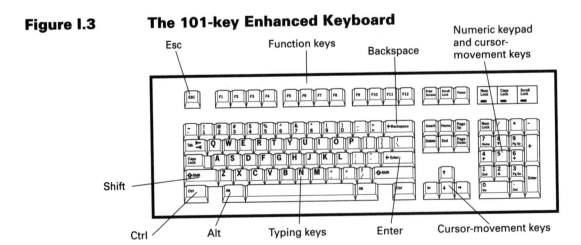

numeric data entry (that is, to keep Num Lock on) and still have access to cursor-movement keys.

 MOUSE OR OTHER TYPE OF TRACKING DEVICE

You need a mouse or other type of tracking or pointing device to work through the activities in this book. Any standard PC mouse or tracking device (a trackball, for example) will do.

Note: Throughout this book, we direct you to use a mouse. If you have a different tracking device, simply use your device to perform all the mousing tasks: pointing, clicking, dragging, and so on.

 PRINTER

Although you don't absolutely need a printer to work through the activities in this book, we strongly recommend that you have one. A laser printer is ideal, but an ink-jet or dot-matrix will do just fine. Your printer must be selected for use with Word for Windows; for help, see Appendix A.

CONVENTIONS USED IN THIS BOOK

The following conventions used in this book will help you learn Word 6.0 for Windows easily and efficiently.

- Each chapter begins with a short introduction and ends with a summary that includes a quick-reference guide to the techniques introduced in the chapter.

- Main chapter topics (large, capitalized headings) and subtopics (headings preceded by a cube) explain Word for Windows features.

- Hands-on activities allow you to practice using these features. In these activities, keystrokes, menu choices, and anything you are asked to type are printed in boldface. Here's an example from Chapter 2:

4. Choose **File, Open** to display the Open dialog box.

- Activities adhere to a *cause-and-effect* approach. Each step tells you what to do (cause) and then what will happen (effect). From the example above,

  Cause: Choose the menu command **File, Open**.

  Effect: The Open dialog box is displayed.

- A plus sign (+) is used with the Shift, Ctrl, and Alt keys to indicate a multi-key keystroke. For example, "press **Ctrl+F10**" means "Press and hold down the Ctrl key, then press the F10 key, and then release them both."

- To help you distinguish between steps presented for reference purposes (*general procedures*) and steps you should carry out at your computer as you read (*specific procedures*), we use the following system:

  - A bulleted step, like this, is provided for your information and reference only.

  1. A numbered step, like this, indicates one in a series of steps that you should carry out in sequence at your computer.

CREATING YOUR WORK DIRECTORY

Throughout this book, you will be creating, editing, and saving several files. In order to keep these files together, you need to create a work directory for them on your hard disk. (A hard drive functions much like a filing cabinet; a *directory* is like a hanging folder in that cabinet storing a group of related files.) Your work directory will also hold the sample files contained on the enclosed Data Disk.

Follow these steps to create your work directory. (**Note:** If Word 6.0 for Windows is not currently installed on your computer, please install it now, *before* you create your work directory. See Appendix A for instructions.)

1. Turn on your computer. After a brief internal self-check, your *operating environment* will load. If you are in Windows, go to step 2. If you are in DOS, skip to step 4. If you are in a non-Windows, non-DOS environment (GeoWorks or a menu system, for example), exit to DOS and then skip to step 4; for help exiting to DOS, follow the on-screen instructions, or refer to your user's guide. If you don't know what operating system you are in, ask a colleague or technician for help.

2. Within Windows, locate *Program Manager*. It can appear in two forms: as a *window* (rectangular box) with "Program Manager" in its overhead title bar; or as an *icon* (small picture) with "Program Manager" beneath it. If your Program Manager appears as a window, go to step 3. If your Program Manager appears as an icon, use the mouse to move the on-screen pointer to this icon, and then double-click (press the **left mouse button** twice in rapid succession) to open it into a window.

3. Use the mouse to move the on-screen pointer to the Program Manager's *Control-menu box,* the small, square box in the upper-left corner of the Program Manager window. Double-click (press the **left mouse button** twice in rapid succession) on the horizontal bar within the Control Menu box. A box entitled "Exit Windows" will appear. Click the mouse pointer once on the **OK** within this box. You have now exited from Windows to DOS. Skip to step 10.

4. You may see this prompt:

```
Current date is Tue 02-18-1994
Enter new date (mm-dd-yy):
```

(Your current date will be different.) If you do not see a date prompt, skip to step 7.

5. If the current date on your screen is wrong, type the correct date. Use a dash (-) to separate the month, day, and year (for example, 6-19-94).

6. Press **Enter**. After you type a command, you must press the Enter key to submit your command to the computer.

7. You may see this prompt:

```
Current time is 0:25:32:56p
Enter new time:
```

(Your current time will be different.) If you do not see a time prompt, skip to step 10.

8. If the current time on your screen is wrong, type the correct time. Use the 24-hour format *hh:mm* (for example, 10:58 for 10:58 a.m., and 22:58 for 10:58 p.m.).

9. Press **Enter** to send the time you specified to the computer's internal clock.

10. The DOS prompt will appear:

```
C:\>
```

(Your DOS prompt may differ somewhat from this.)

11. Type **dir** and press **Enter**. The contents of the current disk directory are displayed, followed by a final line reporting the number of free bytes on your hard disk. If you have 1,000,000 or more free bytes, go to step 12. If you have fewer than 1,000,000 free bytes, you will not be able to create your work directory and perform the hands-on activities in this book. Before you go any further, you must delete enough files from your hard disk to increase the free-byte total to at least 1,000,000. For help doing this, refer to your DOS reference manual, or better yet, enlist the aid of an experienced DOS user. (**Note:** Make sure to back up all your important files before deleting them!)

12. Remove the Data Disk from its envelope at the back of this book. Insert the Data Disk (label up) into the appropriately sized disk drive. Determine whether this is drive A or drive B. (On a single floppy-disk system, the drive is generally designated as A. On a double floppy-disk system, the upper drive is generally designated as A and the lower as B.)

13. Type **a:** if the Data Disk is in drive A, or type **b:** if the Data Disk is in drive B. Press **Enter** to change the current drive to that of the Data Disk.

14. Type **install c: winword wrkfiles** without pressing Enter. (Make sure to type a space between each of the four items.) To create your work directory on a hard-disk drive other than drive C, substitute your hard-disk drive letter for the *c* in this command. For example, to create your work directory on a drive-D hard disk, you would type *install d: winword wrkfiles*. The four items of this command specify the following: *install* is the name of the command; *c:* and *winword* are the drive and directory on which your Word 6.0 program is stored; and *wrkfiles* is the name of your work directory.

15. Press **Enter** to create your work directory. If all goes well, the message

```
Work directory under construction.
Please wait ....................
```

will appear, followed by a list of files that are being copied. When the procedure is complete, the message

```
Work directory successfully completed!
Your work directory is wrkfiles
```

will appear. (The last line reports the name of your work directory.) If these messages appear, skip ahead to **Important Note** following the next step. If all does not go so well, go to step 16.

16. If your work directory has not been successfully completed, one of three messages will appear. The first message is

```
Installation failed! c: drive does not exist.
Reenter the INSTALL command using the correct drive.
```

(Your drive letter may be different.) This message indicates that the hard drive you specified in your step 14 INSTALL command does not exist on your computer. If you get this message, simply repeat steps 14 and 15, making sure to specify the correct letter of your hard drive.

The second message is

```
Installation failed! c:\winword does not exist.
Reenter the INSTALL command using the correct Word 6.0
directory name.
```

(Your drive letter and/or directory name may be different.) This message indicates that the Word 6.0 drive and/or directory you specified in step 14 (c: winword) does not exist on your computer. If you get this message, find out your correct Word 6.0 drive and directory (for help, enlist the aid of an experienced DOS user), then repeat steps 14 and 15, using the correct drive and directory names. For example, if your Word 6.0 drive were D and the directory were winword, you would type *install d: winword wrkfiles* in step 14.

The third message is

```
Installation failed! c:\winword\wrkfiles directory
already exists.
Reenter the INSTALL command using a different work
directory name.
```

(Your drive letter and/or directory name may be different.) This message indicates that the work directory you specified in step 14 (wrkfiles) already exists on your specified hard disk. If you get this message, repeat steps 14 and 15, specifying a new work directory name of your choice instead of *wrkfiles*. Your work directory name can be up to eight letters long. Do not use spaces, periods, or punctuation marks. For example, you might type *install c: winword workdir* or *install c: winword word6wrk*, and so on.

Important Note: The hands-on activities in this book assume that your work directory is on drive C and is named WRKFILES. If you specified a different hard-disk drive or a different work directory name, remember to substitute this drive and/or name whenever we mention drive C or WRKFILES.

SETTING YOUR DEFAULTS TO MATCH OURS

Word 6.0 for Windows is a customizable program. Depending on how its *defaults* (standard settings) have been set—by you or, perhaps, a colleague—your Word for Windows program may look and behave quite differently from ours. To avoid the confusion these differences might create, follow these steps to set your Word for Windows defaults to match ours. This way, our two programs will look and behave identically.

1. Type **a:** if the Data Disk is in drive A, or type **b:** if the Data Disk is in drive B. Press **Enter** to change the current drive to that of the Data Disk.

2. Type **setdefs c:** without pressing Enter. If your Windows and Word 6.0 for Windows programs are stored on a hard-disk drive other than drive C, substitute your hard-disk drive letter for the *c* in this command. For example, if your Windows and Word 6.0 for Windows programs were stored on a drive-D hard disk, you would type *setdefs d:*.

3. Press **Enter** to set your defaults to match ours. If all goes well, the following two messages will appear:

```
WINWORD.INI defaults successfully established!
NORMAL.DOT defaults successfully established!
```

If both—not just one!—of these messages appear, skip ahead to the next section "Resetting Your Original Defaults." If you don't see both messages, go to step 4.

4. If all does not go so well, one or more of the following three messages will appear. The first message is

```
Procedure failed! c: drive does not exist.
Reenter the SETDEFS command using the correct drive.
```

(Your drive letter may be different.) This message indicates that the hard drive you specified in your step 2 SETDEFS command does not exist on your computer. If you get this message, simply repeat steps 2 and 3, making sure to specify the correct letter of your hard drive.

The second message is

```
Procedure failed! c:\windows directory does not exist.
```

(Your drive letter may be different.) This message indicates that the C:\WINDOWS directory does not exist on your computer. If you get this message, perform the following two steps (**Note:** If necessary, find an experienced DOS user to help you):

- Locate your \WINDOWS directory, and within this directory, copy WINWORD.INI to WIN6SAVE.INI.

- Copy WINWORD.INI from the \SETDEFS directory of the Data Disk to your \WINDOWS directory.

The third message is

```
Procedure failed! c:\winword\template directory does not
exist.
```

(Your drive letter may be different.) This message indicates that the C:\WINWORD\TEMPLATE directory does not exist on your computer. If you get this message, perform the following two steps (**Note:** If necessary, find an experienced DOS user to help you):

- Locate your \WINWORD\TEMPLATE directory, and within this directory, copy NORMAL.DOT to NORMSAVE.DOT.

- Copy NORMAL.DOT from the \SETDEFS directory of the Data Disk to your \WINWORD\TEMPLATE directory.

 RESETTING YOUR ORIGINAL DEFAULTS

After you've finished working through this book, you may want to reset your original Word for Windows defaults; that is, the defaults that were in effect before you changed them to match ours in the previous section. Here's how to do this:

Note: Do not do this now! Wait until you're done with the book.

- In your \WINDOWS directory, copy WIN6SAVE.INI to WINWORD.INI.

- In your \WINWORD\TEMPLATE directory, copy NORMSAVE.DOT to NORMAL.DOT.

BEFORE YOU START

Each chapter's activities proceed sequentially. In many cases, you cannot perform an activity until you have performed one or more of the activities preceding it. For this reason, we recommend that you allot enough time to work through an entire chapter in one continuous session.

Feel free to take as many breaks as you need. Stand up, stretch, take a walk, drink some de-caf. Don't try to absorb too much information at one time. Studies show that people assimilate and retain information most effectively when it is presented in digestible chunks and followed by a liberal amount of hands-on practice.

You are now ready to begin. Good learning and...*bon voyage!*

CHAPTER 1: GETTING STARTED

Welcome to Word for Windows 6.0—from here on referred to simply as Word—and the exciting world of word processing! We'll begin this first chapter by getting you up and running in Word and introducing you to the Word working environment. Then we'll lead you through one complete Word work session; you'll start the Word program, create and edit a document, save and print this document, create and save a new document, and finally exit Word. This, in a nutshell, is the procedure you'll use in your day-to-day word processing work with Word.

When you're done working through this chapter, you will know

- How to use the mouse
- How to start Word
- How to enter text
- How to insert, delete, and replace text
- How to save and name a document
- How to print and close a document
- How to create a new document
- How to exit Word

A QUICK REVIEW OF MOUSING SKILLS

The mouse is a hand-operated device that enables you to communicate with Word by manipulating (selecting, deselecting, moving, deleting, and so on) graphical and text objects that are displayed on your computer screen. When you move the mouse across the surface of your mouse pad, a symbol called the *mouse pointer* moves across the screen. You use this mouse pointer to point to the on-screen object that you want to manipulate. The mouse has two or more buttons. You use these buttons to communicate with Word in various ways, as detailed in Table 1.1.

Note: Read through the following table to familiarize yourself with standard Word mousing techniques. Do not, however, try to memorize these techniques. Instead, use this table as a quick-reference guide, referring back to it whenever you need to refresh your mousing memory.

Table 1.1   **Mousing Techniques**

Technique	How to Do It
Point	Move the mouse until the tip of the mouse pointer is over the desired object. "Point to the word *File*" means "move the mouse until the tip of the mouse pointer is over the word *File*."

Table 1.1   **Mousing Techniques (Continued)**

Technique	How to Do It
Click	Press and release the left or right mouse button. When we want you to click the left mouse button, we'll simply say "click." For example, "click on the word *File*" means "point to the word *File* and then press and release the left mouse button." When we want you to click the right mouse button, we'll explicitly say so. For example, "point to the Standard toolbar and click the right mouse button."
Double-click	Press and release the left mouse button twice in rapid succession. "Double-click on the file name PREVIEW1.PPT" means "point to the file name PREVIEW1.PPT and then press and release the left mouse button twice in rapid succession."
Choose	Click on a menu command or a dialog-box button. "Choose File, Open" means "click on the word *File* (in the menu bar), and then click on the word *Open* (in the File menu)."
Drag	Press and hold the left mouse button while moving the mouse. "Drag the scroll box upward" means "point to the scroll box, press and hold the left mouse button, move the mouse upward, and then release the mouse button."
Scroll	Click on a scroll arrow or within a scroll bar, or drag a scroll box.
Select	Click on an object (to select the entire object), or drag over part of a text object (to select part of the text). "Select the file CHAP2.DOC" means "click on the file name CHAP2.DOC." "Select the first four letters of the title *Global Travel*" means "drag over the letters *Glob*."

Table 1.1   **Mousing Techniques (Continued)**

Technique	How to Do It
Check	Click on a check box to check (turn on) that option. "Check the Match Case option" means "click on the Match Case check box to check it."
Uncheck	Click on a check box to uncheck (turn off) that option. "Uncheck the Match Case option" means "click on the Match Case check box to uncheck it."

INTRODUCTION TO WORD

A *word processor* (such as Word) is a computer program that enables you to create, edit, print, and save documents for future retrieval and revision. You enter text into the computer by using a keyboard. As you type, your words are displayed on a *monitor*, or screen, and are stored temporarily in computer memory as you are creating the document (and permanently on disk once you save it) rather than on paper.

One of the chief advantages of a word processor over a conventional typewriter is that a word processor enables you to make changes to a document without retyping the entire document. For example, you can create a letter in a word processor and then, after you are finished, go back and change margins, add sentences, delete words, move paragraphs, correct spelling errors, and so on. You can do all of this without retyping the original text.

 STARTING WORD

Before you start Word, both Microsoft Windows 3.1 and Word for Windows 6.0 must be installed on your hard disk. If either of these programs is not installed, please install it now. For help installing Microsoft Windows 3.1, see your Windows documentation. For help installing Word for Windows 6.0, see Appendix A of this book.

You also need to have created a work directory on your hard disk and copied the files from the enclosed Data Disk to this directory. If you have not done this, please do so now; for instructions, see "Creating Your Work Directory" in the Introduction.

Finally, you need to have set your Word defaults to match ours. If you have not done this, please do so now; for instructions, see "Setting Your Defaults to Match Ours" in the Introduction.

Note: In this book, we present two types of procedures: bulleted and numbered. A *bulleted procedure*—one whose steps are preceded by bullets (•)—serves as a general reference; you should read its steps without actually performing them. A *numbered procedure*—one whose steps are preceded by numbers (1., 2., and so on)—is a specific hands-on activity; you should perform its steps as instructed.

Here's the general procedure for starting Word:

- Turn on your computer.

- If you are already in Windows, skip this step. If you are in a non-DOS operating environment, exit to DOS. At the DOS prompt, type *win* and press *Enter* to start Windows.

- Double-click on the *Microsoft Word* program icon.

Let's follow this procedure to start Word:

1. Turn on your computer. After a brief internal self-check, your *operating environment* will automatically load. If you are in Windows, skip the rest of this activity (steps 2 through 9) and continue with the next activity. If you are in DOS, continue with step 2 of this activity. If you are in a non-DOS operating environment (for example, GeoWorks or a menu system), exit from this environment to DOS and continue with step 2. (For help exiting to DOS, see the reference manuals for your operating environment.)

2. You may see this prompt:

   ```
   Current date is Tue 10-18-1994
   Enter new date (mm-dd-yy):
   ```

   (**Note:** Your current date will be different.) If you do not see a date prompt, skip to step 5.

3. If the current date on your screen is wrong, type the correct date. Use a hyphen (-) to separate the month, day, and year (for example, 11-18-94).

4. Press **Enter**. Remember that after you type a command, you must press the Enter key to send this command to the computer.

5. You may see this prompt:

    ```
    Current time is 0:25:32:56
    Enter new time:
    ```

    (Your current time will be different.) If you do not see a time prompt, skip to step 8.

6. If the current time on your screen is wrong, type the correct time. Use the 24-hour format *hh:mm* (for example, 10:30 for 10:30 a.m., and 22:30 for 10:30 p.m.).

7. Press **Enter** to set your computer's internal clock.

8. The DOS prompt will appear:

    ```
    C:\>
    ```

    (Your DOS prompt may differ somewhat from this.)

9. Type **win** and press **Enter** to start Windows. After a few moments of furious hard-disk activity (indicated by your blinking hard-disk drive pilot light), Windows appears on your screen.

Now that Windows is running, you can start Word for Windows 6.0. To do this, you must locate the program icon entitled "Microsoft Word." A *program icon* is a small on-screen picture that represents a program. Windows is a customizable program. For this reason, we cannot know the details of your Windows setup. So please bear with us as we search for your Microsoft Word program icon:

1. Observe your screen. You need to locate a Windows program named Program Manager. If Program Manager is running as an *icon* (a small picture with "Program Manager" beneath it, as shown in Figure 1.1), double-click on this icon (move the mouse until the tip of the mouse pointer is over the icon, and then press the **left mouse** button twice in rapid succession) to open it into a window. If Program Manager is already running as a window (as shown in Figure 1.2), click (press the **left mouse** button once) on the window's *title bar* (the horizontal bar in which "Program Manager" appears) to activate it.

Figure 1.1   **Program Manager running as an icon**

Figure 1.2   **Program Manager running as a window**

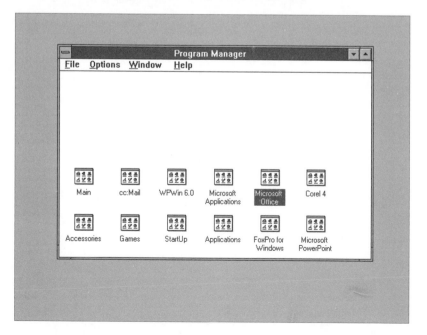

2. Look for the Microsoft Word program icon depicted in Figure 1.3. If you see this icon on your screen right now, skip directly to step 5.

3. Program icons are stored in *program groups*; program groups are, in turn, stored in the Program Manager. Program groups can appear as windows ("Microsoft Applications" in Figure 1.3) or as icons ("Main," "Applications," "Accessories," "StartUp," "Games," and "Music" in Figure 1.3). Normally, the Microsoft Word program icon is stored in a program group entitled "Microsoft Applications." If you see a program-group window entitled "Microsoft Applications," click on its title bar to activate it, and skip to step 5. If you see a program-group icon entitled "Microsoft Applications," double-click on the icon to open it into a window, and skip to step 5.

Figure 1.3   **The Microsoft Word program icon**

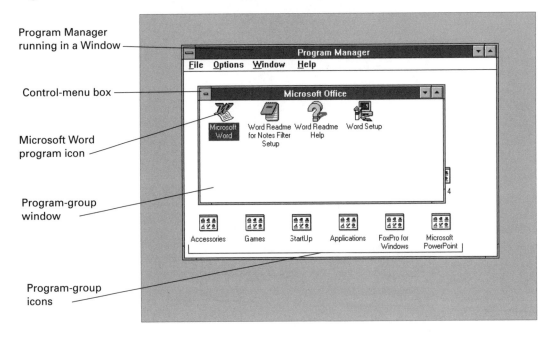

4. If you do not have a program-group window or icon entitled "Microsoft Applications" in your Program Manager window, you'll have to search further for your Microsoft Word program icon. Look for a program-group window or icon with a title that seems appropriate for an application program like Word ("Applications" or "Windows Applications" would be good candidates). If this is a window, click on its title bar to activate it; if this is an icon, double-click on it to open it into a window. If you see the Microsoft Word program icon somewhere inside this window, skip to step 5. If not, double-click on the program-group window's *Control-menu box* (the box containing a horizontal bar in the upper-left corner of the program-group window, as shown in Figure 1.3) to close the window. Repeat this step as many times as you need to find your elusive Microsoft Word program icon. Don't despair: If Word is installed on your computer, its program icon must be stored somewhere within Program Manager! It just may take a while to find it.

5. Double-click on the **Microsoft Word** program icon to start Word. Your screen should match—or closely resemble—that shown in Figure 1.4.

6. Observe the Tip of the Day dialog box in the middle of your screen, as shown in Figure 1.4. (Depending on how your Word program is set up, this dialog box may not appear.)

7. Take a moment to read the tip, and then click on **OK** to close the dialog box. We'll take a closer look at the Tip of the Day feature in Chapter 2.

THE WORD APPLICATION AND DOCUMENT WINDOWS

Word is built around a set of *interactive windows*—rectangular, on-screen boxes through which you communicate with the Word program and create your documents. When you start Word, two windows appear on the screen, one nestled snugly within the other. The larger of these, called the *application window*, frames the entire screen; you use it to communicate with the Word program. (The terms *program* and *application* are synonymous.) The smaller window, called the *document window*, fits seamlessly within the application window; you use it to create and edit your Word documents.

Figure 1.4   **Word, after start-up**

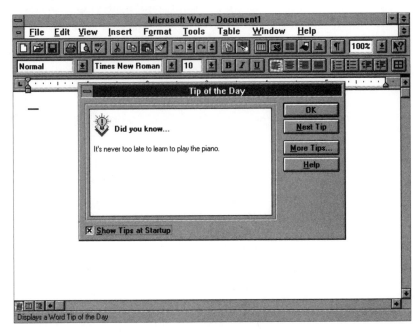

Table 1.2 and Figure 1.5 show the screen elements with which you need to be familiar when using Word.

Table 1.2   **Screen Elements of Word**

Term	Definition
Application window	The larger of the two start-up windows; it provides an interface between the user and Word
Document window	The smaller of the two start-up windows; it holds the currently active Word document
Control-menu boxes	Located in the upper-left corner of the screen; they control the size and position of the application window (upper box) and document window (lower box)

Table 1.2   **Screen Elements of Word (Continued)**

Term	Definition
Title bar	Located at the top of the screen; it displays the name of the application (Microsoft Word) and the active document (Document1, in this case)
Maximize/Restore buttons	Located in the upper-right corner of the screen; they control the size of the application window (upper box) and document window (lower box)
Minimize button	Located to the left of the application Maximize/Restore button; it reduces the application window to an icon
Menu bar	Located below the title bar; it lists the Word menu options
Standard toolbar	Located below the menu bar; it provides quick access to Word's most frequently used commands and utilities
Formatting toolbar	Located below the Standard toolbar; it provides quick access to Word's most frequently used formatting commands
Ruler	Located below the Formatting toolbar; it provides ongoing page measurement as well as quick access to margins, tabs, and indents
Scroll bars	Located along the right side and bottom of the document window; they are used to display different areas of the active document (each scroll bar contains a pair of directional scroll arrows)

Table 1.2   **Screen Elements of Word (Continued)**

Term	Definition
View buttons	Located to the left of the horizontal scroll bar; they are used to change the document display to Normal view (leftmost button), Page Layout view (middle button), and Outline view (rightmost button)
Status bar	Located along the bottom of the screen; it displays a variety of information relating to the active document

Figure 1.5   **Screen elements of Word**

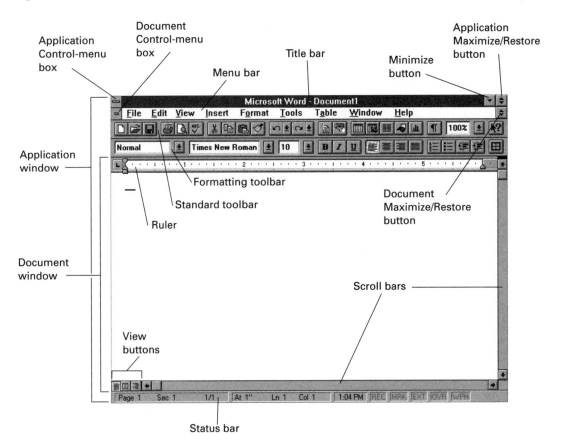

Let's take a closer look at some of these screen elements. (We'll discuss the remaining elements over the next few chapters.)

1. Click on the application-window **Control-menu** box (the upper of the two boxes containing a horizontal bar in the upper-left corner of your screen) to open its *drop-down menu*. (Do not double-click on the Control-menu box, as this would cause you to exit Word.) Note the Control menu options: Restore, Move, Size, Minimize, and so on.

2. Click on the application-window **Control-menu** box again to close its drop-down menu.

3. Now click on the document-window **Control-menu** box (the lower of the two boxes in the upper-left corner of the screen) to open its drop-down menu. Note that the document-window Control menu options are very similar to the application-window Control menu options you saw in the previous step.

4. Click on the document-window **Control-menu** box again to close its drop-down menu.

5. Click on the application-window **Maximize/Restore** button (the upper of the two buttons containing an up/down arrow in the upper-right corner of the screen) to *restore* (shrink) the application window. Note that the Maximize/Restore button now contains an up arrow alone, indicating that its function is to maximize (rather than to restore) the window.

6. Click on the application-window **Maximize/Restore** button again to maximize the application window to fill the entire screen.

7. Now click on the document-window **Maximize/Restore** button (the lower of the two buttons in the upper-right corner of the screen) to restore the document window. Note that the Maximize/Restore button moves to the upper-right corner of the restored (shrunk) document window. Note also that when the document window is restored, it gets its own title bar (Document1).

8. Click on the document-window **Maximize/Restore** button again to maximize the document window to fit snugly within the application window. Note that when the document window is maximized, it loses its title bar, and the document title (Document1) appears in the application-window title bar.

USING THE MENU BAR TO ISSUE COMMANDS

To perform a word processing task (such as retrieving a document from disk, formatting text, printing a document, and so on), you must issue the appropriate Word command. You can do this by:

- Using the mouse to choose the command from the menu bar

- Using the mouse to choose the command from one of the toolbars or the ruler

- Using the mouse to choose the command from a shortcut menu

- Using the keyboard to enter a keyboard shortcut

For example, to italicize text, you could

- Use the mouse to choose the *Font* command from the Format option in the menu bar, and then select the *Italic* option.

- Use the mouse to click on the Italic button on the Formatting toolbar.

- Use the mouse to choose the *Font* command from the short-cut menu, and then select the *Italic* option.

- Use the keyboard to enter *Ctrl+I* (press and hold the *Ctrl* key, press and hold the *I* key, and then release both keys), the keyboard shortcut for italicizing text.

Please do not perform any of these actions now.

The menu bar is the only method that allows you to issue every available Word command. The toolbars and ruler provide a subset of Word's most frequently used commands, as do the shortcut menus and the keyboard. For this reason, we'll begin our exploration of commands by using the menu-bar approach.

Let's issue some commands by using the menu bar:

1. Point to the **File** option; that is, move the mouse pointer until its tip is over the word *File* in the menu bar. Press and hold down the **left mouse** button. (Do not release this button until we tell you to do so in step 4.) The drop-down File menu opens, displaying a set of file-related commands: New, Open, Close, Save, Save As, and so on.

2. Observe the message in the status bar at the bottom of your screen. Word displays a brief description of the currently selected item—the drop-down File menu, in this case.

3. Without releasing the button, drag the mouse pointer down to *highlight* the Save As command. Note that the status bar now displays a brief description of the File, Save As command.

4. Release the mouse button (finally!) to open the Save As dialog box (see Figure 1.6). *Dialog boxes* prompt you to enter information relating to the selected command (File, Save As, in this case). You will work extensively with dialog boxes during the course of this book.

Figure 1.6   **The Save As dialog box**

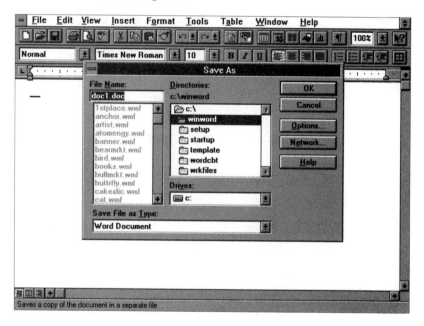

5. Click on the **Cancel** button in the upper-right corner of the Save As dialog box to close it.

6. Click on the **Edit** option in the menu bar. The drop-down Edit menu opens, displaying Word's editing commands. Note that you can either press and hold the mouse button as you did in step 1, or click (press and release) the button as you did here to open a drop-down menu.

7. Observe that several Edit commands are *dimmed* (displayed in light letters): Cut, Copy, AutoText, Links, and so on. Word dims menu commands to show that they are unavailable in the current context. For example, the Copy command is dimmed because you have not selected any text to copy.

8. Observe also that several commands are followed by *ellipses* (Find..., Replace..., Go To..., and so on). When you choose a command with an ellipsis, Word displays a dialog box prompting you for further information; for example, when you choose Find..., Word displays a dialog box prompting you for the word(s) you want to find. When you choose a command without an ellipsis, Word simply carries out the command. For example, when you choose Select All, Word immediately (with no intervening dialog box) selects all the text in the current document. To keep this book easy to read, we chose not to print command ellipses. In step 3 of this activity, for example, we ask you to drag the mouse pointer to the *Save As* command, though *Save As...* is how the command actually appears on your screen.

9. Click on **Edit** again to close the Edit menu.

THE BASICS OF ENTERING TEXT

Word is a *WYSIWYG* (What-You-See-Is-What-You-Get) program; that is, the screen shows you (more or less) exactly how your document will look when you print it. WYSIWYG programs are not subject to the arcane codes and inaccurate page layouts that plague non-WYSIWYG programs. Word's "WYSIWYGness" encourages you to work in a "visual-intuitive" style in which you treat the word processor as a computerized extension of a typewriter.

Over the next several sections, we'll discuss the basics of entering text in a Word document.

 THE TEXT AREA

When you start Word, a new document window automatically opens, providing you with a blank *text area* in which you can type your desired text. Word automatically selects a whole slew of critical document settings, including margins, font and font size, line spacing, tab stops, page dimensions, and many other document attributes. Because Word preselects these settings—which are called *defaults*—you can start to type immediately, without first having to specify any of the settings yourself.

The characters you type are inserted in front of a blinking vertical bar called the *insertion point*. To move the insertion point—and thus change where your typing appears in the document—you simply move the mouse pointer and click at the desired new place in the text.

Let's examine Word's text area (see Figure 1.7):

1. Observe the **insertion point** (the blinking vertical bar). Its location determines where the next character you type will be entered into your document. Note that the insertion point of a new document always appears in the upper-left corner (that is, at the beginning) of the document window.

2. Observe the **end mark**. This is the broad horizontal line that indicates the end of the document. The end mark cannot be formatted or deleted (erased), and you cannot place the insertion point beyond it.

3. Observe the **mouse pointer**. The pointer becomes an *I-beam* (as shown in Figure 1.7) when it is within the text area. When you move it outside the text area, it becomes an arrow. Take a moment to verify this.

WORD-WRAP AND THE ENTER KEY

The Enter key on your keyboard is similar to—but not exactly the same as—the Return key on a typewriter. On a typewriter, you need to hit the Return key whenever you want to end a line. In Word, when a word does not fit on a line, it automatically flows to the beginning of the next line. This feature is called *word-wrap*. However, you do need to press Enter to:

● End a short line (one that doesn't reach the right margin)

● End a paragraph

● Create a blank line

Let's type some text in our new document window and practice using the Enter key. (We'll demonstrate word-wrap in "Using the Backspace Key to Delete Text" later in this chapter.)

Figure 1.7   **The text area**

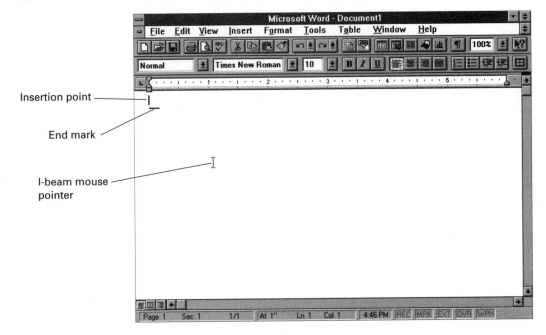

1. Observe the **status bar**. The vertical page position measurement (*At*) and the line number (*Ln*) reflect the current position of the insertion point.

2. Type **Nancy Wright** to enter the characters at the insertion point, and then press **Enter** to end the line. Note that the status bar At and Ln numbers show the new insertion point position.

3. Type **3325 Fillmore Avenue** and then press **Enter**.

4. Type **North Hills, NY 14052** and then press **Enter**.

5. Press **Enter** to create a blank line.

6. Type **Dear Janet:** and then press **Enter** twice to end the line and create one blank line. Your screen should now match Figure 1.8.

Figure 1.8   **Entering text in a document**

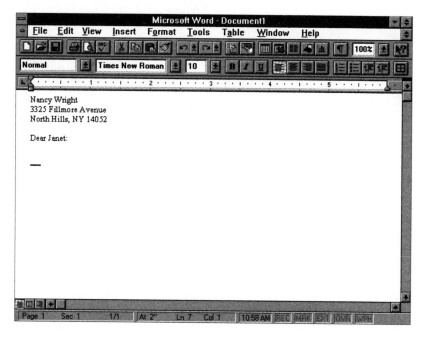

NONPRINTING CHARACTERS

You can choose to have Word display a number of special characters on the screen that show the places in the text where you pressed the spacebar, or the Enter and Tab keys. These *nonprinting characters* (so called because they do not appear on paper when you print the document) are often useful to see. This is particularly true when you are working with heavily formatted documents and need to keep track of your tabs, spaces, blank lines, and so on.

To display Word's nonprinting characters, you click on the Show/Hide button in the Standard toolbar

Let's display the nonprinting characters of your active document:

1. Examine the screen. Each line of text is short, not reaching the right margin. Note that there are no characters marking the ends of these lines.

2. Click on the **Show/Hide** button—the fourth button from the right in the Standard (upper) toolbar, it shows a paragraph mark (¶)—to display Word's special formatting characters.

3. Examine the screen. Each time you pressed Enter in the previous activity, Word placed a paragraph mark (¶) in the document. Each time you pressed the spacebar, Word placed a space mark (•) in the document. These nonprinting characters only appear on the screen when the Show/Hide button is set to Show; they will not appear on your printed document.

4. Click on the **Show/Hide** button again to hide the nonprinting characters. Clicking on this button *toggles* the display between its Show and Hide modes.

5. Click on the **Show/Hide** button again to show your nonprinting characters.

USING THE TAB KEY TO ALIGN TEXT HORIZONTALLY

Tabs enable you to align text horizontally. These lines are properly aligned:

```
Line 1 ....
Line 2 ....
```

These are not:

```
    Line 1 ....
      Line 2 ....
```

Pressing the Tab key moves the insertion point to the next tab stop to the right. *Tab stops* are fixed horizontal positions within a line. By default, Word's tab stops are set at 0.5" increments. Pressing Tab once moves the insertion point 0.5" to the right; pressing Tab again moves it another 0.5", for a total of 1" (0.5" + 0.5") from the left margin; and so on. (We created the properly aligned example just shown by pressing Tab once at the beginning of each line. We created the improperly aligned example by using the spacebar to insert blank spaces at the beginning of each line.)

USING THE BACKSPACE KEY TO DELETE TEXT

You can use the Backspace key to delete text one character at a time. Simply press Backspace to delete the single character immediately to the left of the insertion point.

Let's experiment with Word's Tab, Backspace, and word-wrap features:

1. Press **Tab** to insert a tab at the beginning of the line. This moves the insertion point to the first tab stop, 0.5" to the right. Note that Word displays the tab mark (→), since Show/Hide is still set to Show from our last activity. As with the paragraph and space marks, this tab mark will not appear on the printed page.

2. Press **Tab** again to insert another tab. This moves the insertion point to the second tab stop, 1" from the left margin.

3. Press **Backspace** to remove the second tab character.

4. Type **I have been happy with the service provided by Global Travel.** (Include the period.) Then press the **spacebar** to insert a space before the next sentence.

5. Type **I would like additional information** and then examine the screen. Note that the word *information* automatically wraps to the next line, even though you did not press Enter. This is an example of word-wrap. (**Note:** Depending on the printer you are using, your sentence may wrap at a different place.)

6. Complete the sentence by typing **about your program.** and then press **Enter** twice to end the paragraph and add one blank line before the next paragraph.

PRACTICE YOUR SKILLS

Complete the entire letter as shown in Figure 1.9.

Figure 1.9   **Completed letter in Show mode**

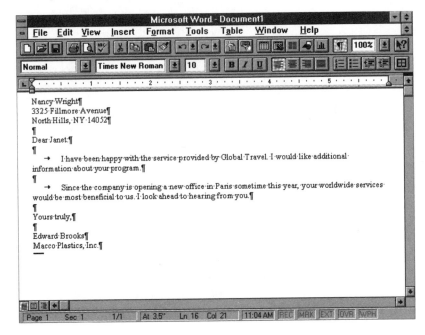

EDITING A DOCUMENT

As mentioned in the introduction to this chapter, one of the strongest arguments for switching from a typewriter to a word processor is the greatly increased ease of editing your documents. In the time it would take you just to pencil in your desired changes to a typewritten document (without actually retyping it), you could incorporate these changes into a word-processed document, print it out, and save it on a hard or floppy disk for future revision.

In the next several sections, we'll discuss the basics of text editing in Word.

INSERTING TEXT

By default, Word runs in *insert mode*; as you type, text to the right of the insertion point is pushed further to the right to make room for your new text. To insert text in a document, perform these two steps:

- Place the insertion point (use the mouse to position the I-beam and click) where you want to insert your new text.

- Type the new text.

Let's practice inserting text in a document:

1. Point to the left of the *p* in *program*, which is located in the second sentence of the paragraph beginning with *I have*. Click the mouse button to place the insertion point directly before the *p* in *program*. (Do not place the insertion point before the space preceding the *p*.) This is where you will insert your new text.

2. Type **corporate travel** and press the **spacebar**. Note that the existing text is pushed to the right of the inserted text.

SELECTING TEXT

At times, you'll find it more convenient to work with a block of text than with a single character. For example, if you needed to underline a sentence in a paragraph, you would not want to underline each character separately (a multistep, tedious task); rather, you would want to underline the entire sentence at once (a single-step, straightforward task).

To work with a block of text, you must first *select* it. In the next activity (in the section "Deleting Text") you'll select text by using the following method:

- Point to the first (or final) character of the text to be selected.

- Press and hold the left mouse button.

- Drag across the text to the final (or first) character to be selected.

- Release the mouse button.

Note: As just indicated, you can select text downward (from the first to the last character) or upward (from the last to the first character). Both methods are equally effective; use whichever you feel more comfortable with.

DELETING TEXT

As you know, Backspace deletes the character to the left of the insertion point. To delete the character immediately to the right of the insertion point, press the Delete key (on the cursor-movement keypad of an enhanced keyboard) or the Del key (on the numeric keypad).

Note: If you use the Del key on the numeric keypad, make sure that Num Lock is off. (To turn Num Lock on/off, press the Num Lock key.) If Num Lock is on, Del functions as a decimal point key; when you press it, Word displays a period (.) on the screen instead of performing the deletion.

To delete a block of selected text:

- Select the text.

- Press *Del* (or *Delete*).

Let's begin by deleting text one character at a time:

1. Place the insertion point directly to the left of the *A* in *Avenue*, which is located in the heading at the top of the page.

2. Press **Del** (or **Delete**) six times to delete the word *Avenue*. (To keep things simple, we'll only mention the Del key from here on. Feel free, however, to use the Delete key instead, if you wish.)

3. Type **Circle**.

4. Place the insertion point to the right of the *y* in *happy*, located in the paragraph beginning with *I have*.

5. Press **Backspace** five times to delete the word *happy*.

6. Type **very pleased**.

Now let's delete a block (in this case, a single word) of selected text:

1. Point to the left of the *m* in *most* in the first sentence of the paragraph beginning *Since the company*.

2. Press and hold the **left mouse** button. Then drag over **most** and the *trailing space* (the space that follows the *t* of *most*) to select the text. Do not select the space before *most*.

3. Release the mouse button.

4. Press **Del** to delete the selected text.

REPLACING TEXT

You already learned how to insert new text within a document. At times, however, you may want to replace existing text with new text. For example, you may want to replace the standard letter salutation *Dear Sir or Madam* with *To Whom It May Concern.* One way you can do this is by inserting the new text and then deleting the old text. This, however, doubles your work and can grow very tiresome, particularly when you are replacing many blocks of text. Fortunately, Word provides a more convenient solution.

To replace existing text with new text:

- Select the text to be replaced.

- Type the new text.

Let's use this technique to replace some text in our letter:

1. Select the name **Janet** in the salutation *Dear Janet:* (be careful not to include the *:* in the selection).

2. Type **Nancy** to replace *Janet* with *Nancy.*

PRACTICE YOUR SKILLS

Make the following additional corrections to your letter:

1. Delete **the** (in the paragraph *Since the company*) and replace it with **our.**

2. Delete **ahead** (in the same paragraph) and replace it with **forward.**

3. Delete **Yours truly** in the closing and replace it with **Sincerely.**

4. Check your work against Figure 1.10.

Figure 1.10   **Final (corrected) letter**

Nancy Wright
3325 Fillmore Circle
North Hills, NY 14052

Dear Nancy:

      I have been very pleased with the service provided by Global Travel. I would like additional information about your corporate travel program.

      Since our company is opening a new office in Paris sometime this year, your worldwide services would be beneficial to us. I look forward to hearing from you.

Sincerely,

Edward Brooks
Macco Plastics, Inc.

SAVING A DOCUMENT

Before you save it, a document exists only in computer memory, a temporary storage area. For permanent storage, you must save the document as a file on a hard or floppy disk. Word provides two commands you can use to save your documents: *File, Save As* and *File, Save*. Let's explore the differences between these commands.

THE FILE, SAVE AS COMMAND

You use the File, Save As command to save a document for the first time, to save a document with a new name, or to save a document in a different location (on another disk or in another directory).

To save a document using File, Save As:

- Choose *File, Save As* (that is, choose the Save As command from the File menu) to open the Save As dialog box.

- In the Drives and Directories list boxes, select the location (drive and directory) in which you wish to save the document, if this location is not already selected.

- In the File Name text box, type the name of the file.

- Click on *OK*.

- If the Summary Info dialog box appears, fill it in (if desired), and then click on *OK*.

Note: When you save a document, Word adds the .DOC file-name extension to identify the file as a document file. Your hard disk or floppy disks can hold many other types of files, such as .EXE program files, .NUM spreadsheet files, .DBF database files, and so on. Do not add the .DOC (or any other) extension yourself; let Word do it automatically.

THE FILE, SAVE COMMAND

You use the File, Save command (rather than File, Save As) to save a document with its current name and in its current location. File, Save *updates* a saved document; it replaces the last-saved version of the document with the new version of the document on your screen. For example, let's say you'd used File, Save As to save a business report to your reports directory as REPORT1, and then you'd gone back and revised the report by adding an extra closing paragraph. If you then chose File, Save, the new (extra paragraph) report version would replace the last-saved (no extra paragraph) version on the disk. Once you've used File, Save As to name and save a document, you should generally use File, Save for all subsequent updates of that document. However, if you later want to rename it or save it in a different location (while retaining a copy of the original file in the current location), you should use File, Save As.

SAVING GUIDELINES

You should save your active documents frequently; every 10 to 15 minutes is a good rule of thumb. That way, if something happens to your computer memory (for example, a power failure, which erases the contents of memory), you will have a recent copy of the document safely stored on disk. This precaution will keep your eventual retyping to a minimum.

Word provides an automatic save option. When this option is turned on, Word automatically saves all your active documents at a specified time interval (for example, every 10 minutes), making it unnecessary for you to save your documents manually (by issuing File, Save commands). This feature is a godsend for those who just can't seem to remember to save as often as they should.

Let's take a moment to make sure that your automatic save option is turned on:

1. Choose **Tools, Options** (click on **Tools** in the menu bar, and then click on **Options** in the drop-down Tools menu) to open the Options dialog box.

2. Click on the **Save** tab (in the left column of tabs) to display the Save options.

3. Observe the *Automatic Save Every* _____ *Minutes* option. If this option is unchecked (turned off)—that is, if the square box preceding *Automatic* is empty—check it (turn it on) by clicking on the square box to fill it with an X.

4. If the rectangular box between *Every* and *Minutes* does not contain the value 10, select its current value (by dragging over it), and then type **10**.

5. Your option should now read *Automatic Save Every 10 Minutes.* This means that Word will automatically save all your active documents every ten minutes.

6. Click on **OK** to close the Options dialog box.

NAMING A DOCUMENT

When you save a document for the first time, you must name it. Follow these guidelines when naming documents:

• A file name can contain from one to eight letters, numbers, or the following special characters: ! @ # $ % ( ) - { } ' ~

• A file name cannot contain spaces.

• A file name should be descriptive so that you can remember the file's contents (for example, JANREPT rather than X117-A).

SUMMARY INFO

Word provides an option called *Prompt for Summary Info.* When this option is turned on, the first time you save a new document, Word displays a Summary Info dialog box. This box prompts you for supplementary information about the document, including the subject, author, keywords, comments, and a descriptive title. Summary Info allows for quite a bit of detail in describing a document; you can enter up to 255 characters for each information category. You can also choose to skip any, or all, of these categories. Summary Info is especially useful for keeping track of author names and for storing comments and notes relating to a document.

Let's begin this activity by turning on the Prompt for Summary Info option. Then we'll save the active document and examine the Summary Info dialog box that appears:

1. Choose **Tools, Options** (click on **Tools** and then click on **Options**) to open the Options dialog box.

2. Click on the **Save** tab to display the Save options.

3. Observe the *Prompt for Summary Info* option. If this option is unchecked, check it by clicking on the box preceding it.

4. Click on **OK** to close the Options dialog box.

5. Choose **File, Save As** (click on **File** and then click on **Save As**) to open the Save As dialog box. Since your document is new (unsaved, as of yet) we're using File, Save As—rather than File, Save—to save it.

6. Scroll to the end of the list of available directories by clicking repeatedly on the **down scroll** arrow in the lower-right corner of the Directories list box (as shown in Figure 1.11). Your *wrkfiles* directory should appear at the bottom of the list. If you don't see it at first, double-click on **winword** to display the entire list of directories under winword. Double-click on **wrkfiles** to select it. This is the work directory you created in the Introduction; it is here that you will store and retrieve all of the documents you work with in this book.

7. Select (drag over) the contents of the File Name text box. Type **mychap1a** to name the document MYCHAP1A (Word ignores capitalization when you type document names). Your screen should now look like Figure 1.11.

Figure 1.11   **Saving MYCHAP1A to the WRKFILES directory**

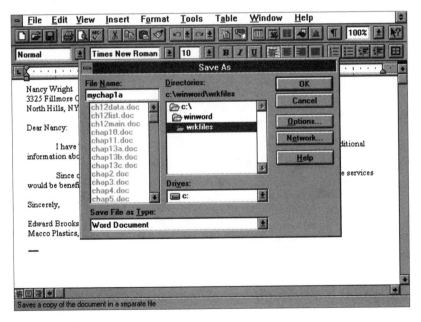

8. Click on **OK** to save the document as a disk file in your WRK-FILES directory.

9. Observe the **Summary Info** dialog box. As mentioned earlier, this box appears the first time you save a new document.

10. The contents of the Title text box should be selected (highlighted); if not, please select it. Type **My first document** to replace the selected text. (You can enter spaces in a Summary Info text box.)

11. Press **Tab** twice to select the contents of the Author text box. (You can't substitute Enter for Tab here. Pressing Enter is the keyboard method of choosing the default (assumed) option in a dialog box, in this case the OK button.) If necessary, type your name to replace the selected text. (When installing Word, you are asked to enter your name. The name that you entered appears in the Author text box, so you may not need to change this text.)

12. Click on **OK** to finish saving the document.

13. Observe the title bar. Note that it has changed to display the document's name, MYCHAP1A.DOC. (As mentioned earlier, when you save a document, Word automatically adds the extension .DOC to its name.)

PRINTING A DOCUMENT

By default, Word prints one copy of the entire active document. You can, however, choose to print the current page only, multiple pages, multiple copies, or selected text. You can also print to a document rather than to a printer, or print nondocument items such as Summary Info. (We'll discuss these print options in Chapter 6.)

To print the active document:

- Choose *File, Print.*
- Select the desired options from the Print dialog box.
- Click on *OK.*

Now let's print MYCHAP1A.DOC:

1. Choose **File, Print** to open the Print dialog box (see Figure 1.12).

Figure 1.12   **The Print dialog box**

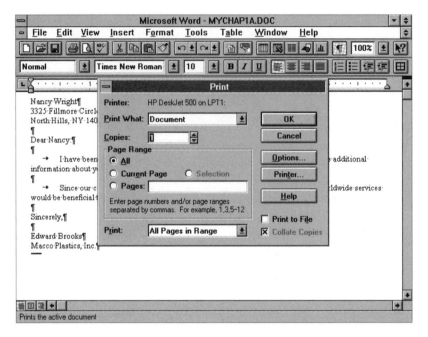

2. Click on **OK** to print the document. (Or, if you do not have a printer, click on **Cancel** to cancel the File, Print command and return to your document.) Compare your printout with Figure 1.10. Depending on the printer you are using, your printout may vary slightly from the one depicted in the figure.

3. If your document failed to print, make sure your printer is online, then try again. If it still won't print, refer to Appendix A for help selecting your printer.

CLOSING A DOCUMENT

When you're finished working with a document—that is, after you've completed, saved, and (if desired) printed it—you should close the document window. To do this, choose File, Close (or double-click on the document window Control-menu box).

Let's close MYCHAP1A.DOC, since we've saved and printed it:

1. Choose **File, Close** to close the document and remove it from memory.

2. Observe the screen. Word remains loaded, but there is no active document. The title bar displays only *Microsoft Word*; the menu bar contains only the File and Help choices; and the ruler and scroll bars have disappeared.

CREATING A NEW DOCUMENT

After you've closed the active document, you're ready—if you choose—to create a new document. To do this:

- Choose *File, New*.

- Click on *OK*.

Word will open a new, blank document window.

Let's create a new document and then save it:

1. Choose **File, New** and then click on **OK** to open a new, blank document window.

2. Type **This is my second document**.

3. Choose **File, Save As** to open the Save As dialog box.

4. Type **mychap1b** to name the document. Note that the desired directory (WRKFILES) is still selected; Word remembered it from the last time you selected it, earlier in this chapter.

5. Observe that the OK button has a dark border. This means that OK is the *default button*. As mentioned earlier, to choose a default button, you simply press Enter. Do this now; press **Enter** to choose OK instead of clicking on OK with the mouse.

6. Press **Enter** again (or click on **OK**) to bypass the Summary Info dialog box.

Let's view the default Summary Info for the document you just created:

1. Choose **File, Summary Info** to open the Summary Info dialog box.

2. Click on **Statistics** to open the Document Statistics dialog box. Observe the document statistics.

3. Click on **Close** (or press **Enter**) to close the Document Statistics dialog box.

4. Click on **OK** (or press **Enter**) to close the Summary Info dialog box.

Let's end this activity by turning off the Summary Info option. If you find this option useful, feel free to turn it back on when you are finished working through the book:

1. Choose **Tools, Options** to open the Options dialog box.

2. Click on the **Save** tab to display the Save options.

3. Uncheck the **Prompt for Summary Info** option.

4. Click on **OK** to close the Options dialog box.

5. Double-click on the document window **Control-menu** box (the lower of the two boxes in the upper-left corner of the screen) to close the document. Do not double-click on the application window Control-menu box (the upper of the two boxes), as this would cause you to exit Word. You can choose File, Close or you can double-click on the Control-menu box to close a document window.

EXITING WORD

Your final step of every Word session is to exit Word. Never turn off your computer before doing so, as this could result in the loss of one or more documents. To exit Word and return to Windows, choose File, Exit.

As a safeguard, if you have not saved the latest version of an active document, Word will prompt you to do so before exiting.

Let's exit Word:

1. Choose **File, Exit**. The Word application window (and any open document windows) disappears, and the Windows Program Manager is displayed.

PRACTICE YOUR SKILLS

You've learned a great deal in this first chapter. The following two activities allow you to apply this knowledge to practical word processing tasks. Please don't think of these activities as tests, but rather as opportunities to hone your Word skills. It is only through repetition that you'll internalize the techniques you've learned.

In this activity, you will create and edit the document shown in two different stages in Figures 1.13 and 1.14. Then you'll produce the final document shown in Figure 1.15.

1. Start Word and click on **OK** (or press **Enter**) if you see a Tip of the Day dialog box.

2. Enter the text shown in Figure 1.13. Where the text *(today's date)* appears, enter the current date.

3. Edit the letter as shown in Figure 1.14.

4. Save the document to your WRKFILES directory under the name **myprac1a**.

5. Print the document and compare the results to Figure 1.15.

6. Close the document window.

In the next activity, you will create and edit the document shown in two stages in Figures 1.16 and 1.17 to produce the final document shown in Figure 1.18.

1. Open a new document window.

2. Enter the text shown in Figure 1.16.

3. Edit the letter as shown in Figure 1.17.

4. Save the document to your WRKFILES directory under the name **myprac1b**.

5. Print the document and compare the results to Figure 1.18.

6. Close the document window.

7. Exit Word.

Figure 1.13   **The first draft of MYPRAC1A.DOC**

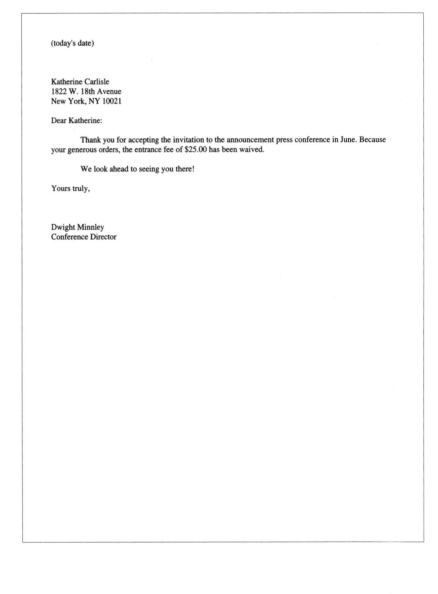

(today's date)

Katherine Carlisle
1822 W. 18th Avenue
New York, NY 10021

Dear Katherine:

      Thank you for accepting the invitation to the announcement press conference in June. Because your generous orders, the entrance fee of $25.00 has been waived.

      We look ahead to seeing you there!

Yours truly,

Dwight Minnley
Conference Director

Figure 1.14   **Editing MYPRAC1A.DOC**

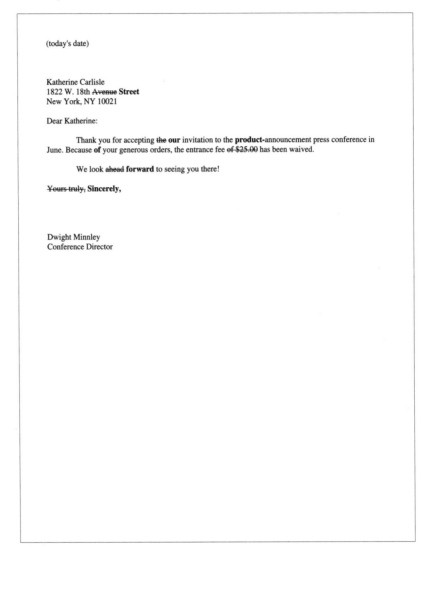

(today's date)

Katherine Carlisle
1822 W. 18th ~~Avenue~~ **Street**
New York, NY 10021

Dear Katherine:

Thank you for accepting ~~the~~ **our** invitation to the **product-**announcement press conference in June. Because **of** your generous orders, the entrance fee ~~of $25.00~~ has been waived.

We look ~~ahead~~ **forward** to seeing you there!

~~Yours truly,~~ **Sincerely,**

Dwight Minnley
Conference Director

Figure 1.15   **The corrected MYPRAC1A.DOC**

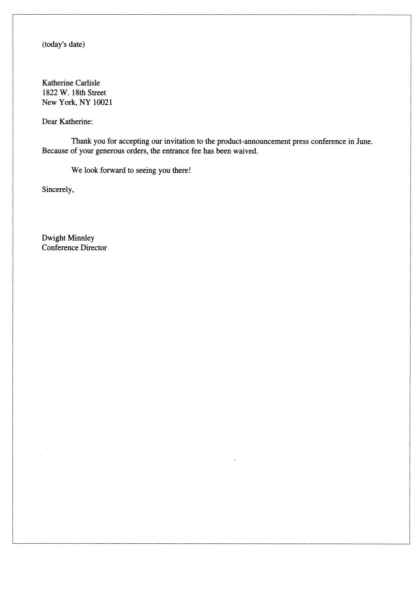

(today's date)

Katherine Carlisle
1822 W. 18th Street
New York, NY 10021

Dear Katherine:

Thank you for accepting our invitation to the product-announcement press conference in June.
Because of your generous orders, the entrance fee has been waived.

We look forward to seeing you there!

Sincerely,

Dwight Minnley
Conference Director

Figure 1.16   **The first draft of MYPRAC1B.DOC**

(today's date)

Jayne L. Corkley
1029 Bodera Drive
Baltimore, MD 21227

Dear Jayne:

Please accept this as a reminder to attend our product-announcement press conference in June. Because you are a valued customer, we want to make all effort to provide you with the support and services you need to make the conference a surreal one.

Attached you will find a map to your hotel and the conference center. After you sign up at our registration desk, on the first day of the conference, your name will be entered into our mailing list. This will ensure that you receive product information and dates for future press conferences.

Thank you for your interest and welcome to our growing list of customers.

Sincerely,

Dwight Minnley

Figure 1.17   **Editing MYPRAC1B.DOC**

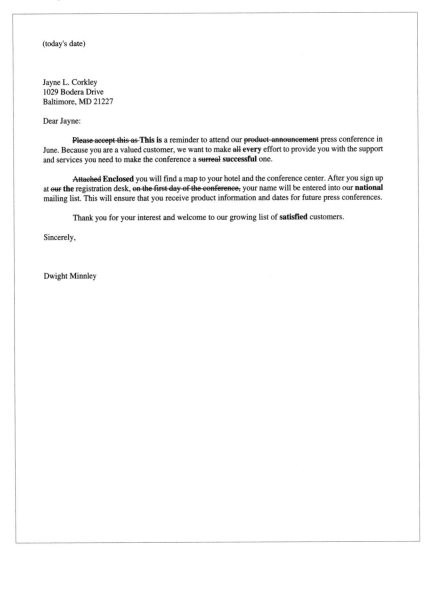

(today's date)

Jayne L. Corkley
1029 Bodera Drive
Baltimore, MD 21227

Dear Jayne:

~~Please accept this as~~ **This is** a reminder to attend our ~~product announcement~~ press conference in June. Because you are a valued customer, we want to make ~~all~~ **every** effort to provide you with the support and services you need to make the conference a ~~surreal~~ **successful** one.

~~Attached~~ **Enclosed** you will find a map to your hotel and the conference center. After you sign up at ~~our~~ **the** registration desk, ~~on the first day of the conference,~~ your name will be entered into our **national** mailing list. This will ensure that you receive product information and dates for future press conferences.

Thank you for your interest and welcome to our growing list of **satisfied** customers.

Sincerely,

Dwight Minnley

Figure 1.18   **The corrected MYPRAC1B.DOC**

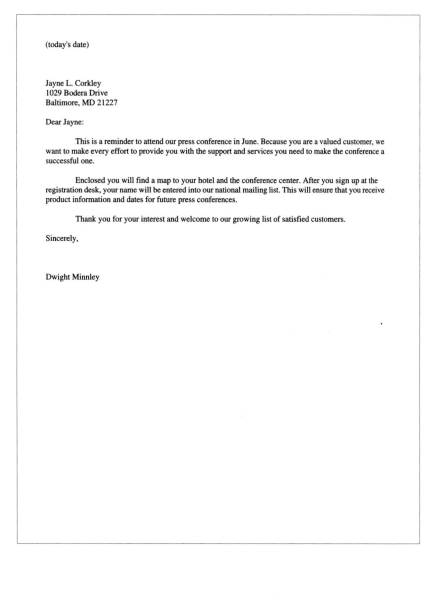

(today's date)

Jayne L. Corkley
1029 Bodera Drive
Baltimore, MD 21227

Dear Jayne:

This is a reminder to attend our press conference in June. Because you are a valued customer, we want to make every effort to provide you with the support and services you need to make the conference a successful one.

Enclosed you will find a map to your hotel and the conference center. After you sign up at the registration desk, your name will be entered into our national mailing list. This will ensure that you receive product information and dates for future press conferences.

Thank you for your interest and welcome to our growing list of satisfied customers.

Sincerely,

Dwight Minnley

SUMMARY

In this chapter, you learned the basics of the document creation-revision-saving-printing cycle, a procedure you'll use frequently in your daily word processing work. You now know how to start and exit Word; how to enter, insert, delete, and replace text; how to save, name, print, and close a document; and how to create a new document. Congratulations! You're well on your way to mastering Word.

Here's a quick reference guide to the Word features introduced in this chapter:

Desired Result	**How to Do It**
Start Word	Start Windows, double-click on the **Microsoft Word** icon.
Maximize/Restore a window	Click on the document or application **Maximize/Restore** button.
Minimize the application window	Click on the **Minimize** button.
Choose a menu command	Click on the menu-bar entry to display the drop-down menu; click on the command. Or, press and hold the **left mouse** button on the menu-bar entry; drag down to the command; and release the mouse button.
End a paragraph or short line	Press **Enter**.
Create a blank line	Press **Enter**.
Display/remove nonprinting characters	Click on the **Show/Hide** button.
Align text horizontally	Use the **Tab** key.
Delete character to the left of the insertion point	Press **Backspace**.

Desired Result	How to Do It
Select text	Point to the first (or final) character of the text; press and hold the **left mouse** button; drag across the text to the final (or first) character; release the mouse button.
Delete character to the right of the insertion point	Press **Del**.
Delete selected text	Select text; press **Del**.
Replace selected text	Select text; type the new text.
Save a document for the first time	Choose **File, Save As**.
Rename a document or save a document as a document in a new location	Choose **File, Save As**.
Save a previously saved document with the same name/location	Choose **File, Save**.
Turn on the automatic save option	Choose **Tools, Options**; click the **Save** tab; check the **Automatic Save Every _____ Minutes** option; if desired, change the number of minutes between auto-saving; click on **OK**.
Print the active document	Choose **File, Print**.
Close the active document	Choose **File, Close**. Or, double-click on the document window **Control-menu** box.
Create a new document	Choose **File, New**; click on **OK**.
Choose a default button	Press **Enter**.
View Summary Info for the active document	Choose **File, Summary Info**.

Desired Result	**How to Do It**
Turn on/off the Summary Info option	Choose **Tools, Options**; click on the **Save** tab; check/uncheck the **Prompt for Summary Info** option; click on **OK**.
Exit Word	Choose **File, Exit**.

In the next chapter, we'll show you how to navigate in Word. You'll learn how to obtain helpful Word tips, open a file (a document stored on a disk), display different portions of a document, search for text in a document, control document magnification, and obtain on-line help.

A NOTE ON HOW TO PROCEED

If you wish to stop here, please feel free to do so now. If you feel energetic and wish to press onward, please proceed directly to the next chapter. Remember to allot enough time to work through an entire chapter in one sitting.

CHAPTER 2:
NAVIGATING IN WORD

Obtaining Word
Tips

Using File, Open
to Open a File

Scrolling through
a Document

Moving through a
Document

Using Word Help
to Obtain On-Line
Help

In Chapter 1 you learned how to use the mouse to move around within a one-page document. In this chapter, you'll learn how to use the mouse *and* the keyboard to navigate through a multipage document. It's essential for you to master these navigational techniques as early as possible in your Word career. The more comfortable you feel moving around within a document, the more you'll be able to concentrate on the contents of the document itself.

When you're done working through this chapter, you will know

- How to obtain Word tips

- How to open a file

- How to use the mouse to scroll through a document

- How to use the keyboard and menus to move through a document

- How to use Edit, Find to search for text

- How to use the Zoom Control box to change the document magnification

- How to use Word Help to obtain on-line help

OBTAINING WORD TIPS

Before we delve into the heart of this chapter, navigating in Word, we'll take a few minutes to explore the Tip of the Day dialog box that appears when you start Word:

1. If you are already running Word, please exit it now.

2. Restart Word. (For help, see "Starting Word" in Chapter 1.)

3. If the Tip of the Day dialog box does not appear, choose **Help, Tip of the Day** to open it.

4. Observe the buttons on the right side of the Tip of the Day dialog box. You have four choices: clicking on OK closes the dialog box; clicking on Next Tip displays another Word tip; clicking on More Tips displays a comprehensive list of tips; and clicking on Help displays a Tip of the Day command Help menu.

5. Click on **Next Tip** to display another Word tip. Repeat this to display several more tips. You can use this flashcard-like technique to obtain random information about Word.

6. Click on **More Tips** to open a *Help window* that displays the Tip of the Day contents. (You'll learn more about Help windows later in this chapter.) Click on the first topic, **Navigating in Word**, to display a list of navigational tips. Take a moment to browse through the list (use the up/down arrows on your keyboard), and then exit Help by double-clicking on its

Control-menu box (the box in the upper-left corner of the Help window). The Tip of the Day dialog box reappears.

7. Click on **Help** to open a Help window that displays the Tip of the Day command Help menu, which briefly describes the Tip of the Day features. Close the Help window by double-clicking on its **Control-menu** box.

8. Observe the **Show Tips at Startup** option at the bottom of the Tip of the Day dialog box. When this option is checked, the Tip of the Day dialog box automatically appears every time you start Word. While these tips are certainly edifying, you may not want to see them every single time you start Word.

9. Uncheck the **Show Tips at Startup** option (remove the X in the option box by clicking on it); then click on **OK.** The Tip of the Day dialog box will now no longer automatically appear when you start Word.

If you find the Tip of the Day feature helpful, feel free to activate it anytime during a Word session (by choosing Help, Tip of the Day) or to turn the Show Tips at Startup option back on when you're done working through this book (by choosing Help, Tip of the Day and checking the Show Tips at Startup option).

USING FILE, OPEN TO OPEN A FILE

In Chapter 1 you learned how to create, modify, and save a document. Here you'll learn how to *open* (retrieve) a *file* (a document that is stored on a disk). This way, you'll be able to revise previously saved documents and then reprint and resave them. (**Note:** The terms *file* and *document* are two different ways of looking at the same thing. When referring to a text object on your screen, we call it a *document;* when referring to this same text object stored on a disk, we call it a *file.*)

To open a file:

• Choose *File, Open* to display the Open dialog box.

• Select the desired drive (in the Drives list box) and directory (in the Directories list box), if necessary.

• Click on the desired file (in the File Name list box) and then click on OK; or, simply double-click on the desired file.

When you open a file, Word places a copy of the file in a document window on your screen. Because this is a *copy* of the file, and not the file itself, you can revise it to your heart's content without changing the original document stored on your disk. You will, however, change the original document if you save your revised document as a file with the same name, and in the same location, as the original. For this reason, if you want to preserve the original document, make sure to give your revised file a new name.

Word also provides a convenient file-opening shortcut; it keeps track of the last four files that you worked on and displays their names at the bottom of the drop-down File menu. To open one of these documents, simply choose File and click on the desired document name.

Let's begin by opening a file that is stored in your WRKFILES directory:

1. Choose **File, Open** to display the Open dialog box (see Figure 2.1).

2. Select your **WRKFILES** directory. (To do this, scroll down to the wrkfiles entry in the Directories list box, and then double-click on **wrkfiles**. Or, if necessary, double-click on **winword** to select it, and then double-click on **wrkfiles**.) You must tell Word where to find a file before you open it.

Figure 2.1   **The Open dialog box**

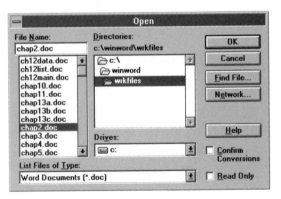

3. In the File Name list box, click once on **chap2.doc**. Note that this file name is automatically inserted in the File Name text box. (A *list box* displays a list of options; a *text box* contains text that is either entered automatically or that you can enter when prompted.)

4. Click on **OK** (or press **Enter**) to open the file. A copy of the file appears in an active document window. Note the title bar, Microsoft Word - CHAP2.DOC (see Figure 2.2).

Figure 2.2   **CHAP2.DOC, newly opened**

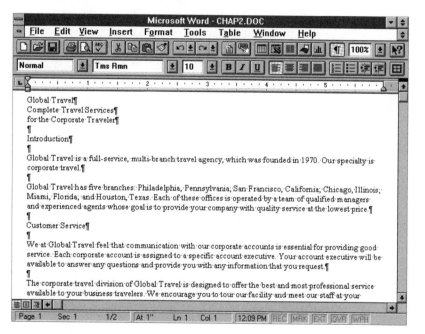

Now let's try the shortcut method for opening this same file. First we'll close it:

1. Double-click on the document window (*not* the application window) **Control-menu** box to close CHAP2.DOC.

2. Click (once) on **File** to display the drop-down File menu. Note that CHAP2.DOC appears in the recently accessed files section at the bottom of the menu.

3. Click on **CHAP2.DOC** to open it.

SCROLLING THROUGH A DOCUMENT

At normal (100%) magnification, a Word document window can only display about half of a standard business-size (8.5 by 11-inch) page on the screen at any one time. To view the remainder of the page (or other pages within the document), you can use the mouse in conjunction with the vertical and horizontal scroll bars to *scroll* through the document. The vertical scroll bar controls up-down scrolling; the horizontal scroll bar controls side-to-side scrolling.

Scrolling through a document changes the document display, but does *not* change the position of the insertion point. For example, if the insertion point is at the top of page 2 and you use the vertical scroll bar to scroll down to page 8, the contents of page 8 will be displayed on the screen, but the insertion point will still be at the top of page 2. If you then begin to type, your text is entered at the insertion point on page 2, not on page 8. (You'll learn how to change both the document display *and* the insertion point position in the next section.)

Table 2.1 lists Word's vertical and horizontal scrolling options and how to perform them. Figure 2.3 identifies screen elements used for scrolling.

Table 2.1   **Vertical and Horizontal Scrolling Options**

To Scroll	Do This
Up or down one line at a time	Click on the up or down scroll arrow.
To the top, bottom, or middle of a document	Drag the vertical scroll box to the top, bottom, or middle of the scroll bar.
Up or down a screen at a time	Click in the shaded area above or below the vertical scroll box.
Left or right a character at a time	Click on the left or right scroll arrow.

Table 2.1   **Vertical and Horizontal Scrolling Options (Continued)**

To Scroll	Do This
To the left edge, right edge, or middle of a document	Drag the horizontal scroll box to the left, right, or middle of the scroll bar.
Left or right a screen at a time	Click in the shaded area to the left or right of the horizontal scroll box.

Figure 2.3   **Scrolling terminology**

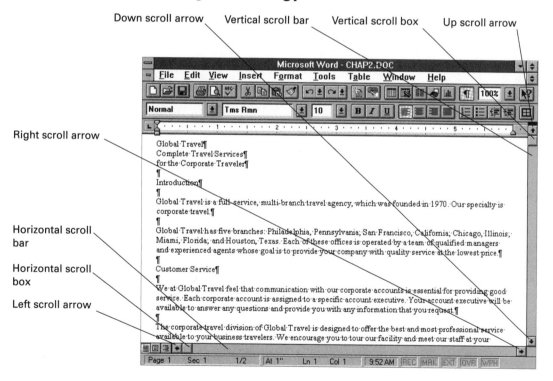

Let's practice scrolling through the active document, CHAP2.DOC:

1. Click on the **down scroll** arrow several times to scroll down through the document one line at a time. Note that the insertion point does not move.

2. Click on the **up scroll** arrow several times to scroll up through the document.

3. Drag the **vertical scroll** box to the bottom of the scroll bar to scroll to the bottom of the document.

4. Drag the **vertical scroll** box to the middle of the scroll bar to scroll to the middle of the document.

5. Observe the *page break*—the dotted line marked *Page Break* that indicates where one page ends and the next begins. (You may have to scroll to see this.) Because CHAP2.DOC is a two-page document, the page break is located about half-way through the document.

6. Drag the **vertical scroll** box to the top of the scroll bar to scroll to the top of the document. Note that, throughout all of your scrolling, the insertion point has remained at the top of the document.

7. Click in the **vertical scroll** bar below the vertical scroll box to scroll one screen length down through the document.

8. Repeat step 7 as many times as necessary to scroll to the bottom of the document.

9. Click in the **vertical scroll** bar above the vertical scroll box to scroll one screen length up through the document.

10. Repeat step 9 as many times as necessary to scroll to the top of the document.

Let's take a moment to observe a common scrolling mistake. Assume you wanted to enter your initials at the end of the active document:

1. Drag the **vertical scroll** box to the bottom of the scroll bar to display the end of the document.

2. Type your initials. The text is inserted at the top of the document (where your insertion point is located), not at the end (where you scrolled to). Note that Word automatically repositions the document to display the inserted text. To avoid making such a mistake, remember these two things: Text that you type is always inserted at the insertion point; and, the insertion point does not move when you use the mouse to scroll through your document.

3. Use **Backspace** to erase your initials.

MOVING THROUGH A DOCUMENT

When you *scroll* through a document, you change the document display but not the insertion point. When you *move* through a document, you change both the document display *and* the insertion point. For this reason, you should scroll when you just want to view different parts of a document, and you should move when you want to view and modify a document.

USING THE KEYBOARD TO MOVE THROUGH A DOCUMENT

Table 2.2 lists several ways to move through a document by using the keyboard.

Table 2.2   **Keyboard Movement Techniques**

To Move	Press
Up one screen	PgUp (or Page Up on enhanced keyboards)
Down one screen	PgDn (or Page Down)
To the top of the document	Ctrl+Home
To the end of the document	Ctrl+End
To the beginning of a line	Home
To the end of a line	End

Now let's practice using the keyboard to move—rather than to scroll—through a document.

Note: If you intend to use the PgDn and PgUp keys on the numeric keypad, make sure that Num Lock is off.

1. Press **PgDn** (or **Page Down**) twice to move two screen lengths down through the document. Note that the insertion point has moved along with the document display.

2. Press **PgUp** (or **Page Up**) twice to move two screen lengths up through the document. Note that the insertion point has moved.

3. Press **Ctrl+End**—that is, press and hold down the **Ctrl** key, press the **End** key, and then release both keys—to move to the end of the document.

4. Press **Ctrl+Home** (press **Ctrl**, press **Home**, and then release both) to move to the beginning of the document.

Let's redo our initial-writing task, this time using the correct method:

1. Press **Ctrl+End** to move to the end of the document.

2. Type your initials. They now appear in the desired location, because you used Ctrl+End (not the scroll bar) to move the insertion point along with the document display.

USING EDIT, GO TO TO MOVE TO A PAGE

You can use the Edit, Go To command to move to the top of a specified page in the active document. This technique is particularly useful when you are moving through a long (multipage) document.

To move to the top of a page:

- Choose *Edit, Go To* or press *F5.*

- Type the page number and then click on *Go To* (or press *Enter*).

- To move to a different page, repeat the previous step.

- When you're finished using Go To, click on *Close* (or press *Esc*).

As indicated in the first of the above bulleted steps, you can issue a Go To command by pressing the F5 shortcut key instead of choosing Edit, Go To from the menu bar. *Shortcut keys* allow you to issue frequently used commands directly from the keyboard. (For a list of Word's shortcut keys, see Appendix B.)

Let's use the Edit, Go To command to move through a document. First we'll choose Edit, Go To from the menu bar; then we'll use the F5 key:

1. Choose **Edit, Go To** to open the Go To dialog box (see Figure 2.4).

Figure 2.4   **The Go To dialog box**

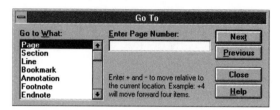

2. In the Enter Page Number text box, type **2** to specify the destination page. Then click on **Go To** to move (the document display and the insertion point) to the top of page 2. Note that your current page number is displayed in the status bar. The Go To dialog box remains on the screen, allowing you to move to another page.

3. *Enter* **1**—that is, type **1** and then press **Enter**—to move to the top of page 1. (From here on, we'll use "enter text" to mean "type *text* and then press *Enter*.")

4. Click on **Close** to close the Go To dialog box.

5. Click on **Edit** to display the drop-down Edit menu. Observe the shortcut key for the Go To command, F5. Click on **Edit** again to close the Edit menu.

6. Press **F5** to open the same Go To dialog box you opened in step 1 by choosing Edit, Go To.

7. Enter **2** (type **2** and press **Enter**) to move to the top of page 2.

8. Enter **1** to move to the top of page 1.

9. Press **Esc** to close the Go To dialog box.

PRACTICE YOUR SKILLS

1. Use **Edit, Go To** to move to the top of page 2, and then close the Go To dialog box.

2. Use **F5** to move to the top of page 1, and then attempt to move to the top of page 3. Since CHAP2.DOC does not have a page 3, Word moves you to the top of the final page (2).

USING EDIT, FIND TO SEARCH FOR TEXT

One of Word's most powerful features is its ability to locate a specific word or phrase in a document. You can use this feature to move rapidly to any desired document location. For example, you can move to the sentence containing the phrase "We would like to establish...," even if you have no idea on which page this sentence appears.

To use Edit, Find to search for text within a document:

- Choose *Edit, Find* or press *Ctrl+F* to open the Find dialog box.

- In the Find What text box, type the *search text* (the text that you want to find).

- Select any desired search options (as explained in the paragraph following this bulleted procedure).

- Click on *Find Next* (or press *Enter*); Word finds and highlights the first occurrence of your search text.

- Repeat the previous step as many times as necessary until you have searched through the entire document (or cancel your search at any time by clicking on *Cancel*).

- When Word has finished searching the document, it displays a message informing you so. Click on *OK* (or press *Enter*) to close this message box.

- If desired, perform another search by repeating the previous five steps.

- When you are finished searching, click on *Cancel* to close the Find dialog box.

Edit, Find provides several options that allow you to refine your text searches. By checking (turning on) the *Match Case* option, you can locate only words that exactly match the case (capitalization) of your search text. By checking the *Find Whole Words Only* option, you can tell Find to locate only whole words that match your search text. By checking the *Search Up* option, you can search from the insertion point upward, instead of in the default downward direction.

Let's experiment with the Edit, Find command:

1. Your insertion point should be at the top of page 2. If it is not, use **Edit, Go To** (or **F5**) to move it there.

2. Choose **Edit, Find** to open the Find dialog box (see Figure 2.5).

Figure 2.5 **The Find dialog box**

3. In the Find What text box, type **vacation**. This is the word we're going to search for. Before we actually perform the search, we need to verify that the search options are correctly set.

4. Uncheck all of the following options: **Match Case, Find Whole Words Only, Use Pattern Matching**, and **Sounds Like**. Verify that the Search option box is set to *All* (if not, select this option by clicking on the **down arrow** next to the Search list box and then clicking on **All**); this option tells Word to search the entire document. If the **No Formatting** button is active—that is, if it is not dimmed—click on it; this tells Word to ignore the formatting (font, style, and so on) of your search word (*vacation*).

5. Click on **Find Next** (or press **Enter**) four times, pausing each time to examine the found word; when a word is found, it is highlighted in the document. Word finds the following occurrences of *vacation*:

Vacations

vacation

Vacation

Vacation

Word found the second occurrence (*vacation*) because it exactly matches your search text (*vacation*). It found the last two occurrences (*Vacation*), because by unchecking the Match Case option, you told it to ignore capitalization. It found the first occurrence (*Vacations*), because by unchecking the Find Whole Words Only option, you told it to find not just vacation, but to find all words that contain *vacation* (*Vacations* contains *vacation*).

6. Click on **Find Next** (or press **Enter**) again. A *message box* appears, informing you that Word has finished searching the document. Click on **OK** (or press **Enter**) to close this box.

7. Click on **Cancel** (or press **Esc**) to close the Find dialog box.

Now let's refine our search by using the Match Case and Find Whole Words Only options:

1. If necessary, move the insertion point back to the top of page 2.

2. Press **Ctrl+F** (or **Ctrl+f**—you do not need to capitalize shortcut-key letters) to open the Find dialog box. Ctrl+F is the shortcut key for the Edit, Find command.

3. Check the **Find Whole Words Only** option.

4. Click on **Find Next** (or press **Enter**) three times, pausing to examine each found word. This time, only three occurrences are found: *vacation*, *Vacation*, and *Vacation*. *Vacations* is not found, because you told Word to find only whole-word matches of *vacation*.

5. Click on **Find Next** (or press **Enter**) again; the end-of-document message box appears. Click on **OK** to close this box, but do not close the Find dialog box.

6. Check the **Match Case** option; both Match Case and Find Whole Words Only should now be checked. Click on **Find Next** (or press **Enter**) two times. Only one occurrence of your search text is found: *vacation*. *Vacation* is not found, because you told Word to find only case-matching occurrences of *vacation*.

7. Click on **OK** to close the search-finished message box.

PRACTICE YOUR SKILLS

1. Uncheck the **Match Case** and **Find Whole Words Only** options, and search your entire active document for *news*. There are three matches.

2. Check the **Find Whole Words Only** option and repeat this search. There is one match.

3. Uncheck **Find Whole Words Only,** check **Match Case**, and repeat the search. There are two matches.

4. Close the Find dialog box.

USING THE ZOOM CONTROL BOX TO CHANGE DOCUMENT MAGNIFICATION

Word allows you to change the level of magnification at which your documents are displayed on the screen. By default, documents are displayed at 100 percent magnification (where the screen display matches the actual document size), but you can adjust this magnification to anywhere from 10 percent to 200 percent.

Lower magnifications (from 99 percent to 10 percent) shrink the on-screen document, allowing you to view more of a page at once. Higher magnifications (from 101 percent to 200 percent) enlarge the on-screen document, allowing you to view text and graphics close up to perform detail work.

To change the magnification of the active document:

• Click on the *down arrow* next to the *Zoom Control* list box to open a drop-down list of magnification options.

• Click on your desired magnification. Clicking on the *Page Width* option shrinks a page so that its extra-wide text lines fit on-screen.

Let's change the magnification of CHAP2.DOC:

1. If necessary, move the insertion point to the top of the document.

2. Observe the Zoom Control box (the box that contains a percentage, near the right edge of the Standard toolbar). Note that it reads *100%*, meaning that the active document is displayed at 100 percent (actual-size) magnification.

3. Click on the **down arrow** next to the Zoom Control list box to open its drop-down list of magnification options.

4. Click on the **50%** option to shrink the document to half its actual size.

5. Using the technique outlined in the previous two steps, change the magnification to **150%** (see Figure 2.6). Note how much less of the text fits on-screen.

Figure 2.6 **Changing the magnification to 150%**

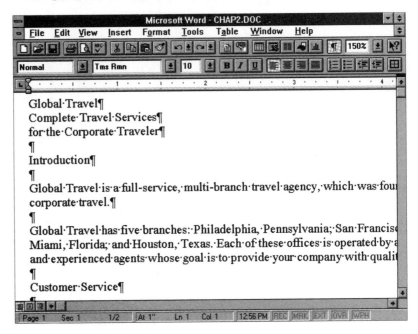

6. Change the magnification back to **100%**.

7. Open the Zoom Control drop-down list and click on the **Page Width** option. Note that your screen display does not change. If, however, CHAP2.DOC had one or more lines that were too wide to fit on-screen, clicking on Page Width would have shrunk the document to the size where all its lines fit widthwise on-screen.

8. Verify that the magnification is set to 100%.

USING WORD HELP TO OBTAIN ON-LINE HELP

Word Help is an extensive on-line help system that provides you with "how-to" information on every aspect of the Word program. The beauty of Word Help is its accessibility. No matter what you are doing in Word (choosing a command from the menu, editing a document, filling in a dimalog box, and so on), Help is only a keystroke—or mouse click—away.

USING THE WORD HELP CONTENTS WINDOW TO OBTAIN HELP

The Word Help Contents window provides an overview of the topics for which Help information is available. To use the Word Help Contents window:

* Choose *Help*, *Contents* to open the Word Help Contents window.

* To open a Help window for an underlined topic, click on that topic.

* To open a *pop-up definition* of a dotted-underlined term, click on that term; to close the definition, click again.

* To exit Word Help, double-click on its *Control-menu* box.

Let's use the Word Help Contents window to get help for typing and revising documents:

1. Choose **Help, Contents** to open the Word Help Contents window. Click on the window's **Maximize/Restore** button to maximize it (see Figure 2.7).

2. Point to the underlined topic **Using Word**. Note that the mouse pointer changes to a hand. Click on **Using Word** to open the Using Word window, which displays a list of topics grouped together under the heading *Using Word*.

3. Click on the underlined topic **Typing and Revising** to open the Typing and Revising window.

4. Click on the topic **Overview** to open the Overview of Typing and Revising window. Maximize this window and skim the contents.

5. Click on the dotted-underlined term **insertion point** to open its pop-up definition. Skim it, and then click again to close the pop-up definition.

6. Exit Word Help by double-clicking on its **Control-menu** box.

Figure 2.7   **The Word Help Contents window, maximized**

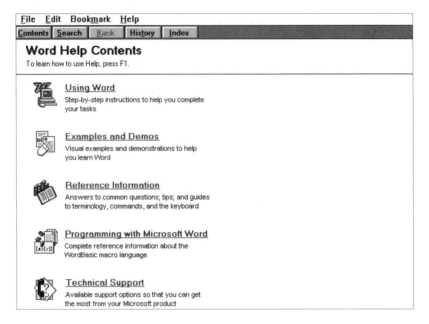

USING THE F1 KEY TO OBTAIN CONTEXT-SENSITIVE HELP

Word Help also offers you *context-sensitive* help—help related to your current working context. For example, if a dialog box is open and you ask for context-sensitive help, Help displays information about that particular dialog box. Used in this manner, Help can quickly provide information about specific dialog boxes, menu commands, or areas of the screen. You can use either of the following methods to obtain context-sensitive help:

- Press *F1*; Word displays the Help window related to your current working context.

- Press *Shift+F1*; the mouse pointer changes to an arrow with a question mark attached. Make any menu choice, or click on any button or any part of the application window, and Word will open the related Help window.

Let's use the F1 key to obtain context-sensitive help:

1. Choose **Edit, Go To** to open the Go To dialog box.

2. Press **F1** to open the Help window for the Go To command, and maximize the window, if necessary (see Figure 2.8). This is an example of context-sensitive Help, in which Word provides help relative to your current working context.

Figure 2.8   **Help window for the Go To command**

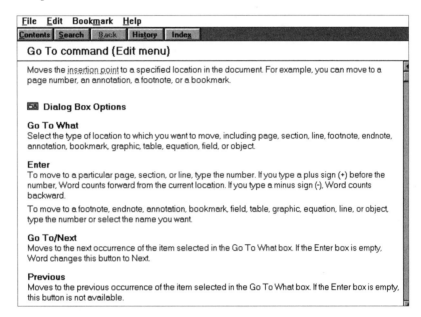

3. Exit Help (by double-clicking on its **Control-menu** box).

4. Click on **Close** to close the Go To dialog box.

Now let's use the Shift+F1 method to obtain context-sensitive Help:

1. Press **Shift+F1** to activate context-sensitive Word Help. Note that the mouse pointer now has a question mark attached to it (see Figure 2.9).

Figure 2.9   **Context-sensitive Help pointer**

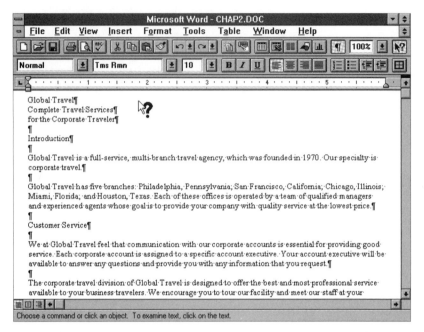

2. Choose **File, Summary Info** to open the Help window on the Summary Info command.

3. Exit Help.

4. Press **Shift+F1** to reactivate context-sensitive Help.

5. Click on a blank area (between buttons) of the Standard (upper) toolbar to open its Help window.

6. Exit Help.

7. Double-click on the document window **Control-menu** box to close the document. If prompted whether you want to save the changes, click on **No**.

SUMMARY

In this chapter, you learned the basics of navigating in Word. You now know how to obtain Word tips, open a file, scroll and move through a document, search for text, control document magnification, and obtain on-line help.

Here's a quick reference guide to the Word features introduced in this chapter:

Desired Result	How to Do It
Obtain Word tips	Choose **Help, Tip of the Day**.
Open a file	Choose **File, Open**; select the drive and directory; click on the file name, and then click on **OK** (or double-click on the file name).
Open a recently used document	Choose **File**; click on the document name at the bottom of the File menu.
Scroll up or down one line	Click on the **up** or **down scroll** arrow.
Scroll to the top, bottom, or middle of a document	Drag the **vertical scroll** box to the top, bottom, or middle of the scroll bar.
Scroll up or down a screen	Click in the **vertical scroll** bar above or below the vertical scroll box.
Scroll left or right a column	Click on the **left** or **right scroll** arrow.
Scroll to the left edge, right edge, or middle of a document	Drag the **horizontal scroll** box to the left, right, or middle of the scroll bar.
Scroll to the left or right a screen at a time	Click in the **horizontal scroll** bar to the left or right of the horizontal scroll box.
Move up one screen	Press **PgUp**.
Move down one screen	Press **PgDn**.
Move to the top of the document	Press **Ctrl+Home**.

Desired Result	How to Do It
Move to the end of the document	Press **Ctrl+End**.
Move to the beginning of a line	Press **Home**.
Move to the end of a line	Press **End**.
Move to the top of a page	Choose **Edit, Go To** or press **F5**; type the page number and click on **OK**; repeat the previous step, if desired; when finished, click on **Close**.
Search for text	Choose **Edit, Find** (or press **Ctrl+F**); type the search text; select any desired search options; click on **Find Next** (or press **Enter**); if desired, perform another search; when finished, click on **Close**.
Change the document magnification	Open the Zoom Control list box; click on your desired magnification option.
Open the Word Help Contents window	Choose **Help, Contents**.
Open a Help window for a topic	Click on the underlined Help topic.
Open a pop-up definition of a term	Click on the dotted-underlined term.
Obtain context-sensitive Help	Press **F1**. Or, press **Shift+F1**; make any menu choice, or click on any button or part of the application window.
Exit Word Help	Double-click on its **Control-menu** box.

In the next chapter, you'll learn how to edit text. The editing process includes replacing found text, moving text, and copying text. You'll also be introduced to a handy way to undo an action when you change your mind about an editing decision.

IF YOU'RE STOPPING HERE

If you need to break off here, please exit Word (for help, see "Exiting Word" in Chapter 1). If you want to proceed directly to the next chapter, please do so now.

CHAPTER 3:
EDITING TEXT

Techniques for Selecting Text

Using Edit, Replace to Replace Found Text

Moving and Copying Text

Using Undo to Reverse Your Last Operation

In Chapter 1, you learned the basics of editing—how to insert, select, replace, and delete text. In this chapter we'll introduce you to some of Word's more advanced editing techniques. You'll learn sophisticated ways to select text and then move and copy this text to other locations in your document. You'll find out how to use the Edit, Replace command (Edit, Find's more powerful cousin) to find text and replace it with new text of your choice. Finally, we'll show you how to use the Undo command to rescue yourself from a potentially catastrophic word processing mistake.

When you're done working through this chapter, you will know

- How to use the mouse, the keyboard, and menus to select text
- How to use the Edit, Replace command to replace found text
- How to move and copy text
- How to use the Undo command to reverse your last operation

TECHNIQUES FOR SELECTING TEXT

Before you can move or copy text, you must select it. You can do this by using the mouse, the keyboard, or menus. Table 3.1 lists Word's text selection techniques.

Table 3.1   **Text Selection Techniques**

Selection Technique	How to Do It
Dragging	Point at one end of the text you want to select. Press and hold the mouse button. Move (drag) the mouse pointer to the other end of the text. Release the mouse button. All the text between the two ends is selected.
Using Shift	Place the insertion point at one end of the text. Press and hold Shift, and then click at the other end of the text you want to select (do not drag). Release Shift. All the text between the two ends is selected.
Selecting a word	Point anywhere inside the word and double-click the mouse button. The trailing space is automatically selected along with the word.

Table 3.1   **Text Selection Techniques (Continued)**

Selection Technique	How to Do It
Selecting a sentence	Point anywhere inside the sentence. Press and hold the Ctrl key, and then click the mouse button. Release Ctrl. End punctuation and trailing spaces are automatically selected along with the sentence.
Selecting a line	Point in the *selection bar* area (the blank vertical bar on the left side of the document window) next to the line and click the mouse button. All the text on that line is selected.
Selecting multiple lines	Point in the selection bar next to the first or last line of text you want to select. Press and hold the mouse button; then drag down or up. Release the mouse button. All the lines you "dragged" are selected.
Selecting a paragraph	Point in the selection bar next to the paragraph and double-click the mouse button. The ending paragraph mark is selected along with the paragraph.
Selecting an entire document	Choose Edit, Select All. Or point anywhere in the selection bar, press and hold Ctrl, click the mouse button, and then release Ctrl.
Extending an existing selection	While holding Shift, click beyond the existing selection. The selection extends to that point.

Table 3.1   **Text Selection Techniques (Continued)**

Selection Technique	How to Do It
Shortening an existing selection	While holding Shift, click inside the existing selection. The selection shortens to that point.
Deselecting an existing selection	Make another selection, or click the mouse button in the text area anywhere outside the existing selection.

If you are not running Word, please start it now (for help, see "Starting Word" in Chapter 1). Let's begin this chapter's activities by opening a new document file and then using the mouse-dragging method to select text:

1. Click on the **Open** button (second from the left in the toolbar; it shows a file folder being opened) to display the Open dialog box. Clicking on the Open button is equivalent to choosing the File, Open command from the menu.

2. If your WRKFILES directory is not already selected, select it now.

3. In the File Name list box, double-click on **chap3.doc** to open the document file. Double-clicking on a list-box item is often equivalent to clicking once on the item and then clicking on OK (or pressing Enter).

4. Point to the left of the *C* in *Corporate* in the third line of the document.

5. Drag to the right to select **Corporate** and the trailing space.

6. Release the mouse button. Your screen should resemble Figure 3.1.

Now let's use the whole-word selection technique:

1. Point to the word *five* in the first paragraph of the document.

2. Double-click the mouse button to select the entire word **five**. Note that selecting *five* deselects *Corporate*.

3. Examine the selected text. The trailing space after *five* is also selected.

Figure 3.1   **Dragging the mouse to select text**

Open button

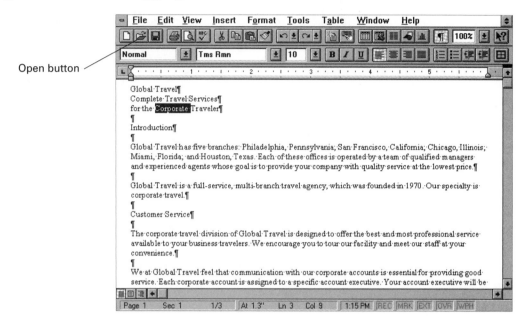

Now let's use the selection bar to select text:

1. Move the mouse pointer into the selection bar—the blank vertical bar between the left edge of the document window and the left edge of the document text (see Figure 3.2). Note that the pointer changes from an I-beam into an arrow.

2. Point in the selection bar next to the line beginning with *Global Travel is a full-service.* Click the mouse button to select the entire line.

3. Point in the selection bar next to *Global Travel has five branches.* Double-click the mouse button to select the entire paragraph.

4. Point in the selection bar next to *Introduction.* Press and hold the mouse button, and then drag down to the paragraph mark before *Customer Service* to select multiple lines of text. Release the mouse button.

Figure 3.2   **The selection bar**

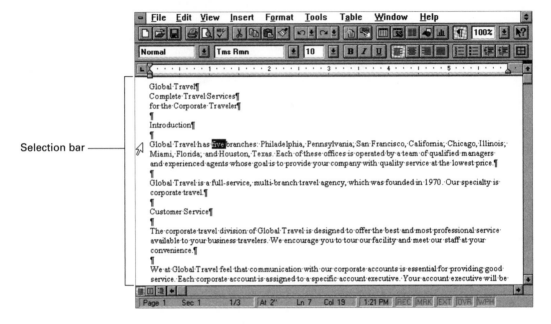

Selection bar

Let's use the Shift key to select a block of text and then extend and shorten this selection:

1. Place the insertion point before the *C* in *Corporate* in the third line of the document.

2. Press and hold **Shift**; then click the mouse pointer in the space after *five* to select all the text from *Corporate* to *five*. Release **Shift** (see Figure 3.3).

3. Point to the right of the *s* in *Texas* in the next line down (but do *not* click). Press and hold **Shift**; then click the mouse button to extend the selection through to the end of *Texas*. Release **Shift**.

4. Point to the left of the *P* in *Philadelphia*. Note that the pointer appears as an arrow (instead of an insertion point) when you point to selected text. Press and hold **Shift**; then click the mouse button to shorten the selection. Release **Shift**.

Figure 3.3   **Selecting text with the mouse and the Shift key**

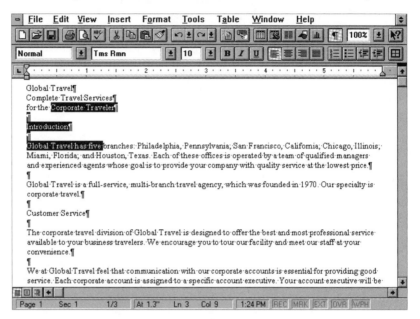

Finally, let's use the menu to select the entire document:

1. Choose **Edit, Select All** to select the entire document.

2. Click anywhere within the text area to *deselect*.

PRACTICE YOUR SKILLS

1. Select the first sentence of the paragraph beginning with *Global Travel is a full-service*, using the mouse-dragging technique.

2. Deselect.

3. Select the same sentence as in step 1, this time using the mouse in conjunction with **Ctrl** to select the entire sentence without dragging. (For help, refer to Table 3.1, earlier in this chapter.)

4. Use the double-clicking technique to select each of the following words in the first paragraph: *Global*, *Philadelphia*, *Texas*, *qualified*, *price*. Note that double-clicking selects the trailing space after a word, but not the trailing comma (as in *Philadelphia*,) or period (as in *Texas*. and *price*.).

5. Use the selection-bar technique to select the first line of the document. Extend the selection to include the first four lines. Shorten the selection to include the first two lines.

USING EDIT, REPLACE TO REPLACE FOUND TEXT

In Chapter 2, you learned how to use Edit, Find to search for text in a document. Here you'll learn how to use the Edit, Replace command to search for text and replace it with new text of your choice.

Edit, Replace is one of Word's most powerful commands. Let's say you typed a 100-page document that made frequent reference to a man named *Pablo Sitauskus* and then you found out that the correct spelling was *Sitauskis*. Normally you'd have to find each occurrence of *Sitauskus* and retype it—an ugly task considering the length of the document. Using Edit, Replace, however, you could issue a single command that would automatically (and rapidly) replace every occurrence of *Sitauskus* with *Sitauskis*.

To use Edit, Replace to replace found text in a document:

- Choose *Edit, Replace* to open the Replace dialog box.

- In the Find What text box, type the *search text* (the text you wish to find).

- In the Replace With text box, type the *replace text* (the text you wish to replace the search text).

- If necessary, check your desired search option(s)—*Match Case, Find Whole Words Only, Use Pattern Matching,* or *Sounds Like*.

- If necessary, click on the Search list box and select *Down* (to search from the insertion point to the end of the document), *Up* (to search fromn the insertion point to the beginning of the document), or *All* (to search the entire document).

- Click on *Find Next* (or press *Enter*); Word highlights the first occurrence of your search text.

- Click on either *Replace* (to replace the found text and search for the next occurrence), *Find Next* (to leave the found text unchanged and search for the next occurrence), or *Replace All* (to replace all occurrences of the search text throughout the rest of the document).

- Repeat the previous step as many times as necessary until you have searched through the entire document, or cancel your search at any time by clicking on *Cancel*.

- Close the Replace dialog box.

Let's use the procedures just described to find and replace some text in the active document:

1. Choose **Edit, Replace** to open the Replace dialog box (see Figure 3.4).

2. In the Find What text box, type **20**. This is the text we will search for and replace.

Figure 3.4   **The Replace dialog box**

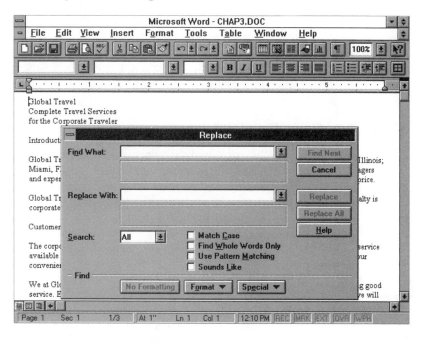

3. Press **Tab** to select the Replace With text box and then type **50**. This is the text that will replace the search text (*20*).

4. Uncheck (deselect) the **Find Whole Words Only** and **Match Case** options, if necessary.

5. If necessary, click on **All** in the Search list box to search the entire document.

6. Click on **Find Next** to find the first occurrence of *20*.

7. Click on **Replace** to replace *20* with *50* and to search for the next occurrence of *20*.

8. Click on **Find Next** to leave *20-30%* unchanged and search for the next occurrence of *20*.

9. Click on **Replace** to replace *20* with *50* and search for the next occurrence of *20*. The message

   ```
   Word has finished searching the document.
   ```

   is displayed.

10. Click on **OK** to remove the message. Because there are no more occurrences of *20*, the insertion point moves back to where it was when you began the search.

11. Click on **Close** to close the Replace dialog box.

You'll have a chance to use the Replace All command in the "Practice Your Skills" section at the end of this chapter.

MOVING AND COPYING TEXT

Another of Word's powerful editing features is its ability to move and copy text within a document. You can, for example, quickly and easily move a table of numbers from the top of the fifth page of a business report to the bottom of the 11th page, or copy a four-line address to several different locations within the body of a letter.

THE CLIPBOARD

Windows provides a temporary storage area called the *Clipboard* for those times when you move or copy text. When selected text is *cut* (removed) or copied, it is placed on the Clipboard. *Pasting* inserts a copy of the Clipboard contents before the insertion point. You'll notice that the Paste button, which is the ninth from the left on the toolbar, resembles a clipboard. Entries remain on the Clipboard, either until you cut or copy another entry to it, or until you exit from Windows.

MOVING TEXT

To move text within a document:

- Select the text to be moved.

- Choose *Edit, Cut* (or click on the *Cut* button—seventh from the left in the toolbar; it shows a pair of scissors) to cut the selected text from the document and place it on the Clipboard. See the previous section for a discussion of the Clipboard.

- Place the insertion point where you want to move this text.

- Choose *Edit, Paste* (or click on the *Paste* button) to paste the cut text before the insertion point.

Let's practice moving text from one location to another within a document:

1. If you aren't at the beginning of the document, press **Ctrl+Home** to move there, and then drag in the selection bar to select the paragraph beginning with *Global Travel is a full-service* and the trailing blank line.

2. Choose **Edit, Cut** to remove the selected text from the document and place it on the Windows Clipboard.

3. Place the insertion point before the *G* in *Global Travel has five*.

4. Choose **Edit, Paste** to paste a copy of the Clipboard contents before the insertion point (see Figure 3.5).

COPYING TEXT

To copy text within a document:

- Select the text to be copied.

- Choose *Edit, Copy* (or click on the *Copy* button—eighth from the left in the toolbar; it shows two identical pages) to copy the selected text to the Clipboard.

Figure 3.5   **Page 1 of CHAP3.DOC, after pasting**

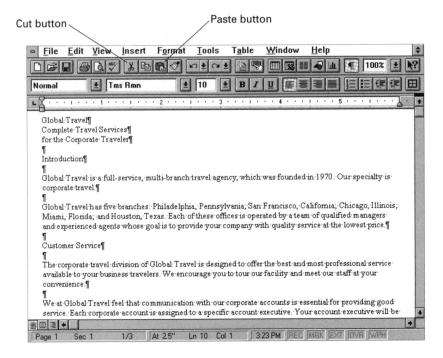

Cut button

Paste button

- Place the insertion point where you want to copy this text.

- Choose *Edit, Paste* (or click on the *Paste* button) to paste the Clipboard text before the insertion point.

Now let's practice copying text within a document:

1. Select the first four lines of the document (the three-line page heading and the trailing blank line).

2. Choose **Edit, Copy** to place a copy of the selected text on the Clipboard. Note that the selected text is not removed from the document, as it was when you chose Edit, Cut.

3. Use **F5** (Go To) to place the insertion point at the top of page 2.

4. Choose **Edit, Paste** to paste a copy of the Clipboard contents before the insertion point (see Figure 3.6).

Figure 3.6   **Page 2 of CHAP3.DOC, after pasting**

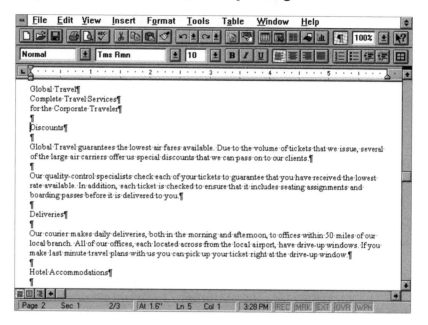

As demonstrated earlier, you can also use the toolbar to paste text from the Clipboard. Let's try this out:

1. Place the insertion point at the top of page 3.

2. Click on the **Paste** button (the one showing a clipboard). Because a copy of the text is still on the Clipboard, you do not need to copy the text again before pasting.

3. Use **File, Save As** to save the document as *mychap3*.

USING UNDO TO REVERSE YOUR LAST OPERATION

Word provides an Undo command that allows you to reverse (undo) one or more of the most recent operations that you have performed.

Use either of the following Undo methods to reverse your last operation:

*   Choose *Edit, Undo*.

*   Click on the *Undo* button (11th from the left in the toolbar, it shows an arrow moving counterclockwise).

You can also repeat an action that you've canceled (with Undo) by using the Redo command. This is the equivalent of choosing the Repeat option from the Edit menu. To repeat an action that you've undone, click on the Redo button (to the right of the Undo button) in the toolbar.

Note: It is possible to Undo or Redo any of several actions, not just the most recent one. To list several of the most recent procedures that you've performed or undone, click on the down arrow button immediately to the right of the Undo or Redo button, respectively. Then drag to select the operation that you wish to undo or redo.

Let's delete a block of text from MYCHAP3.DOC and then use the Undo feature to undelete this text:

1. Select the heading *Flight Insurance* near the top of page 3.

2. Press **Del** to delete the text. (Because you used Del rather than Edit, Cut or Edit, Copy, the text has not been placed on the Clipboard.)

3. Click on **Edit** to display the Edit drop-down menu. Observe the Undo option at the top; it reads *Undo Clear.* The Edit, Undo option changes to reflect the operation to be undone.

4. Choose **Undo Clear** to restore your deleted text.

Now let's use the toolbar Undo button to reverse a potentially catastrophic text-replacement mistake:

1. Select the entire document. (Choose **Edit, Select All.**)

2. Type your first initial. Word prompts:

   ```
   Are you sure you want to replace the current
   selection?
   ```

   This prompt is intended as a safeguard to prevent you from accidentally replacing (thus deleting) the entire contents of your document. For now, we'll ignore its warning.

3. Press **Enter** (or click on **Yes**) to replace the entire document with your first initial. Surprise! All that's left in the document window is a single letter. We should have taken Word's warning more seriously.

4. Click on the **Undo** button (the 11th one from the left) to restore the original text. All is well.

5. Deselect to avoid deleting the entire document again.

6. Choose **File, Save** to update the document—that is, to save it with the same name and in the same location.

7. Close the document window.

PRACTICE YOUR SKILLS

In Chapters 2 and 3, you've learned how to navigate within a document, and how to select, replace, move, and copy text. The following two Practice Your Skills activities give you the opportunity to apply these techniques to realistic word processing situations.

Follow these steps to produce the final document shown in Figures 3.7 and 3.8 from the original document PRAC3A.DOC:

1. Open **PRAC3A.DOC** (Chapter 2). (You'll have to scroll through your WRKFILES directory.)

2. Replace all occurrences of *Mayco* with **Macco**. (**Hint:** Select **Replace All** in the Replace dialog box.)

3. Move the second paragraph on page 1 (beginning with *Congratulations to all*), and the trailing blank line, to before the first paragraph on page 1 (beginning with *As we expected*).

4. Copy the three-line heading and the trailing blank line on the top of page 1 to the top of page 2.

5. Save the document as **myprac3a** (Chapter 2).

6. Print the document and compare it to Figures 3.7 and 3.8 (Chapter 1).

7. Close the document (Chapter 1).

Follow these steps to produce the final document shown in Figures 3.9 and 3.10 from the original document PRAC3B.DOC:

1. Open **PRAC3B.DOC** (Chapter 2).

2. Replace all case-matching occurrences of *Territory* with **Region** (Chapter 3).

3. Move the heading *3. Computer Study* and the subsequent paragraph and paragraph marks on page 1 to before the heading *2. Regional Updates* (Chapter 3).

4. Change *3. Computer Study* to **2. Computer Study** (Chapter 1).

Figure 3.7   **Page 1 of the completed document MYPRAC3A.DOC**

Macco Plastics Inc.
Quarterly Sales Report
First Quarter

1. Introduction

Congratulations to all of you! An initial review of the sales figures for the nation reveals a surge in sales in all of Macco's sales areas. Major new clients have been added and many new products are on the way.

As we expected when we entered the field, computer-related products, such as keyboard housings and protective carrying cases, are accounting for a major portion of this upswing.

2. Regional Updates

Midwestern Territory

After several years of falling sales due to the slump in the auto industry, Blair Williams and his folks have something to celebrate. The recent boom in auto manufacturing has led to renewed demand of Macco Products in Detroit.

Northeastern Territory

John Martinson and his group are doing a great job in Nashua. They have secured major contracts for a wide range of new and existing products. Much of this business is coming from Computer Equipment Corporation, a major client of Macco's.

Southern Territory

Mark Daley and his group have done a fine job of maintaining relations with Becker's Product Development Division in Boca Raton. They have been working closely with Becker to decrease manufacturing costs.

3. Computer Study

A companywide study will begin in March, under the direction of Cathy Donaldson and Bill Schuster in data processing, to determine how to most effectively implement automation in our firm. We will be making a large commitment to productivity gains via computerization sometime late this year.

Figure 3.8   **Page 2 of the completed document MYPRAC3A.DOC**

Macco Plastics Inc.
Quarterly Sales Report
First Quarter

4. Quarterly Meeting

The quarterly meeting will take place in Memphis this time. You will find the agenda attached to this report.

5. Conclusion

If the recovery continues at the current pace, this year should be a banner year for all of us at Macco. We want to thank all of you for the outstanding jobs you have done and, most important, for standing by Macco in hard times. Keep up the good work!

John Smith
Regional Coordinator
Macco Plastics Inc.

Figure 3.9   **Page 1 of the completed document MYPRAC3B.DOC**

Macco Plastics Inc.
Quarterly Sales Report
First Quarter
February 27, 1994

1. Introduction

Congratulations to all of you! An initial review of the sales figures for the nation reveals a surge in sales
in all of Macco's sales regions. Major new clients have been added and many new products are on the
way.

As we expected when we entered the field, computer-related products, such as keyboard housings and
protective carrying cases, are accounting for a major portion of this upswing.

2. Computer Study

A companywide study will begin in March, under the direction of Cathy Donaldson and Bill Schuster in
data processing, to determine how to most effectively implement automation in our firm. We will be
making a large commitment to productivity gains via computerization sometime late this year.

3. Regional Updates

Midwestern Region

After several years of falling sales due to the slump in the auto industry, Blair Williams and his folks
have something to celebrate. The recent boom in auto manufacturing has led to renewed demand of
Macco Products in Detroit.

Northeastern Region

John Martinson and his group are doing a great job in Nashua. They have secured major contracts for a
wide range of new and existing products. Much of this business is coming from Computer Equipment
Corporation, a major client of Macco's.

Southern Region

Mark Daley and his group have done a fine job of maintaining relations with Becker's Product
Development Division in Boca Raton. They have been working closely with Becker to decrease
manufacturing costs.

Figure 3.10   **Page 2 of the completed document MYPRAC3B.DOC**

Macco Plastics Inc.
Quarterly Sales Report
First Quarter
February 27, 1994

4. Quarterly Meeting

The quarterly meeting will take place in Memphis this time. You will find the agenda attached to this
report.

5. Conclusion

If the recovery continues at the current pace, this year should be a banner year for all of us at Macco. We
want to thank all of you for the outstanding jobs you have done and, most important, for standing by
Macco in hard times. Keep up the good work!

John Smith
Regional Coordinator
Macco Plastics Inc.

5. Change *2. Regional Updates* to **3. Regional Updates** (Chapter 1).

6. Add the current date as a fourth line to the three-line heading on the top of page 1 (Chapter 1).

7. Copy the entire date line into the heading on the top of page 2 (Chapter 3).

8. Save the document as **myprac3b** (Chapter 2).

9. Print the document and compare it to Figures 3.9 and 3.10 (Chapter 1).

10. Close the document (Chapter 1).

SUMMARY

In this chapter, you learned how to use the mouse, keyboard, and menus to select text; how to use the Edit, Replace command to replace found text; how to move and copy text; and how to use the Undo command to reverse one or more of your most recent operations.

Here's a quick reference guide to the Word features introduced in this chapter:

Desired Result	How to Do It
Select text by dragging	Point at one end of the text to be selected; press and hold the mouse button; drag the mouse pointer to the other end of the text; release the mouse button.
Select text by using Shift	Place the insertion point at one end of the text; press and hold **Shift**; click at the other end of the text; release **Shift**.
Select a word	Point anywhere inside the word and double-click the mouse button.
Select a sentence	Point anywhere inside the sentence; press and hold **Ctrl**; click the mouse button; release **Ctrl**.

Desired Result	How to Do It
Select a line	Point in the selection bar next to the line and click the mouse button.
Select multiple lines	Point in the selection bar next to the first or last line of text to be selected; press and hold the mouse button; drag down or up; release the mouse button.
Select a paragraph	Point in the selection bar next to the paragraph and double-click the mouse button.
Select an entire document	Choose **Edit, Select All**; or, point anywhere in the selection bar; press and hold **Ctrl**, click the mouse button; and then release **Ctrl**.
Extend an existing selection	While holding **Shift**, click beyond the existing selection.
Shorten an existing selection	While holding **Shift**, click inside the existing selection.
Deselect an existing selection	Make another selection; or, click the mouse button in the text area anywhere outside the existing selection.
Replace found text in a document	Choose **Edit, Replace**; type the search text in the Find What text box; type the replace text in the Replace With text box; select your desired search options; click on **Find Next** (or press **Enter**) to find the first occurrence; then click on either **Replace, Find Next**, or **Replace All**; repeat the above step as many times as necessary until you have searched through the entire document (or cancel your search at any time by clicking on **Cancel**); close the **Replace** dialog box.

Desired Result	How to Do It
Move text within a document	Select the text to be moved; choose **Edit, Cut** (or click on the toolbar **Cut** button); place the insertion point where you want to move this text; choose **Edit, Paste** (or click on the toolbar **Paste** button).
Copy text within a document	Select the text to be copied; choose **Edit, Copy** (or click on the toolbar **Copy** button); place the insertion point where you want to copy this text; choose **Edit, Paste** (or click on the toolbar **Paste** button).
Undo your last operation	Choose **Edit, Undo** (or click on the toolbar **Undo** button).

In the next chapter, you'll learn the basics of character formatting—how to apply and remove character styles (such as bold and italic) and how to change fonts (typestyles) and point sizes of your text.

IF YOU'RE STOPPING HERE

If you need to break off here, please exit from Word. If you want to proceed directly to the next chapter, please do so now.

CHAPTER 4: CHARACTER FORMATTING

Applying Font
Styles

Applying Fonts
and Point Sizes

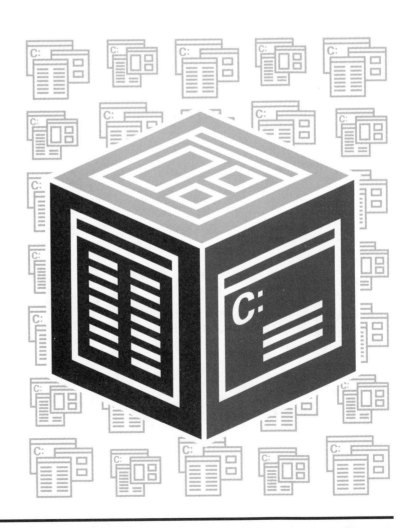

The overall effectiveness of a document is directly related to the way it looks. A brilliantly written business report, for example, can be severely undermined by an inappropriate typestyle, print too small to read comfortably, a dizzying barrage of italics or underlining, tables whose columns don't line up, an overbusy page layout, and so on. These next three chapters are devoted to *formatting*—controlling the way your documents look. We'll proceed logically: This chapter covers Word's smallest formatting units, *characters*; Chapter 5 covers its intermediate units, *paragraphs*; and Chapter 6 covers its largest units, *pages*.

When you're done working through this chapter, you will know

- How to apply and remove font styles
- How to change fonts and point sizes

APPLYING FONT STYLES

You can enhance the appearance of your documents and emphasize selected text through the application of font styles (bold, italic, underline, and so on). In this book, for example, we chose to bold certain headings (such as **Desired Result** and **How to Do It**, which appear in each chapter's Summary) and italicize new terms (such as *font styles*). Word provides two methods for applying font styles: the Font dialog box (accessed by issuing the Format, Font command) and the font style buttons in the Formatting toolbar.

 ### USING THE FONT DIALOG BOX TO APPLY FONT STYLES

To use the Font dialog box to apply font styles:

- Select the desired text.
- Choose *Format, Font* to open the Font dialog box.
- Click on the tab of the Font folder, if necessary.
- Select your desired font style options.
- Click on *OK* (or press *Enter*) to apply your chosen styles.

To use the Font dialog box to remove font styles, follow the procedure just described, selecting Regular in the Font Style list.

If you are not running Word, please start it now. Let's begin by opening a new document and modifying its font styles:

1. Click on the **Open** button (the toolbar button showing an open file folder) to display the Open dialog box.

2. If your WRKFILES directory is not already selected, select it now.

3. In the File Name list box, double-click on **chap4.doc** to open the document.

4. Select **Introduction**, near the top of the document.

5. Choose **Format, Font** to open the Font dialog box. Notice that the Font dialog box contains two folders: the Font folder and the Character Spacing folder (see Figure 4.1). (If you cannot see the contents of the Font folder, click on its tab to display them.) Under Font Style, the current selection is *Regular*. The Preview box, in the lower-right portion of the dialog box, displays the currently selected text.

Figure 4.1   **The Font dialog box**

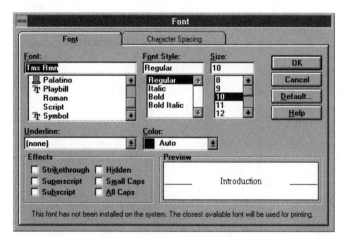

6. In the Font Style list box, select (click on) the **Bold** option. Note that the Preview box shows you how your style choice (Bold) will look when applied to the selected text.

7. Click on **OK** (or press **Enter**) to bold your selected text and return to the document.

8. Deselect **Introduction** to verify that it is bolded. You can see font styles better when the text is deselected.

9. Select **Customer Service**, the next heading on page 1.

10. Choose **Format, Font** to open the Font dialog box. Under Font Style, select the **Bold** option, and then click on **OK** (or press **Enter**) to bold *Customer Service.*

Now let's see how to remove the font style that you just applied and then restore it:

1. If **Customer Service** is not selected, select it now.

2. Choose **Format, Font**.

3. Under Font Style, select **Regular**, and then click on **OK** (or press **Enter**) to unbold *Customer Service.*

4. Choose **Edit, Undo Font Formatting** to reverse step 3—that is, to rebold *Customer Service.*

Let's use the Font dialog box to apply multiple styles (italic and underline) to your document's first line:

1. Select **Global Travel**, the first line.

2. Choose **Format, Font**.

3. Under Font Style, select **Italic**. Observe the Preview box text; the text is italicized.

4. Click on the **down arrow** next to the Underline list box to display Word's underline options. Click on **Single** to apply a single underline. Observe the Preview box; the text is now italicized *and* underlined.

5. Click on **OK** (or press **Enter**) to italicize and underline your selected text, *Global Travel*. Deselect the text to see the multiple styles more clearly.

6. Select **Global Travel** again.

7. Choose **Format, Font**.

8. Select the **Regular** font style, and then click on **OK** to remove the italic character style. Deselect *Global Travel* to verify that the italics (but not the underline) have been removed, as shown in Figure 4.2.

 ## USING THE FORMATTING TOOLBAR TO APPLY FONT STYLES

Located just below the toolbar, the Formatting toolbar provides quick access to font style options, including bold, italic, and underline.

To use the formatting toolbar to apply font styles:

- Select the desired text.

Figure 4.2   **Global Travel, after removing italics**

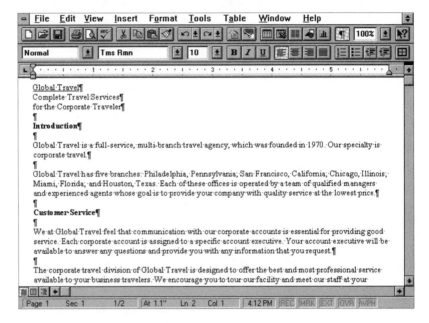

- Click on the desired font style button.

To use the Formatting toolbar to remove font styles:

- Select the desired text.

- Click on the button of the font style you wish to remove.

When you wish to remove all font styles from your selected text, use this shortcut: Press *Ctrl+Spacebar.*

Let's practice using the Formatting toolbar to apply font styles:

1. Move to the top of the document.

2. Select the paragraph beginning with *Global Travel has five branches* (double-click in the selection bar). Do not include the trailing blank line.

3. Click on the Bold button (the button with a bold **B**, in the middle of the Formatting toolbar) to bold the entire paragraph. Note that the button now appears to be pushed in.

4. Choose **Format, Font**. Note that the Bold font style is selected. Regardless of how you apply font styles—by using

the Formatting toolbar or the Font dialog box—these styles are reflected in both places.

5. Select the **Regular** font style, and then click on **OK**. Observe the Bold button; it no longer appears pushed in.

6. Click on the **Bold** button to rebold the selected text.

7. Click on the **Italic** button (the button with an italicized *I* to the right of the Bold button) to italicize the text.

8. Click on the **Underline** button (the button with an underlined U to the right of the Italic button) to single-underline the text (see Figure 4.3).

Figure 4.3   **Selected text, after applying bold, italic, and underline font styles**

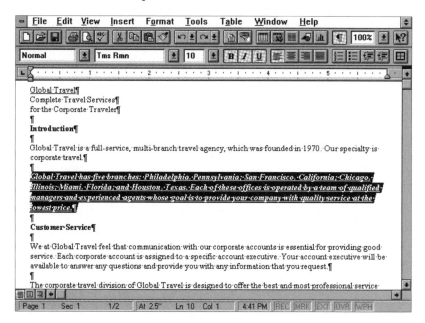

Now let's use the Ctrl+Spacebar technique to remove all font styles from your selected text:

1. If the paragraph *Global Travel has five branches* is not selected, select it now.

2. Press **Ctrl+Spacebar** to remove all font styles from the selected text. Note that this removal is reflected in the font style buttons on the Formatting toolbar.

PRACTICE YOUR SKILLS

1. Verify that your font style removal is also reflected in the Font dialog box.

2. Select the entire document and then italicize it.

3. Use the **Undo** command to reverse step 2.

4. Remove the underline from the first line of the heading (Global Travel); then bold and italicize it.

COPYING FONT STYLES

Once you have applied one or more font styles to your selected text, you can easily reapply (repeat) these styles to newly selected text. To do this:

- Select the new text.

- Choose *Edit, Repeat Font Formatting*, or press the *F4* (Repeat) shortcut key.

Note: If you wish to use the technique just described to repeat multiple font styles (for example, bold *and* italic), you must have applied these font styles through the Font dialog box. If you attempt to repeat multiple font styles that you applied by using the Formatting toolbar, only the last font style will be repeated.

Let's use the F4 key to repeat font styles:

1. Scroll to the bottom of the document. (Drag the vertical scroll box to the bottom of the scroll bar.)

2. Select **Flight Insurance**.

3. Choose **Format, Font**.

4. Select the **Italic** font style. In the Underline list box, click on **Single**. Then click on **OK** to italicize and underline the selected text.

5. Select **Telex**.

6. Open the Edit menu (click on **Edit**). Observe the shortcut key for the Repeat Font Formatting command—it is Ctrl+Y. Close the Edit menu (click on **Edit** again).

7. Press **F4** (Repeat) to repeat your last font style. Note that the selected text (*Telex*) is now italicized and underlined.

8. Use **F5** (Go To) to move to the top of page 2.

9. Select **Complete Travel Services**. Click on the **Bold** button, then click on the **Italic** button to bold and italicize the selected text.

10. Move to the top of the document and select **Complete Travel Services**.

11. Press **F4** (Repeat) to attempt to repeat your bold/italic styles. Deselect and observe the text. Because you used the Formatting toolbar, pressing F4 repeated only the *last* font style: italic. To ensure that *all* font styles are repeated, you should apply multiple font styles through the Font dialog box.

12. Reselect **Complete Travel Services** and click on the **Bold** button to correct the style.

13. Use **File, Save As** to save the disk file as **mychap4**.

PRACTICE YOUR SKILLS

1. Bold the heading **International Travel**.

2. Use **F4** (Repeat) to bold the remaining headings: **Corporate Profiles, Worldwide Services, Discounts, Deliveries, Auto Rentals, Hotel Accommodations, Additional Services, Personal Vacations, Flight Insurance,** and **Telex**.

3. Remove the italics and underlining from **Flight Insurance** and **Telex**.

4. Use the **Font** dialog box to bold and italicize (choose the **Bold Italic** option) **for the Corporate Traveler** at the top of page 1.

5. Use **F4** to repeat these multiple styles to **Global Travel** and **for the Corporate Traveler** at the top of page 2.

6. Compare your document to the printouts depicted in Figures 4.4 and 4.5.

7. Update the disk file (use **File, Save**).

Figure 4.4   **Page 1 of MYCHAP4.DOC**

Global Travel
Complete Travel Services
for the Corporate Traveler

Introduction

Global Travel is a full-service, multi-branch travel agency, which was founded in 1970. Our specialty is corporate travel.

Global Travel has five branches: Philadelphia, Pennsylvania; San Francisco, California; Chicago, Illinois; Miami, Florida; and Houston, Texas. Each of these offices is operated by a team of qualified managers and experienced agents whose goal is to provide your company with quality service at the lowest price.

Customer Service

We at Global Travel feel that communication with our corporate accounts is essential for providing good service. Each corporate account is assigned to a specific account executive. Your account executive will be available to answer any questions and provide you with any information that you request.

The corporate travel division of Global Travel is designed to offer the best and most professional service available to your business travelers. We encourage you to tour our facility and meet our staff at your convenience.

International Travel

We offer complete international itinerary assistance. We maintain a supply of passport and visa applications so that we can provide the necessary papers to our clients with minimum delay. Our International Rate Program guarantees you fast and accurate pricing, no matter how complicated the itinerary.

Corporate Profiles

Your company profile will be stored in our computer, and individual profiles will be maintained on each frequent traveler. Each profile will contain information regarding passport information, seating preference, car rental preference, frequent-flyer membership number, and corporate discount numbers. This information ensures that we can provide frequent travelers fast, cost-effective itineraries.

Worldwide Services

Global Travel's Reservation Center will handle all of your weekend and after-hour reservations and changes. The reservation center can be dialed toll-free 24 hours a day. The worldwide service emergency numbers will be clearly marked on your travel itineraries.

Figure 4.5   **Page 2 of MYCHAP4.DOC**

Global Travel
Complete Travel Services
for the Corporate Traveler

Discounts

Global Travel guarantees the lowest air fares available. Due to the volume of tickets that we issue, several of the large air carriers offer us special discounts that we can pass on to our clients.

Our quality-control specialists check each of your tickets to guarantee that you have received the lowest rate available. In addition, each ticket is checked to ensure that it includes seating assignments and boarding passes before it is delivered to you.

Deliveries

Our courier makes daily deliveries, both in the morning and afternoon, to offices within 20 miles of our local branch. All of our offices, each located across from the local airport, have drive-up windows. If you make last minute travel plans with us you can pick up your ticket right at the drive-up window.

Auto Rentals

We guarantee the lowest prices on all car rentals. We will match the type of car with the information provided in the profile for each of your frequent travelers. Each car that is rented through Global Travel carries an extra $50,000 worth of liability insurance.

Hotel Accommodations

Our Corporate Hotel Program is the most competitive and comprehensive program in the world, offering corporate travelers cost savings and extra amenities in most business locations. Global Travel has access to more than 10,000 hotels worldwide, with a range of rooms from economy to luxury. This selection offers your corporate travelers the accommodations they want with a cost savings of 10-30% off the regular rates.

Additional Services

Global Travel also provides the following services for our corporate customers:

Personal Vacations

Our corporate clients are invited to discuss their vacation and personal travel plans with an agent from Global Travel's Vacation Division. Our Vacation Division is skilled in both domestic and international travel.

Flight Insurance

We will supply all clients with $250,000 worth of flight insurance for every trip arranged through Global Travel.

Telex

Service is available for international hotel confirmations.

APPLYING FONTS AND POINT SIZES

You can change the shape and size of your selected text by changing the text's *font* and *point size*. The font determines the shape (typestyle) of the text; the point size determines the size of the font (one point equals ¹/₇₂ of an inch). The sentence you are reading, for example, is printed in 10-point Univers font. You can use the Font dialog box or the Formatting toolbar to apply fonts and point sizes.

Note: The specific fonts and point sizes that Word makes available for your use are dependent upon your currently selected printer. PostScript-type laser printers, for example, offer a large variety of fonts and point sizes, whereas low-end dot-matrix printers offer a much more limited selection.

USING THE FONT DIALOG BOX TO APPLY FONTS AND POINT SIZES

To use the Font dialog box to apply fonts and point sizes:

* Select the desired text.
* Choose *Format, Font* to open the Font dialog box.
* Select your desired font and/or point size.
* Click on *OK* (or press *Enter*).

Let's select some text and use the Font dialog box to change its font and point size:

1. Move to the top of the document.

2. Select the lines **Complete Travel Services** and **for the Corporate Traveler** in the heading at the top of page 1.

3. Choose **Format, Font**.

4. Scroll through the Font list box to view your available fonts. Note that the font names are listed in alphabetical order. Observe the current font (*Tms Rmn*, short for Times Roman) and the representative text in the Preview box.

5. Select **Helvetica**. You may need to scroll up through the list to find it. Observe the change in the Preview box text.
   Note: If Helvetica is not available, choose Arial, which is a similar font. In fact, you should feel free to select Arial font whenever we suggest Helvetica for the remainder of this book.

6. Scroll through the Size list box to view the available point sizes for the Helvetica font.

7. Select **12**. Observe the change in the Preview box text.

8. Click on **OK** to apply your chosen font and point size to the selected text. Deselect and compare your screen to Figure 4.6.

Figure 4.6   **Lines 2 and 3 of the heading, after changing the font and point size**

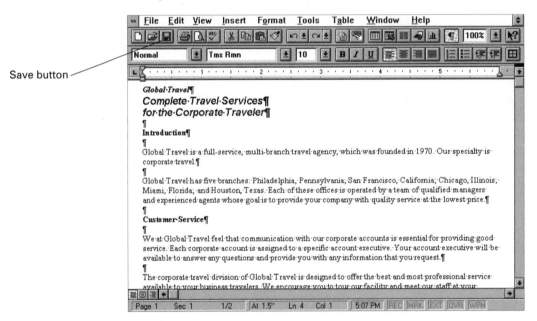

In a previous activity, you used F4 (Repeat) to repeat font styles. Now let's use F4 to repeat the font and point size:

1. Move to the top of page 2.

2. Select **Complete Travel Services** and **for the Corporate Traveler**, lines 2 and 3 in the page heading.

3. Press **F4** to repeat your last font style. Because you used the Font dialog box instead of the Formatting toolbar when you applied the font and point size on page 1, the selected text changes to Helvetica *and* 12 point.

4. Click on the **Save** button (the third from the left in the tool-bar, it shows a floppy disk) to update the document.

USING THE FORMATTING TOOLBAR TO APPLY FONTS AND POINT SIZES

To use the Formatting toolbar to apply fonts and point sizes:

• Select the desired text.

• Click on the down arrow of the *Font* or *Size* list boxes (respectively, the second and third boxes from the left in the Formatting toolbar).

• Select your desired font or point size.

Let's use the Formatting toolbar to change the font and point size:

1. Select **Global Travel**, the first line on page 2.

2. Open the Font list box in the Formatting toolbar (click on the **down arrow** to the right of the box). Note that the box currently displays *Tms Rmn* (or *Times New Roman*). Select **Helvetica**.

3. Open the Size list box in the Formatting toolbar. Note that the box currently displays *10*. Select **24** (you'll need to scroll).

PRACTICE YOUR SKILLS

1. Move to the top of page 1.

2. Change the font and point size of the first line, *Global Travel,* to **Helvetica** and **24**. (Hint: Use the Formatting toolbar.)

3. Deselect and compare your screen to Figure 4.7.

4. Save the disk file and close the document.

SUMMARY

In this chapter, you learned the basics of character formatting. You now know how to apply and remove font styles, and how to change fonts and point sizes.

Figure 4.7   **Global Travel, after changing the font and point size**

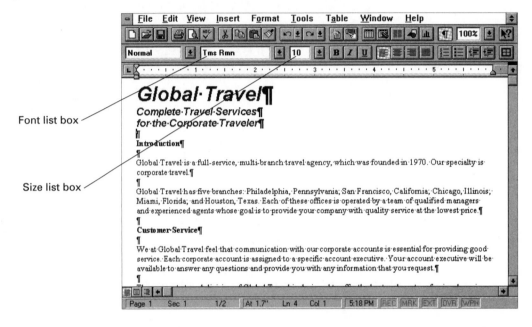

Font list box

Size list box

Here's a quick reference guide to the Word features introduced in this chapter:

Desired Result	How to Do It
Use the Font dialog box to apply font styles	Select the desired text; choose **For-mat, Font**; select your desired font style options; click on **OK** (or press **Enter**).
Use the Font dialog box to remove font styles	Follow the procedure just described, and choose the **Regular** font style option.
Use the Formatting tool-bar to apply font styles	Select the desired text; click on the de-sired font style button.
Use the Formatting tool-bar to remove font styles	Select the desired text; click on the button of the font style you wish to remove.

Desired Result	How to Do It
Remove all font styles from your selected text	Press **Ctrl+Spacebar**.
Repeat font formatting	Select the new text; choose **Edit, Repeat Font Formatting** (or press **F4**).
Use the Font dialog box to apply fonts and point sizes	Select the desired text; choose **Format, Font**; select your desired font and/or point size; click on **OK** (or press **Enter**).
Use the Formatting toolbar to apply fonts and point sizes	Select the desired text; click on the **down arrow** of the Font or Size boxes; select your desired font or point size.

In the next chapter, you will learn the basics of paragraph formatting. You'll find out how to work with tab stops and paragraph indents, create new lines within a paragraph, align paragraphs, and set line spacing.

IF YOU'RE STOPPING HERE

If you need to break off here, please exit Word. If you want to proceed directly to the next chapter, please do so now.

CHAPTER 5: PARAGRAPH FORMATTING

Working with Tabs

Setting Indents and Line Breaks

Using Shift+Enter to Create a New Line

Setting Paragraph Alignment

Setting Line Spacing

In Chapter 4, you learned the basics of character formatting. In this chapter, we'll move on to Word's intermediate unit of formatting: the paragraph. Many important document layout features are controlled at the paragraph level, including tab stops, indents, text alignment, and line spacing. Mastering paragraph formatting will greatly assist you in presenting professionally laid out, attractive documents.

When you're done working through this chapter, you will know

- How to set, change, and clear tab stops
- How to set and repeat paragraph indents
- How to create new lines within a paragraph
- How to align paragraphs
- How to set line spacing

WORKING WITH TABS

As you learned in Chapter 1, you use tabs to align text at preset tab stops across the page. This type of alignment is particularly important in tables, where several categories of information must line up in precise columns. In the first part of this chapter, you'll learn how to set, change, and clear custom tab stops.

SELECTING PARAGRAPHS FOR PARAGRAPH FORMATTING

Before you set custom tab stops, you must first select the desired paragraph or paragraphs. As you learned in the last chapter, when you select a paragraph for character formatting (character styles, font, point size, and so on), you must select the entire paragraph. However, when you select a paragraph for *paragraph formatting* (tab stops, indents, line spacing, and so on), you *do not* have to select the entire paragraph. To select a *single* paragraph for paragraph formatting, place the insertion point anywhere in the paragraph. You do not have to select (highlight) any characters. To select *multiple* paragraphs for paragraph formatting, select (highlight) a portion of each paragraph.

The techniques just described are paragraph selection shortcuts. If you feel more comfortable selecting entire paragraphs for paragraph formatting, please do so.

TAB TYPES

There are four types of tab stops available in Word. Figure 5.1 illustrates how tab stops align on your computer screen, and Table 5.1 defines each tab type.

Figure 5.1   **Tab types**

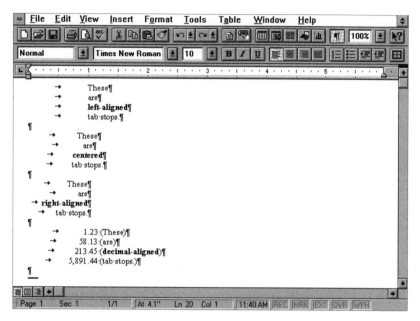

Table 5.1   **The Four Tab Types**

Type	How Tab Affects Text
Left-aligned	Text flows to the right of the tab stop.
Centered	Text is centered on the tab stop.
Right-aligned	Text flows to the left of the tab stop.
Decimal-aligned	Text aligns on the decimal point (used for numbers).

Note: By default, left-aligned tab stops are set at 0.5" increments between the margins (0.5", 1", 1.5", and so on). These default tab stops are displayed as small vertical lines at the bottom of the ruler (examples shown shortly).

SETTING CUSTOM TAB STOPS

Word allows you to create your own custom tab stops, and in doing so, to clear its default tab stops. To set custom tab stops:

- Select the desired paragraph(s).

- Click on the *Tab Alignment* button at the left of the tab ruler until the desired tab type is displayed (see Figure 5.2).

- Point at the desired tab-stop position in the ruler, and click the mouse button.

Figure 5.2   **Default tab stops and the Tab Alignment button**

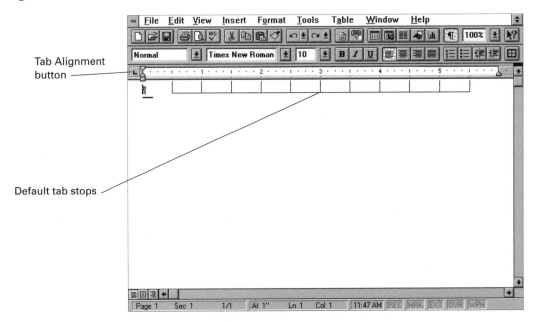

Your custom tab stop is set and all default tab stops to the left of your custom stop are automatically cleared.

As you click on the Tab Alignment button, it changes to indicate the type of tab: *left-aligned, centered, right-aligned,* or *decimal-aligned.* This is illustrated in Figure 5.3.

Figure 5.3 **The four tab indicators**

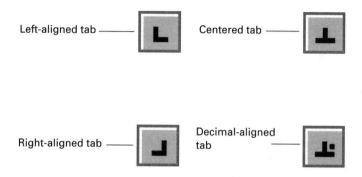

Left-aligned tab

Centered tab

Right-aligned tab

Decimal-aligned tab

If you are not running Word, please start it now.

Note: The further you progress in this book, the more succinct our activity instructions tend to be. For example, instead of saying "Click on the Open button, select the WRKFILES directory, and then double-click on CHAP5.DOC to open it," we now simply say "Open CHAP5.DOC from your WRKFILES directory." If you are unsure of how to perform a certain Word task, use the Index, the end-of-chapter quick reference guides, or Word Help to jog your memory.

Let's open a new document and begin our exploration of tabs by adding text to a tabbed table:

1. Open **chap5.doc** from your WRKFILES directory.

2. Move to the top of page 2.

3. Scroll down and examine the tabbed table following the heading *Discounts*. Note that the Paris and Sydney savings percentages (*20%* and *10%*) are misaligned. We will fix this in the next activity.

4. Place the insertion point in the first blank line after the tabbed table.

5. Press **Tab** to move the insertion point to the first tab stop (0.5" to the right) and then type **Hong Kong**.

6. Press **Tab** to move to the second tab stop (1" to the right) and then type **25%**.

7. Press **Enter** to create a new blank line. Compare your screen to Figure 5.4.

Figure 5.4   **Adding text to the Discounts tabbed table**

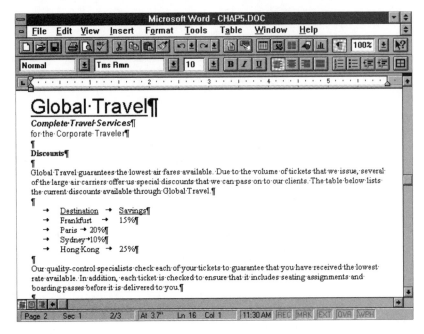

Now let's set some new left-aligned tab stops to fix the Paris and Sydney savings-percentage misalignments. First we need to select the entire table (all five lines). Let's use our multiple paragraph selection shortcut to do this:

1. Select all the text from *Savings* (in the first line) up to and including *Hong* (in the last line). Even though the first and last lines of the table are only partially highlighted, they are fully selected. Any paragraph formatting changes you now make will apply equally to all five lines.

2. Observe the ruler. Note that Word's default tab stops are set every half inch (0.5").

3. Observe that the Tab Alignment button is currently set to create a left-aligned tab (see Figure 5.3). Text flows to the right of a left-aligned tab stop. The Tab Alignment button

determines the alignment of the *next* tab stop that you set; a left-aligned tab stop is the default.

4. Point directly at the **1"** tick mark in the ruler. Click the mouse button to set a left-aligned tab stop at 1". Note that the default tab stop to the left of 1" has automatically been cleared.

5. Observe the text. The first column in the tabbed table is now 1" from the left margin.

PRACTICE YOUR SKILLS

1. Set a second left-aligned tab stop at **2.5"**. The second column in the table is now properly aligned.

2. Deselect the table, and compare your screen to Figure 5.5.

Figure 5.5   **Setting tab stops for the Discounts table**

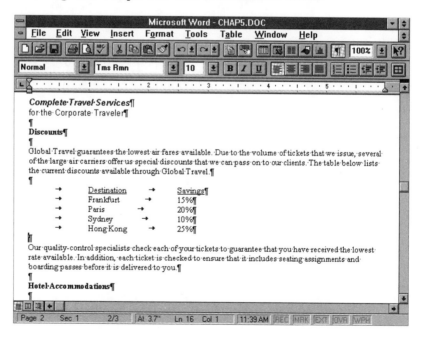

SETTING DIFFERENT TYPES OF TABS

As mentioned in the previous section, Word provides four types of tab stops: left-aligned, centered, right-aligned, and decimal-aligned. Let's use the ruler and the tab buttons to experiment with these:

1. Scroll down to the tabbed table following the heading *Hotel Accommodations*, near the middle of page 2.

2. Use the multiple paragraph selection shortcut to select the body (lower four lines) of the tabbed table.

3. Click once on the **Tab Alignment** tab button. It is now set to insert a centered tab (see Figure 5.3). Click a second time; it is now set to insert a right-aligned tab. Click a third time; it is set to insert a decimal-aligned tab. Click once again; the Tab Alignment button cycles back to the left-alignment setting.

4. Click twice on the **Tab Alignment** button to right-align the next tab stop you set.

5. Set a right-aligned tab stop at **3.5"**.

6. Click on the **Tab Alignment** button to decimal-align the next tab stop you set. Notice the decimal point in the button's icon. Decimal tabs are used to align numbers containing decimals.

7. Set a decimal tab stop at **5"**. Notice that the tab markers on the ruler reflect the type of tab set at each location.

PRACTICE YOUR SKILLS

1. Prepare to set tab stops for the heading (top line) of the tabbed table. (**Hint:** Use the single paragraph selection short-cut—place the insertion point anywhere within the heading.)

2. Set a centered tab stop at **2.5"**.

3. Set a right-aligned tab stop at **5"**.

4. Note that the heading and body columns are misaligned (see Figure 5.6). We will fix this in the next activity.

Figure 5.6   **The Hotel Accommodations table, misaligned**

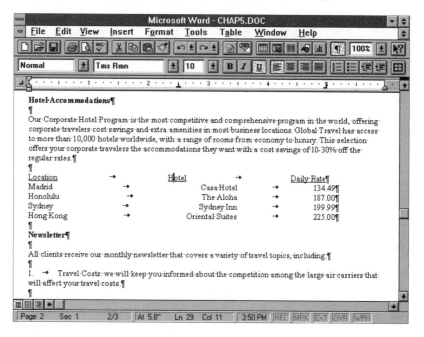

CHANGING THE POSITIONS OF CUSTOM TAB STOPS

Word allows you to quickly and easily change the positions of your custom tab stops. To do this:

- Select the desired paragraph(s).

- In the ruler, drag the custom tab stop to a new position.

CLEARING CUSTOM TAB STOPS

Word also allows you to quickly clear (delete) your custom tab stops. To do this:

- Select the desired paragraph(s).

- Drag the custom tab stop down into the text area.

Now let's fix the Hotel Accommodations table's misalignment by changing and clearing tabs:

1. Select the body (four lines) of the tabbed table.

2. Drag the decimal tab stop at 5" to **4.75"** to adjust the position of the table's numbers.

3. Place a centered tab stop at **2.5"**. Note that this causes a severe misalignment. Why? Because there is now an undesired tab stop in the ruler (the right-aligned tab stop at 3.5"), which prevents the final column of text (*Daily Rate*) from moving to its intended decimal tab-stop location at 4.75".

4. Drag the undesired right-aligned tab stop at 3.5" down off the ruler into the text area, and then release the mouse button to clear this tab stop. Note that the misalignment problem has been fixed.

5. Deselect and compare your screen to Figure 5.7.

6. Save the disk file as **mychap5** (use **File, Save As**).

Figure 5.7   **The Hotel Accommodations table, properly aligned**

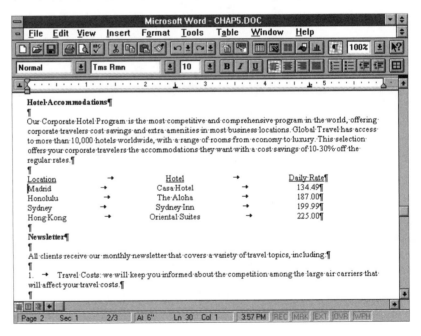

USING THE TABS DIALOG BOX TO MANAGE YOUR CUSTOM TAB STOPS

We've shown you how to use the ruler to manage your custom tab stops. This is generally the preferred method of tab management because it is quick, easy, and provides immediate visual feedback. You can, however, perform all of the tab-management tasks already presented in this chapter (setting, changing, and clearing tab stops) by using the Tabs dialog box (see Figure 5.8).

Figure 5.8   **The Tabs dialog box**

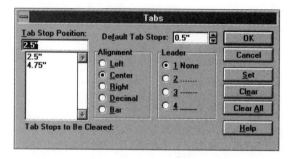

The advantage of using the Tabs dialog box is that you can specify exact tab-stop positions that you couldn't choose by using the mouse and ruler (for example, 3.12" or 6.78"). The disadvantages are that you must type in your tab-stop positions and that you only see how your tab-stop settings affect the selected paragraph(s) when you exit the Tabs dialog box.

To use the Tabs dialog box for managing your custom tab stops:

- Select the desired paragraph(s).

- Choose *Format, Tabs* to open the Tabs dialog box.

Note: The Tabs dialog box in Figure 5.8 reflects the settings for the tabbed table line beginning with *Madrid*.

- Enter your desired settings to change or clear tab stops.

- Click on *OK* (or press *Enter*).

Note: We recommend that you use the ruler for managing your custom tab stops, except in those rare instances when you need to set an exact tab-stop position that you cannot choose with the mouse and the ruler.

SETTING INDENTS AND LINE BREAKS

Margins define the upper, lower, left, and right page boundaries of an entire document (see "Setting Margins" in Chapter 6 for details on this Word feature). *Indents* define the left and right boundaries of selected paragraphs within a document.

By default, a paragraph's left and right indents are set equal to the document's left and right margins. However, you can modify a paragraph's left and/or right indents without changing the document's margins. Figure 5.9 illustrates the relationship between margins and indents.

Figure 5.9   **Margins and indents**

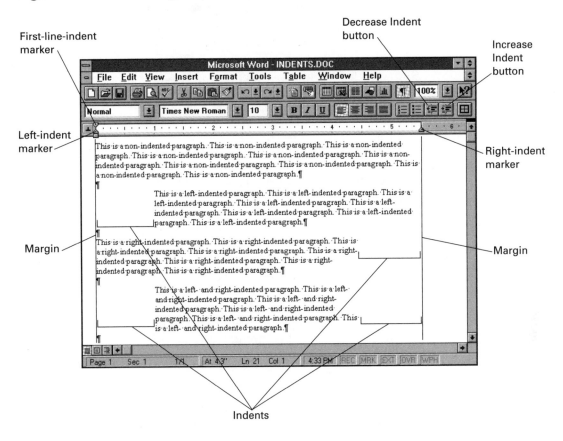

INDENT MARKERS

The ruler provides *indent markers* (displayed as triangles—see Figure 5.9) that you can use to control the positions of a selected paragraph's indents. There are three types of indent markers as shown in Figure 5.9.

Indent Marker Type	Location and Function
First-line indent	Upper-left triangle in the ruler; controls the left boundary for the first line of a paragraph
Left indent	Lower-left triangle in the ruler; controls the left boundary of every line in a paragraph but the first
Right indent	Triangle on the right end of the ruler; controls the right boundary for every line in a paragraph

SETTING INDENTS

Word allows you to quickly and easily set indents. To do this:

- Select the paragraph(s) you wish to indent.

- Drag the appropriate indent marker to your desired new position in the ruler.

By default, if you drag the left-indent marker, the first-line-indent marker does not move along with it. To left-indent every line of a paragraph, move both these markers by dragging the small box below the left-indent marker.

THE INCREASE INDENT AND DECREASE INDENT BUTTONS

If you wish to increase or decrease the left indentation of a paragraph, using existing tabs, you can also use the Increase Indent and Decrease Indent buttons in the Formatting toolbar (see Figure 5.9). The left border of the paragraph automatically moves to the next tab stop in the chosen direction. To do so:

- Select the paragraph(s) you wish to affect.

- To increase the left indent to the next tab stop, click on the *Increase Indent* button. To decrease the left-indent to the previous tab stop, click on the *Decrease Indent* button.

REPEATING PARAGRAPH FORMATTING

In the last chapter, you learned how to repeat character formatting. Word also allows you to repeat paragraph formatting. To do this:

- Format a paragraph.
- Select a new paragraph.
- Choose *Edit, Repeat Formatting* (or press *F4*).

Let's set some indents and then repeat them:

1. Move to the top of page 3.

2. Place the insertion point in the *Personal Vacations* heading. This heading is indented 0.5" from the left margin.

3. Observe the ruler. The left-indent marker and the first-line-indent marker (the lower and upper triangles near the left end of the ruler, respectively) are both at 0.5".

4. Place the insertion point in the paragraph beginning with *Our corporate clients*. This paragraph is not indented. Observe the ruler. The indent markers are set even with the margins.

5. Drag the **right-indent** marker—the triangle at the right end of the ruler—to **5.5"**. (Use the measurement in the center of the ruler as a guide.) A right indent creates a different right boundary for the selected paragraph.

6. Point the tip of the mouse pointer at the **left-indent** marker (the lower-left triangle), and drag the **left-indent** marker to 0.5" to change the left boundary of all lines of the paragraph but the first one.

7. Now, drag the **first-line-indent** marker to 0.5" to also change the left boundary of the first line of the paragraph. The entire paragraph now has a left indent of 0.5".

Now let's repeat our indent formatting:

1. Place the insertion point in the paragraph beginning with *We will supply all clients* (the next multiple-line paragraph on page 3).

2. Choose **Edit, Repeat Formatting** (or press **F4**) to repeat your indent formatting. Observe the new indents.

PRACTICE YOUR SKILLS

1. Format the paragraph beginning with *Telex service is available* with left and first-line indents at **0.5"** and a right indent at **5.5"**. (**Hint:** Use **F4**.)

2. Compare your screen to Figure 5.10.

Figure 5.10   **MYCHAP5.DOC, after indent formatting**

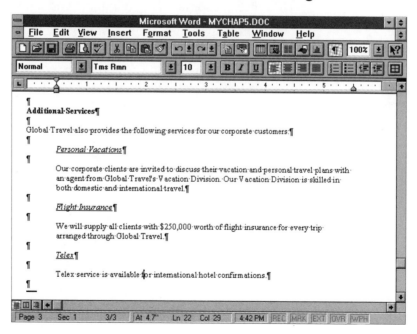

SETTING HANGING INDENTS

The term *hanging indent* is used to describe a format in which a paragraph's first line is left-indented less than all of its subsequent lines. In effect, the first line *hangs* over the rest. Hanging indents are commonly used for the paragraphs in bulleted or numbered lists, such as the list of bulleted instructions that appears next or the lists of numbered instructions in the activities throughout this book.

To create a hanging indent:

- Select the desired paragraph(s).

- If necessary, drag the *first-line indent* marker (the upper-left triangle) to the desired position.

- Drag only the *left-indent* marker (the lower-left triangle—not the small box below it) to the desired position (to the right of the first-line-indent marker).

Now let's set some hanging indents and then repeat them:

1. Scroll up to the heading *Newsletter* (near the bottom of page 2).

2. Place the insertion point in the paragraph beginning with *1. Travel Costs*.

3. Drag the **left-indent** marker (the lower-left triangle in the ruler) to **0.5"**. Observe your hanging indent: The second line is indented to 0.5", while the first line remains at the left margin—that is, unindented.

PRACTICE YOUR SKILLS

1. Repeat a 0.5" hanging indent for the paragraphs beginning with *2. Special Fares* and *3. Travel Basics*. (**Hint:** Use **F4**.)

2. Deselect and compare your screen to Figure 5.11.

Figure 5.11   **Setting hanging indents**

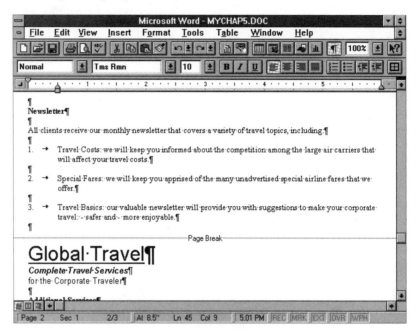

USING THE PARAGRAPH DIALOG BOX TO MANAGE YOUR INDENTS

As you've learned in previous sections of this chapter, you can manage custom tab stops by using the Formatting toolbar and the ruler or the Tabs dialog box. Similarly, you can manage indents by using the ruler or the Paragraph dialog box. The same advantages and disadvantages apply to both situations (you may want to review the section on the Tabs dialog box, earlier in this chapter). Again, we recommend that you use the ruler for managing your indents, except in those instances when you need to set an exact indent position that you cannot choose with the mouse and the ruler.

To use the Paragraph dialog box to manage your indents:

*   Select the desired paragraph(s).

*   Choose *Format, Paragraph* to open the Paragraph dialog box.

*   Enter your desired indent settings.

*   Click on *OK* (or press *Enter*).

USING SHIFT+ENTER TO CREATE A NEW LINE

When you press Enter to create a new line in a document, you also create a new paragraph. At times, this may be undesirable. For example, let's say that you wanted to insert a new line in the middle of a list within a hanging-indent paragraph. If you pressed Enter to create the new line, you would lose your indent. (Remember, pressing Enter creates a new first-line paragraph, and the first line of a hanging-indent paragraph is not indented.) To remedy this problem, Word allows you to use Shift+Enter to create a new line without creating a new paragraph. To do so:

- Place the insertion point where you want to end the current line and create a new line.

- Press *Shift+Enter*; Word inserts a *newline character* (↵) and creates a new line (without creating a new paragraph).

Let's take a moment to observe the difference between new paragraphs and new lines:

1. In the paragraph beginning with *3. Travel Basics*, place the insertion point to the left of the hyphen (-) in - *safer and*.

2. Press **Enter** to create a new paragraph. All text to the right of the insertion point is moved onto the next line. Because you've created a new paragraph, the first (and in this case, the only) line loses its hanging indent and moves back flush with the left margin.

3. Press **Backspace** to delete the paragraph mark and return the text to its original position.

4. Now press **Shift+Enter** to create a new line without creating a new paragraph. Your hanging indent is maintained. Note that pressing Shift+Enter ends the line with a newline character (↵) instead of with the usual paragraph mark (see Figure 5.12).

5. Press **Shift+Enter** to insert a blank line while maintaining the hanging indent. Notice that the newline character is also displayed on the blank line.

Figure 5.12   **Inserting a newline character**

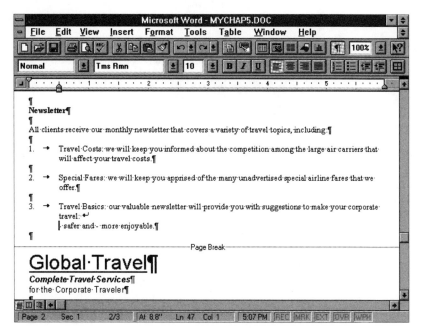

6. Place the insertion point to the left of the second hyphen (-) in the same paragraph, - *more enjoyable*.

7. Press **Shift+Enter** twice to create two new lines.

SETTING PARAGRAPH ALIGNMENT

Paragraph alignment determines how text is positioned between the left and right indents. Word provides four types of paragraph alignment. Figure 5.13 illustrates how paragraph alignment appears on your computer screen, and Table 5.2 defines each type of paragraph alignment.

Figure 5.13   **Paragraph alignment types**

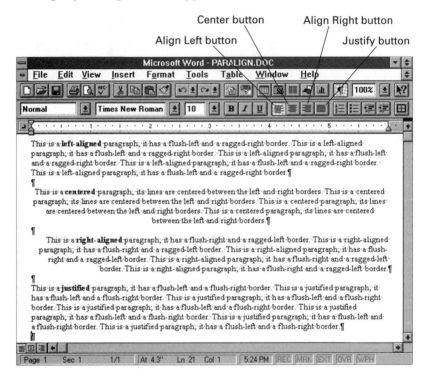

Table 5.2   **The Four Paragraph Alignment Types**

Type	Alignment
Left-aligned	Lines of text are *flush-left* (aligned evenly along the left indent) and *ragged-right* (aligned unevenly along the right indent). Left-aligned is the default paragraph-alignment setting.
Centered	Lines of text are centered between the indents. Both the left and right sides of a centered paragraph are ragged.

Table 5.2   **The Four Paragraph Alignment Types (Continued)**

Type	Alignment
Right-aligned	Lines of text are flush-right and ragged-left, the opposite of left-aligned.
Justified	Lines of text are both flush-left and flush-right. In a justified paragraph, Word adjusts the spacing between words so that they stretch from the left indent to the right indent.

To set paragraph alignment:

* Select the desired paragraph(s).

* Click on the appropriate alignment button in the Formatting toolbar (see Figure 5.13).

Note: You can also use the Alignment option in the Paragraph dialog box to align paragraphs; but, once again, we recommend using the Formatting toolbar.

Let's begin our paragraph-alignment activities by centering some paragraphs:

1. Place the insertion point anywhere within the first line of the document, *Global Travel*. Observe the text-alignment buttons (the four buttons to the left of the tab buttons in the Formatting toolbar). The Align Left text button (the one with the flush-left lines) is selected.

2. Click on the **Center** button in the Formatting toolbar (see Figure 5.13) to center each line of the selected paragraph between the left and right indents. In this example, the paragraph contains only one line.

3. Select lines 2 and 3 of the heading.

4. Click on the **Center** button to center both paragraphs.

5. Deselect and compare your screen with Figure 5.14.

Figure 5.14   **Centering paragraphs**

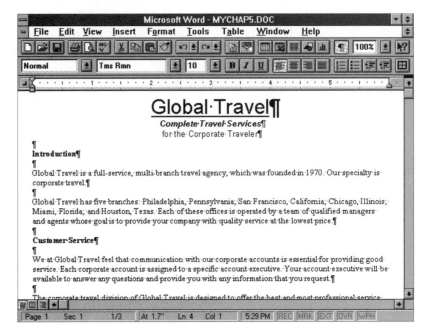

Now let's try the other paragraph alignments:

1. Place the insertion point in the paragraph beginning with *Global Travel has five branches* (the second multiple-line paragraph on page 1). Observe the last word in each line of the selected paragraph: Because the paragraph is left-aligned, text does not always reach the right indent before wrapping to the next line.

2. Click on the **Justify** button (see Figure 5.13). Observe the last word in each line: Word increases the spacing between words in the selected paragraph to fill each line (except the last line, which is too short) so that the text is even with both the left and right indents.

3. Click on the **Align Right** button (see Figure 5.13). Observe the text: Text in the current paragraph now aligns only with the right-indent marker.

4. Click on the **Align Left** button to return the paragraph to its original alignment.

PRACTICE YOUR SKILLS

1. Center all three lines of the heading on the top of page 2.

2. Repeat step 1 for the three-line heading on the top of page 3. (**Hint:** Use **F4.**)

3. Update the disk file (use **File, Save**).

SETTING LINE SPACING

Line spacing is the vertical distance between lines of text. Word provides six line-spacing options:

- *Single* (the default setting) sets the line spacing to one single line; Single always maintains a minimum of 12-point (1/6") spacing.

- *1.5 lines* sets the line spacing to a line-and-a-half.

- *Double* sets the line spacing to two lines.

- *At Least* allows you to specify a custom minimum line spacing.

- *Exactly* allows you to specify exact line spacing that will not adjust according to font size.

- *Multiple* sets the line spacing to accommodate more than one line; the default is three lines.

To set line spacing:

- Select the desired paragraph(s).

- Choose *Format, Paragraph* to open the Paragraph dialog box; you cannot set line spacing by using the Standard toolbar, Formatting toolbar, or ruler.

- Display the Indents and Spacing folder (click on its tab), if necessary.

- Select your desired line-spacing setting from the *Line Spacing* list box.

- Click on *OK* (or press *Enter*).

Let's use the above procedure to change the line spacing of MYCHAP5.DOC:

1. Move to the top of the document.

2. Select the entire document (choose **Edit, Select All**).

3. Choose **Format, Paragraph**. Examine the Indents and Spacing folder (click on its tab to display it, if necessary). Unlike the Formatting toolbar and ruler, the Paragraph dialog box provides access to *all* paragraph-formatting options and allows you to type in exact measurements.

4. Click on the **down arrow** of the **Line Spacing** list box to open the box and display the line-spacing choices.

5. Select **1.5 Lines** and then click on **OK** (or press **Enter**). Observe the text. The line spacing has changed from 1 to 1.5 lines (see Figure 5.15).

6. Choose **Format, Paragraph** and then open the **Line Spacing** list box (click on its **down arrow**).

7. Select **Double** and then click on **OK** (or press **Enter**). Observe the text. The line spacing has changed to 2 lines from its previous value of 1.5 lines.

Figure 5.15   **Changing the line spacing to 1.5 lines**

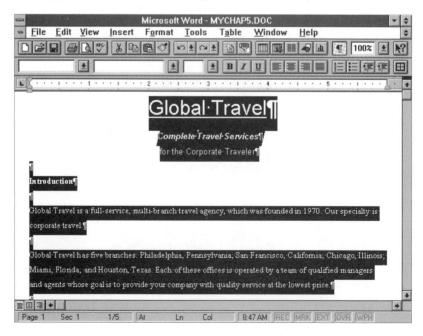

8. Choose **Format, Paragraph** and then open the **Line Spacing** list box.

9. Select **Single** and then click on **OK** (or press **Enter**). Observe the text. The line spacing has returned to its original value of 1 line.

10. Deselect the text to avoid inadvertently deleting the entire document.

Up to now, you've always saved the changes you made to your active document before closing it. However, you can close a document without saving the changes. Let's see how:

1. Choose **File, Close**. Word prompts:

   Do you want to save changes to MYCHAP5.DOC?

2. Click on **No** to save the document without saving the changes.

PRACTICE YOUR SKILLS

In Chapters 4 and 5, you learned the basics of character and paragraph formatting. The following two Practice Your Skills activities give you the opportunity to apply these formatting techniques to realistic word-processing situations.

Follow these steps to produce the final document shown in Figure 5.16 from the original document PRAC5A.DOC:

1. Open **prac5a.doc** (Chapter 2).

2. Select the entire document and remove all of its character formats (Chapters 3 and 4). (**Hint:** Use the **Ctrl+Spacebar** shortcut.)

3. Bold the following headings (Chapter 4):

   1. Introduction

   2. Computer Study

   3. Regional Updates

   4. Quarterly Meeting

   5. Conclusion

Figure 5.16   **The completed document MYPRAC5A.DOC**

Macco Plastics Inc.
Quarterly Sales Report
First Quarter

1. Introduction

Congratulations to all of you! An initial review of the sales figures for the nation reveals a surge in sales in all of Macco's sales regions. Major new clients have been added and many new products are on the way.

As we expected when we entered the field, computer-related products, such as keyboard housings and protective carrying cases, are accounting for a major portion of this upswing.

2. Computer Study

A companywide study will begin in March, under the direction of Cathy Donaldson and Bill Schuster in data processing, to determine how to most effectively implement automation in our firm. We will be making a large commitment to productivity gains via computerization sometime late this year.

3. Regional Updates

Midwestern Region

After several years of falling sales due to the slump in the auto industry, Blair Williams and his folks have something to celebrate. The recent boom in auto manufacturing has led to renewed demand of Macco Products in Detroit.

Northeastern Region

John Martinson and his group are doing a great job in Nashua. They have secured major contracts for a wide range of new and existing products. Much of this business is coming from Computer Equipment Corporation, a major client of Macco's.

Southern Region

Mark Daley and his group have done a fine job of maintaining relations with Becker's Product Development Division in Boca Raton. They have been working closely with Becker to decrease manufacturing costs.

**Figure 5.16   The completed document MYPRAC5A.DOC
(Continued)**

Macco Plastics Inc.
Quarterly Sales Report
First Quarter

4. Quarterly Meeting

The quarterly meeting will take place in Memphis this time. You will find the agenda attached to this report.

5. Conclusion

The following items will be discussed at the next managers' meeting:

A.   Marketing and sales strategies for the introduction of the new System 400 and System 500 product lines.

B.   Current available positions resulting from the early retirement program and normal attrition of personnel.

C.   Development of the new expense form to facilitate the prompt payment of - travel reimbursements - other out-of-pocket expenses and - commissions.

If the recovery continues at the current pace, this year should be a banner year for all of us at Macco. We want to thank all of you for the outstanding jobs you have done and, most important, for standing by Macco in hard times. Keep up the good work!

John Smith
Regional Coordinator
Macco Plastics Inc.

4. Using the Font dialog box, change the font and point size of the three-line heading on the top of page 2 to **12-point Helv** (Chapter 4).

5. Repeat the formatting in step 4 for the three-line heading on the top of page 1 (Chapter 4).

6. Scroll to the bottom of page 1 (Chapter 2).

7. In the paragraph beginning with *After several years* set left and first-line indents at **0.5"** and a right indent at **5.5"**.

8. Repeat the indents in step 7 for the paragraphs beginning with *John Martinson* and *Mark Daley.*

9. Center the three-line heading on the top of pages 1 and 2.

10. Save the disk file as **myprac5a** (Chapter 2).

11. Print the document and compare it to Figure 5.16 (Chapter 1).

12. Close the document (Chapter 1).

Follow these steps to produce the final document shown in Figure 5.17 from the original document PRAC5B.DOC:

1. Open **prac5b.doc** (Chapter 2).

2. Using the Font dialog box, italicize the first line on page 1, *Macco Plastics Inc.*, and change the point size to 24-point (Chapter 4).

3. Repeat the formatting in step 2 for the first line on page 2 (Chapter 4).

4. Single-underline the following subheadings (near the bottom of page 1) (Chapter 4):

   Midwestern Region

   Northeastern Region

   Southern Region

5. Clear (delete) the 2" left-aligned tab stop from the paragraph that begins with *B. Current available positions* (near the top of page 2).

6. Set a 0.5" hanging indent for the paragraph beginning with *A. Marketing and sales.*

Figure 5.17   **The completed document MYPRAC5B.DOC**

Macco Plastics Inc.

Quarterly Sales Report
First Quarter

1. Introduction

Congratulations to all of you! An initial review of the sales figures for the nation reveals a surge in sales in all of Macco's sales regions. Major new clients have been added and many new products are on the way.

As we expected when we entered the field, computer-related products, such as keyboard housings and protective carrying cases, are accounting for a major portion of this upswing.

2. Computer Study

A companywide study will begin in March, under the direction of Cathy Donaldson and Bill Schuster in data processing, to determine how to most effectively implement automation in our firm. We will be making a large commitment to productivity gains via computerization sometime late this year.

3. Regional Updates

Midwestern Region

After several years of falling sales due to the slump in the auto industry, Blair Williams and his folks have something to celebrate. The recent boom in auto manufacturing has led to renewed demand of Macco Products in Detroit.

Northeastern Region

John Martinson and his group are doing a great job in Nashua. They have secured major contracts for a wide range of new and existing products. Much of this business is coming from Computer Equipment Corporation, a major client of Macco's.

Southern Region

Mark Daley and his group have done a fine job of maintaining relations with Becker's Product Development Division in Boca Raton. They have been working closely with Becker to decrease manufacturing costs.

Figure 5.17   **The completed document MYPRAC5B.DOC
(Continued)**

Macco Plastics Inc.
Quarterly Sales Report
First Quarter

4. Quarterly Meeting

The quarterly meeting will take place in Memphis this time. You will find the agenda attached to this report.

5. Conclusion

The following items will be discussed at the next managers' meeting:

A.   Marketing and sales strategies for the introduction of the new System 400 and System 500 product lines.

B.   Current available positions resulting from the early retirement program and normal attrition of personnel.

C.   Development of the new expense form to facilitate the prompt payment of

   - travel reimbursements

   - other out-of-pocket expenses and

   - commissions.

If the recovery continues at the current pace, this year should be a banner year for all of us at Macco. We want to thank all of you for the outstanding jobs you have done and, most important, for standing by Macco in hard times. Keep up the good work!

John Smith
Regional Coordinator
Macco Plastics Inc.

7. Repeat the 0.5" hanging indent for the paragraphs beginning with *B. Current available positions* and *C. Development of the*.

8. In the paragraph beginning with *C. Development of the*, create new lines for:

   - **travel reimbursements**

   - **other out-of-pocket expenses and**

   - **commissions.**

9. Save the disk file as **myprac5b** (Chapter 1).

10. Print the document and compare it to Figure 5.17 (Chapter 1).

11. Close the document (Chapter 1).

SUMMARY

In this chapter, you learned the basics of paragraph formatting. You now know how to set, change, and clear tab stops; how to set and repeat paragraph indents; how to create new lines within a paragraph; how to align paragraphs; and how to set line spacing.

Here's a quick reference guide to the Word features introduced in this chapter:

Desired Result	How to Do It
Select a single paragraph for paragraph formatting	Place the insertion point anywhere in the paragraph.
Select multiple paragraphs for paragraph formatting	Select (highlight) at least a portion of each paragraph.
Create a custom tab stop	Select the desired paragraph(s); select the desired type of tab stop by clicking on the **Tab Alignment** button until the desired tab type appears; point at the desired tab-stop position in the ruler; click the mouse button.

Desired Result	How to Do It
Change the position of a custom tab stop	Select the desired paragraph(s); drag the custom tab stop (in the ruler) to a new position.
Clear (delete) a custom tab stop	Select the desired paragraph(s); drag the custom tab stop down into the text area.
Use the Tabs dialog box to manage custom tab stops	Select the desired paragraph(s); choose **Format, Tabs** to open the Tabs dialog box; enter your desired settings to set, change, or clear tab stops; click on **OK** (or press **Enter**).
Set indents	Select the paragraph(s) you wish to indent; drag the appropriate indent marker to your desired new position in the ruler.
Repeat paragraph formatting	Format a paragraph(s); select a new paragraph(s); choose **Edit, Repeat Formatting** or press **F4**.
Create a hanging indent	Select the desired paragraph(s); if necessary drag the **first-line-indent** marker to the desired position; drag only the **left-indent** marker to the desired position.
Use the Paragraph dialog box to manage your indents	Select the desired paragraph(s); choose **Format, Paragraph** to open the Paragraph dialog box; click on the tab of the Indents and Spacing folder, if necessary; enter your desired indent settings; click on **OK** (or press **Enter**).
Create a new line without creating a new paragraph	Place the insertion point where you want to end the current line and create a new line; press **Shift+Enter**.

Desired Result	How to Do It
Set paragraph alignment	Select the desired paragraph(s); click on the appropriate alignment button in the Formatting toolbar.
Set line spacing	Select the desired paragraph(s); choose **Format, Paragraph** to open the Paragraph dialog box; in the Indents and Spacing folder, select your desired line-spacing setting; click on **OK** (or press **Enter**).

In the next chapter, you will learn the basics of page formatting. You'll find out how to work with headers and footers, how to use Print Preview to preview a printed document, how to set margins, how to use page breaks to paginate a document, how to work in Page Layout view, how to hyphenate text, and how to control the printing of your documents.

IF YOU'RE STOPPING HERE

If you need to break off here, please exit Word. If you want to proceed directly to the next chapter, please do so now.

CHAPTER 6:
PAGE FORMATTING

Creating Headers
and Footers

Using Print
Preview to Preview
a Printed
Document

Setting Margins

Using Page Breaks
to Paginate a
Document

Working in Page
Layout View

Hyphenating Text

Controlling the
Printing of Your
Documents

In Chapters 4 and 5, you learned how to format your documents at the character and paragraph levels. In this chapter, we'll introduce Word's final level of formatting—*page formatting*. Many powerful formatting features are controlled at the page level, including headers and footers, margins, page breaks, hyphenation, and advanced printing options.

We'll also present two new methods for displaying your documents—*Print Preview* and *Page Layout* view—both of which are well-suited for page-level formatting tasks.

When you're done working through this chapter, you will know

- How to create, edit, and view headers and footers

- How to use Print Preview to preview a printed document

- How to set margins

- How to use page breaks to paginate a document

- How to work in Page Layout view

- How to hyphenate text

- How to control the printing of your documents

CREATING HEADERS AND FOOTERS

A *header* is text that is automatically printed at the top of every page in a document, and a *footer* is text that is automatically printed at the bottom of every page. Headers and footers are used extensively in word processing to do such things as number each page in a document, place the current date on each page, print the document title and/or author name on each page, and so on.

To create a header or footer, choose *Header and Footer* from the View menu. Word automatically switches to Page Layout view, opens the Header area, and displays the Header and Footer toolbar (see Figure 6.1). (You'll learn about Page Layout view later in this chapter.)

To open the Footer area from the Header area and vice versa, click on the *Switch Between Header and Footer* button (see Figure 6.1).

To enter header/footer information:

- In the Header or Footer area, type your desired header or footer text, using the Header and Footer toolbar buttons as desired (these buttons are discussed in the next section).

- Click on *Close* to accept the header or footer and close the Header or Footer area

Figure 6.1 **The Header area and Header and Footer toolbar**

Show Previous   Show Next   Page Numbers   Time   Show/Hide Document Text

Switch Between
Header and Footer

Same as Previous   Date   Page Setup

To delete a header or footer:

- Follow the previous procedure to open the Header or Footer area.

- Choose *Edit, Select All* to select the entire contents of the Header or Footer area.

- Press *Del* to delete these contents.

- Click on *Close* to close the Header or Footer area.

THE HEADER OR FOOTER TOOLBAR

You can use the Header and Footer toolbar buttons to insert the page number, the current date, or the current time into your header or footer (see Figure 6.1). When using the Date and Time buttons, keep in mind that your printout will reflect the date and time when you *print* the document, rather than the date and time when you first *created* the document.

The Show Previous, Show Next, and Same as Previous buttons are sometimes used in long documents that consist of more than one section, and in which each section has more than one header and/or footer. (You'll learn about sections in Chapter 11.) The Page Setup button opens the Page Setup dialog box, in which you can control, for example, your document's margins and the size of its pages. The Show/Hide Document Text button allows you to display the document text dimmed in the background (as in Figure 6.1) or to remove it from the screen display.

VIEWING HEADERS AND FOOTERS

Word provides five *views* (screen representations) for your documents: *Normal, Outline, Page Layout,* and *Master Document,* which are available through the View menu; and *Print Preview,* which is located in the File menu. The three most important views, and the ones we'll use in this book, are Normal, Page Layout, and Print Preview.

When you are working in Normal view (the view we've always used up to now), your headers and footers are not shown on-screen, though they will still appear if you print the document. To see your headers and footers on-screen, you must be in Print Preview or Page Layout view. These views will be discussed later in this chapter.

If you are not running Word, please start it now. Let's begin this chapter's activities by opening a new document and creating a header for it:

1. Open **chap6.doc** from your WRKFILES directory.

2. Choose **View, Header and Footer** to open the Header area and display the Header and Footer toolbar (see Figure 6.1).

3. Observe the Header area. Text entered here will automatically appear at the top of every page of your document.

4. Without clicking on any of the buttons, move the mouse pointer to each button. As in the main (Standard) and Formatting toolbars, the name of each button is displayed when you point to it.

5. Type **Global Travel**. Press **Tab** twice and then type **Travel Services**.

6. Observe the header text. Note that *Travel Services* is right-aligned. Observe the ruler. As long as the Header area is open, the ruler refers to the header, *not* to the document. Word has automatically set a centered tab stop at 3" (half-way between the left and right margins) and a right-aligned tab stop at 6" (at the right margin). These preset tab stops enable you to quickly and easily use tabs to center your header text or to align it with the right margin. (To align it with the left margin, you would simply begin typing without pressing Tab, as you did with *Global Travel.*)

7. Click on **Close** in the Header and Footer toolbar to accept your header and close the Header area. Note that the ruler now refers to the document, not to the header. Note also that the header you just created is not displayed on the screen. As mentioned earlier in this section, headers and footers are only visible in Print Preview and Page Layout views.

Now let's create a footer:

1. Choose **View, Header and Footer**. The header you just created is again visible in the Header area.

2. Click on the **Switch Between Header and Footer** button (see Figure 6.1) to open the footer area.

3. Examine the Footer area. It is identical to the Header area. However, the text you type here will be displayed at the *bottom* of every page, instead of at the top.

4. Click on the **Date** button (see Figure 6.1) to insert the current date.

5. Press **Tab** twice to move to the right margin.

6. Type **Page** and then press the **Spacebar**.

7. Click on the **Page Numbers** button (see Figure 6.1) to insert the page number.

8. Close the Footer area (click on **Close**) to accept your footer and return to the document.

USING PRINT PREVIEW TO PREVIEW A PRINTED DOCUMENT

Print Preview provides a miniature view of how a document will look when it is printed. You can use Print Preview to examine and adjust the layout of a document before you actually print it.

You can edit text in Print Preview, but doing so is not very efficient and, depending on the system you are using, the response of the program can be slow. You can, however, control the placement of text on the page by changing the margins. You also can print the active document and view two or more pages at one time.

To use the Print Preview option:

- Choose *File, Print Preview* to open the Print Preview window.

- To print the document, click on the *Print* button in the Print Preview option bar (see Figure 6.2).

Figure 6.2   The Print Preview window

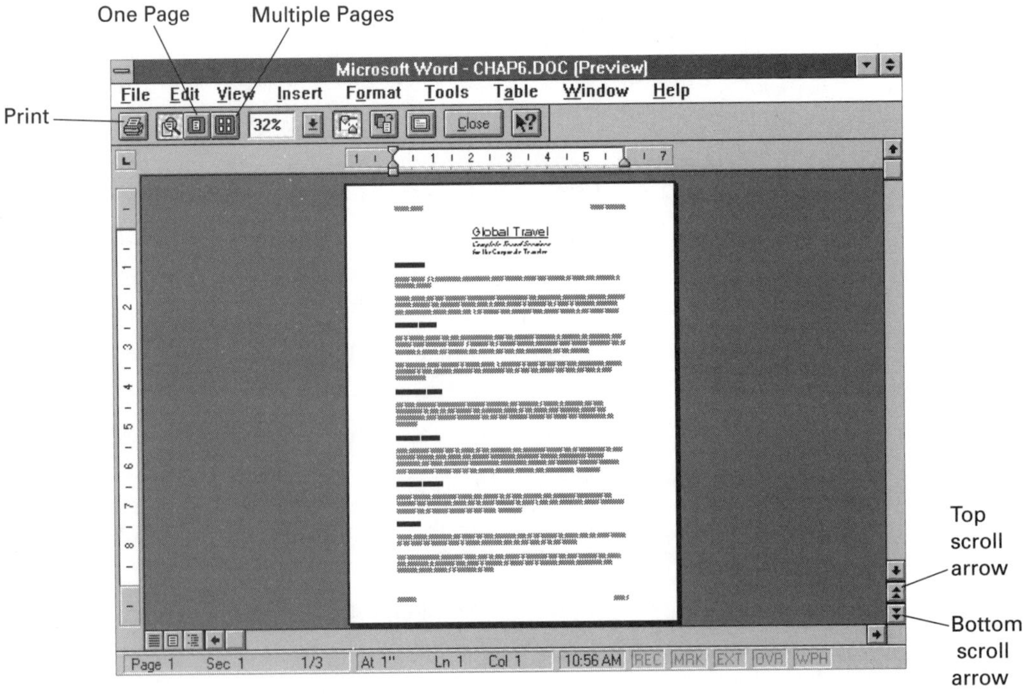

- To view more than one page at a time, click on the *Multiple Pages* button in the Print Preview option bar, and then drag over the grid to select the desired number of pages and their configuration (see the next exercise); to return to single-page view, click on the *One Page* button.

- To close the window, click on the *Close* button in the Print Preview option bar.

Let's use Print Preview to examine our header and footer:

1. Choose **File, Print Preview** to open the Print Preview window (see Figure 6.2). Click on the View Ruler button (the sixth button from the left) to display the horizontal and vertical ruler. Print Preview provides a miniature display of your document as it will print, including headers and footers. Remember, you cannot edit text in this view. Notice that, in addition to the horizontal ruler displayed above the document page, a vertical ruler at the left of the Print Preview window is displayed.

2. Click on the **Multiple Pages** button (see Figure 6.2) to display the Multiple Pages grid.

3. Drag down one row and three "pages" to the right, so that a **1 × 3** grid is selected (see Figure 6.3). Then release the mouse button to display a single row of (all) three pages of the document at one time. Compare your screen to Figure 6.4. Notice that the horizontal ruler, which functions in the same manner as the one in Normal document view, appears above the page that currently contains the insertion point (page 1).

4. Click on the **One Page** button to return to single-page view.

5. Click on the **bottom scroll** arrow (see Figure 6.2) to display page 2 of the document; then click again on the **bottom scroll** arrow to display page 3. In Print Preview, each click scrolls one full page. Notice that the headers and footers appear on every page. CHAP6.DOC is a three-page document. Click once again on the **bottom scroll** arrow to verify this; your computer may beep, and the screen display does not change, since there are no more pages to scroll to.

6. Click on the **top scroll** arrow (see Figure 6.2) twice to return to page 1.

Figure 6.3   **Specifying the number of pages to be previewed**

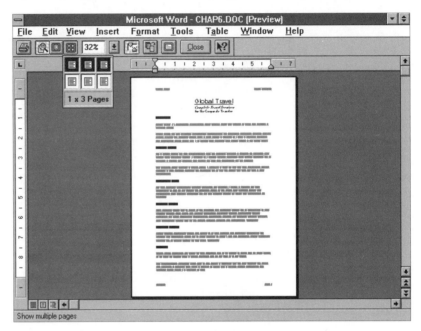

Figure 6.4   **Print Preview in Multiple Pages view**

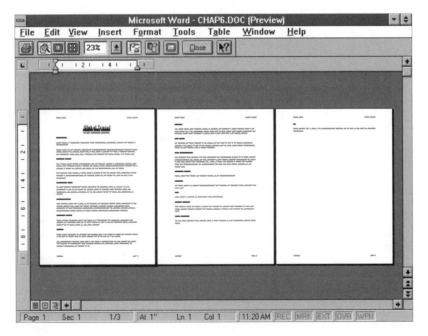

SETTING MARGINS

Margins determine the space between the four edges of the page and the text of the document. Figure 6.5 shows a Print Preview of a sample document with Word's default margin settings—the top and bottom margins are set to 1"; the left and right margins are set to 1.25". Figure 6.6 shows the same document with custom margins set to twice the default values—the top and bottom are set to 2"; the left and right are set to 2.5".

You can set a document's margins either from the Print Preview window (by dragging the margin boundaries) or in Normal or Page Layout view (by using the Page Setup dialog box).

Figure 6.5   **A sample document with default margins**

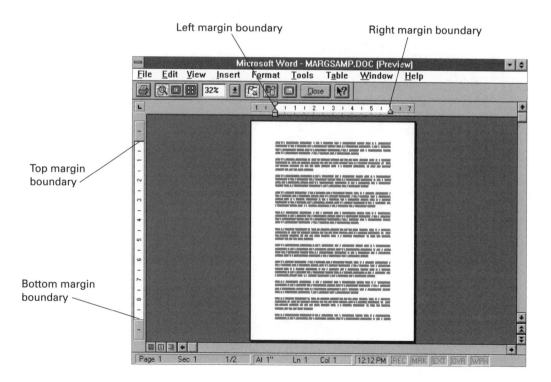

Figure 6.6   **A sample document with custom margins**

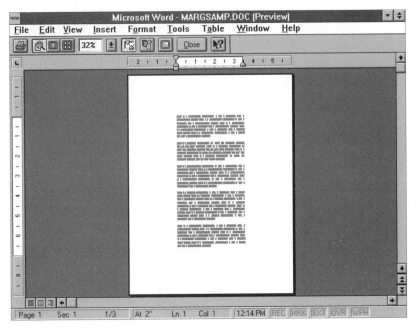

Use the following methods to adjust margins in Print Preview:

- To change the left and right margins, place the mouse pointer over the left margin boundary on the horizontal ruler (between the left-indent and first-line-indent markers) to change the left margin or over the right margin boundary (directly above the right-indent marker) to change the right margin; when the mouse pointer becomes a left- and right-pointing arrow, drag the margin to the desired position.

- To change the top and bottom margins, place the mouse pointer in the vertical ruler, at the top margin boundary to change the top margin, or the bottom boundary to change the bottom margin, until the mouse pointer becomes an up- and down-pointing arrow; then drag the margin to the desired position.

To set margins by using the Page Setup dialog box:

- Choose *File, Page Setup* to open the Page Setup dialog box.

- Display the *Margins* folder (click on its tab), if necessary.

- Enter the new margin settings in the appropriate margin text boxes.

- Click on *OK* (or press *Enter*).

Let's practice changing margins from the Print Preview window:

1. Observe the margin boundaries in the horizontal and vertical rulers (see Figure 6.5).

2. Position the mouse pointer on the top margin boundary, in the vertical ruler. The arrow changes to an up- and down-pointing arrow.

3. Press and hold the mouse button, and then begin to drag the top margin boundary downward. Notice that the top margin measurement appears above the top margin boundary in the vertical ruler. Drag the handle down until the top-margin measurement reads **1.5"**; then release the mouse button. Note that the new margin boundary line is displayed, and the page is reformatted to reflect this new top margin.

4. Click on the **Multiple Pages** button in the option bar, and select a **1 × 2** grid to display a single row of two pages (in this case, the first two) of the document. Then click the mouse pointer in **page 2** of the document to select the page. The horizontal and vertical rulers now refer specifically to this page of the document. (The horizontal ruler is now above page 2.) Notice that page 2 also reflects the new margin setting. It's important to note that margin settings apply to the whole document, not only to the selected page.

5. Hold down the **Alt** key as you drag the bottom margin boundary upward until the bottom-margin measurement indicator reads **1.5"**. Then compare your screen to Figure 6.7. In the status bar, you can see that the margin adjustment has caused the number of pages in the document to increase to 4.

6. Scroll to view pages 3 and 4 of the document (click on the **bottom scroll** arrow). The margins have changed on every page. (Pages 3 and 4 contain very little text because manual page breaks have been inserted in the document.)

7. Click on **Close** to close the Print Preview window.

Now let's change margins by using the Page Setup command:

1. Move to the top of the document, if necessary.

2. Choose **File, Page Setup** to open the Page Setup dialog box, and click on the **Margins** tab, if necessary (see Figure 6.8).

3. Verify that the top and bottom margins are set to **1.5"**.

Figure 6.7   **Changing the margins in Print Preview**

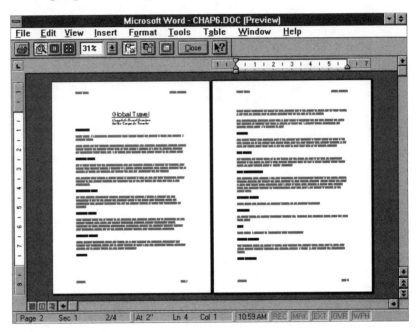

Figure 6.8   **The Margins tab in the Page Setup dialog box**

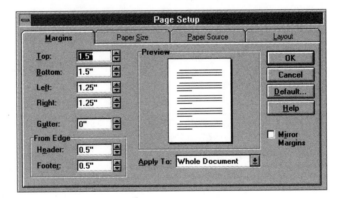

4. Double-click in the **Left** text box to select the current left margin setting (**1.25"**). Type **1** to change the left margin to 1". Note that you do not have to type the inch symbol (").

5. Press **Tab** to select the current right margin setting (**1.25"**). Type **1** to change the right margin to 1".

6. Press **Enter** (or click on **OK**) to accept your margin changes. Due to the extra 0.5" of text width that you gained (by decreasing the left and right margins by 0.25" each), your text lines now run off the right end of the screen (see Figure 6.9). Note that the screen representation of the left margin has not changed. When you are working in Normal view (as opposed to Print Preview or Page Layout view), Word always displays your left margin in the same place (approximately one-quarter inch to the right of the document window edge), no matter how large or small the margin actually is.

7. Save the disk file as **mychap6**.

Figure 6.9   **Overwide text lines**

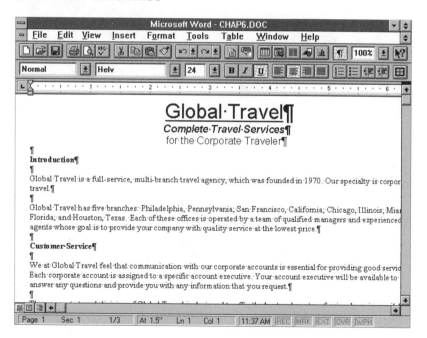

Let's use the Zoom Control feature (covered in Chapter 2) to shrink the display, so that the text lines no longer run off the screen:

1. Observe the status bar. The current magnification level is *100%*.

2. Click on the Zoom Control **down arrow** button to open the Zoom Control list box, and select **Page Width**. Observe the text and the Standard toolbar (see Figure 6.10). The magnification level automatically adjusts to fit the entire width (but not the length) of the page on the screen. In the Zoom Control box, you can see that the program has automatically adjusted the magnification level to *92%*.

Figure 6.10   **Using the Zoom Control Page Width option**

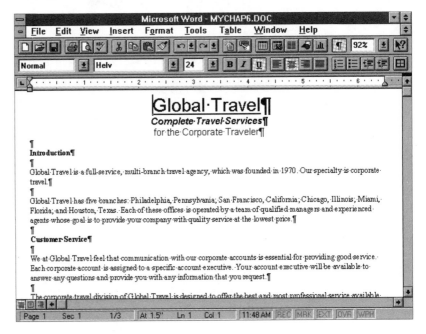

USING PAGE BREAKS TO PAGINATE A DOCUMENT

Pagination is the process of separating a document's text into pages. The separations between pages are called *page breaks*.

There are two types of page breaks in Word:

- *Automatic* page breaks, which Word automatically inserts into a document. An automatic page break appears as a loosely spaced dotted line across the text area.

- *Manual* page breaks, which you insert into the document. A manual page break appears as a tightly spaced dotted line with the words *Page Break* in the center of the line.

To insert a manual page break:

- Place the insertion point immediately to the left of the first character that you want on the new page.

- Choose *Insert, Break*, verify that *Page Break* is selected, and then click on *OK*; or, simply press *Ctrl+Enter*.

To delete a manual page break:

- Move the mouse pointer into the selection bar.

- Select the page break.

- Press *Del*.

You cannot delete automatic page breaks. However, if you insert a manual page break above an automatic page break, Word will remove the automatic page break.

Let's use the above procedure to insert some manual page breaks in MYCHAP6.DOC:

1. Move to the top of page 2, and scroll up one line. Observe the automatic page break before the paragraph beginning with *Our quality control specialists*. It is displayed as a loosely spaced dotted line.

2. Place the insertion point to the left of the *D* in the heading *Discounts*, near the bottom of page 1.

3. Choose **Insert, Break** to open the Break dialog box. Verify that **Page Break** is selected. Point to (but *don't* click on) OK and, while observing the automatic page break between pages 1 and 2, click on **OK**. Word inserts a manual page break (with the words *Page Break*) at your insertion point and then, shortly afterward, deletes the automatic page break. Because you changed the beginning of page 2 to *Discounts*, Word no longer needed to break pages automatically at *Our quality control specialists*.

4. Move to the bottom of page 2. Place the insertion point before the *F* in the heading *Flight Insurance*.

5. Press **Ctrl+Enter** to insert a manual page break. As mentioned earlier in this section, pressing Ctrl+Enter is the keyboard shortcut for using the Insert, Break command.

6. Note that the automatic page break after *Flight Insurance* disappears, but that the manual page break before *Fax* remains (see Figure 6.11). Automatic page breaks are deleted or repositioned automatically, as necessitated by changes you make to the document (resetting margins, changing font size, inserting new page breaks, and so on). Undesired manual page breaks, however, must be deleted manually.

7. In the selection bar, point to the manual page break before *Fax*. Click the mouse button to select the page break.

8. Press **Del** to delete the manual page break.

WORKING IN PAGE LAYOUT VIEW

Word's Page Layout view allows you to view all page areas, including headers, footers, and margins. Page Layout view is like a cross between Normal view (where you can edit and format body text, but cannot view headers and footers) and Print Preview (where you can see headers and footers but cannot edit text).

Note: Page Layout view can be useful for applying the finishing touches to your documents. However, you might find that this view significantly slows the operating speed of Word and makes it awkward to move around in the document. For this reason, we recommend that you do most of your work in Normal view.

Figure 6.11   **Inserting a manual page break**

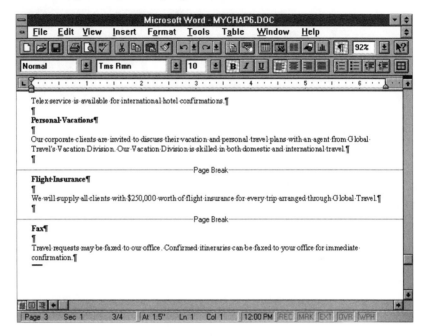

To enter Page Layout view:

- Choose *View, Page Layout*; or click on the *Page Layout View* button (to the left of the horizontal scroll bar; see Figure 6.12).

To return to Normal view:

- Choose *View, Normal*; or click on the *Normal View* button.

To edit a header or footer in Page Layout view:

- Double-click on the (dimmed) header or footer.

- Edit the header or footer text, as desired.

- Click on *Close*.

Let's edit your header and footer in Page Layout view. But first we'll open the Print Preview window to observe a page-positioning problem with the header and footer:

1. Move to the top of the document.

Figure 6.12   **The Normal and Page Layout View buttons**

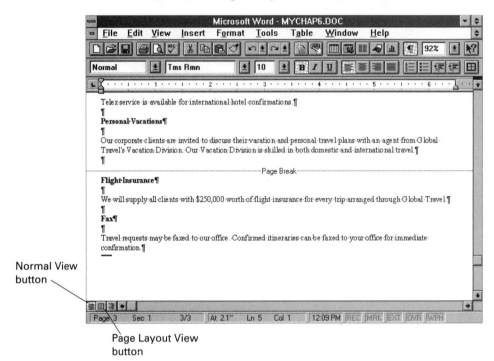

Normal View
button

Page Layout View
button

2. Open the Print Preview window (choose **File, Print Preview**). Notice that the header and footer text no longer aligns with the right margin. Why? Because you changed the document's margins in a previous activity, but did not adjust the position of the right-aligned tab stop in the header and footer. This tab stop does not reach the new right margin. (We'll fix the problem in a moment.)

3. Close the Print Preview window (click on **Close**).

4. Choose **View, Page Layout** to switch to Page Layout view. Notice that the Zoom Control is set to *100%*, which doesn't allow you to view the right margin.

5. Open the Zoom Control list box, and select **Page Width** to automatically adjust the magnification (see Figure 6.13). In Page Layout view, you can both view and edit headers and footers, even though they are currently dimmed and cannot, therefore, be selected.

Figure 6.13   **MYCHAP6.DOC in Page Layout view**

6. Double-click on the dimmed header. Eureka! The Header area is displayed in Page Layout view.

7. Place the insertion point in the header before the *T* in *Travel Services*. Type **Complete** and then press the **Spacebar**.

8. Observe the ruler. The right-aligned tab stop at 6" did not automatically adjust when you changed the margins earlier.

9. Drag the right-aligned tab stop at 6" to **6.5"** to set it even with the right margin.

10. Click on the **Switch Between Header and Footer** button (in the Header and Footer toolbar) to view the footer.

11. Drag the right-aligned tab stop at 6" to **6.5"**. Then close the Footer area (click on **Close**).

12. Open the Print Preview window. Scroll through the document to verify that the headers and footers now align with the right margin on every page. Then close the Print Preview window.

13. Choose **View, Normal** to return to Normal view.

14. Open the Zoom Control drop-down list box, and select **100%** to return to 100% magnification.

15. Update the disk file (use **File, Save**).

HYPHENATING TEXT

Up to now, we have worked exclusively with unhyphenated text: Each of our documents' lines has ended with a whole word, rather than a *hyphenated* word—a word broken into two parts by a hyphen. You may, at times, wish to hyphenate a document to reduce the raggedness of its right margin (with left-aligned text) or to tighten things up by minimizing the blank space between words (with justified text). Word provides two methods for doing this: *manual hyphenation*, in which you can use either the keyboard or the Tools, Hyphenation command; and *automatic hyphenation*, in which you use the Tools, Hyphenation command.

MANUAL HYPHENATION

To hyphenate text manually:

• Place the insertion point between the desired letters of the word you wish to hyphenate.

• Insert your desired hyphen, choosing from the three types shown in the following table:

Type of Hyphen	How and When to Use
Regular	Press the *Hyphen* key (-); use when you always want the hyphen to appear, such as in compound words ("left-aligned," "right-aligned," and so on).
Optional	Press *Ctrl+Hyphen*; use when you only want the hyphen to appear if the word is broken at the end of a line (such as "auto-matic").
Hard	Press *Ctrl+Shift+Hyphen*; use when you always want the hyphen to appear, but you never want the word to be broken at the end of a line, such as with names ("Ann-Marie," for instance).

Let's use the Ctrl+Hyphen technique to insert an optional hyphen into a word:

1. Move to the top of the document, if necessary.

2. Use **File, Page Setup** to change the left and right margins to **1.5"**.

3. Click on the **Show/Hide** button (it shows a ¶ character) to hide nonprinting characters.

4. In the second line of the paragraph beginning with *We at Global Travel* (under the heading *Customer Service*), place the insertion point between the *o* and the *v* of *providing*. Then press **Ctrl+Hyphen** to insert an optional hyphen at the insertion point. Notice that the word *providing* is broken into two parts, *pro-* and *viding* (see Figure 6.14).

Figure 6.14   **Inserting an optional hyphen into *providing***

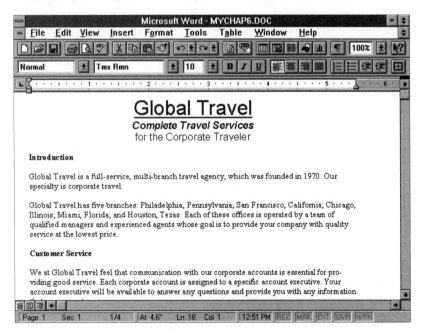

5. Place the insertion point before *essential* (in the same sentence). Type **absolutely** and then press the **Spacebar** to force the entire word *providing* to move to the next line. Note that the optional hyphen disappears when it is not needed.

6. Click on the **Show/Hide** button to show nonprinting characters. Note that the optional hyphen now appears on-screen as a horizontal line with a slightly downturned right end. (Optional hyphens do not appear when you print a document.)

7. Delete **absolutely** (and the trailing space) from the text.

AUTOMATIC HYPHENATION

To hyphenate a document automatically:

- Move the insertion point to the top of the document.
- Choose *Tools, Hyphenation* to open the Hyphenation dialog box.
- Check the *Automatically Hyphenate Document* option.
- Click on *OK* (or press *Enter*) to hyphenate the document.

Now let's use the Tools, Hyphenation command to automatically hyphenate the entire document:

1. Move to the top of the document.

2. Choose **Tools, Hyphenation** to open the Hyphenation dialog box (see Figure 6.15).

3. Check the **Automatically Hyphenate Document** option. Notice that the Hyphenate Words in CAPS option is unchecked. With this option unchecked, when Word encounters any words that contain all capitals, it will not hyphenate them.

Figure 6.15   **The Hyphenation dialog box**

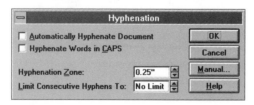

4. Click on **OK** (or press **Enter**) to begin the hyphenation procedure. Scroll the document and observe which words have been hyphenated automatically: *dis-count, is-sue, cost-effective* (which was manually hyphenated, but due to the automatic hyphenation has been interrupted by a line break), *assign-ments,* and *infor-mation.* (Your hyphenated words may vary from these, depending on your margins, and so on.)

CONTROLLING THE PRINTING OF YOUR DOCUMENTS

Several times in this book, you've used the File, Print command to print your active document. Let's revisit this very powerful command and learn how to use some of its more advanced features. In addition to printing a single copy of your entire document, File, Print allows you to print the current page, multiple pages, multiple copies, selected text, or nondocument items such as Summary Info.

To use the Print dialog box to control how your documents print:

- If you wish to print selected text, select that text.
- Choose *File, Print* to open the Print dialog box.
- Choose the desired Print options (see Table 6.1).
- Click on *OK* (or press *Enter*).

 ### PRINT DIALOG BOX OPTIONS

The Print dialog box provides the options shown in Table 6.1.

Table 6.1 **Print Dialog Box Options**

Option	Description
Print What	In this drop-down list box, you choose what you wish to print. The default choice is the current document, but you can also print, for example, summary information (covered later in this section), styles, and AutoText (printing AutoText will be discussed in Chapter 9).

Table 6.1   **Print Dialog Box Options (Continued)**

Option	Description
Copies	In this text box, you enter the number of copies that you wish to print. The default is 1 copy.
Page Range	In this area of the dialog box, you specify the portion of the document that you wish to print. Choose *All* to print the entire document. Choose *Current Page* to print the page where the insertion point is located. If you selected text in your document before issuing the File, Print command, the Selection button becomes active; choose it to print the selected text. Choose *Pages* and enter page numbers in the Pages text box to print a range of pages; separate page numbers with commas (for nonsequential pages) or dashes (for sequential pages)—for example, enter 3, 6, 10-12 to print pages 3, 6, 10, 11, and 12.
Print	From this drop-down list, you can specify the printing of all the pages in a specified range, only the odd-numbered pages, or only the even-numbered pages.

Let's practice using the print options in the Print dialog box. (If you do not have a printer, please skip this activity.)

1. Move to the top of the document.

2. Choose **File, Print** to open the Print dialog box (see Figure 6.16).

3. In the Page Range area of the box, choose the **Current Page** option (click on the radio button to the left of the option). Click on **OK** to print only the current page (the page on which the insertion point is located), which in this case is page 1. After the page has been sent to the printer, the Print dialog box is automatically closed.

4. Choose **File, Print** to reopen the Print dialog box. Note that Page Range has been reset to its default (*All*). Each time you open the Print dialog box, all of its settings are reset to their default values.

Figure 6.16   **The Print dialog box**

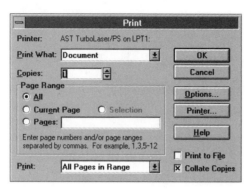

5. In the Page Range area of the box, select the **Pages** option. Type **1-2** in the Pages text box; this informs Word to print only from page 1 through page 2 of the document. Click on **OK** to print these pages.

6. Choose **File, Print** to reopen the Print dialog box. In the Page Range area of the box, notice that the Selection option is currently dimmed, because no text is selected in the document.

7. Select the **Current Page** option. Double-click in the Copies text box to select the current value (**1**); type **2** to tell Word to print two copies of the current page. Click on **OK** to print these copies.

8. Select all text from the heading *Customer Service* up to and including the empty paragraph above *International Travel*.

9. Choose **File, Print** to reopen the Print dialog box. Note that the Copies and Page Range options have been reset to their default values of *1* and *All*, respectively. Note also that the Selection option is now available (see Figure 6.17).

10. Choose the **Selection** option and then click on **OK** to print only your selected text.

11. Press **Ctrl+Home** to deselect and move to the top of the document. Choose **File, Print** to reopen the Print dialog box. Note that the Selection option is once again dimmed (because there is no text selected in the document).

Figure 6.17   **Printing selected text**

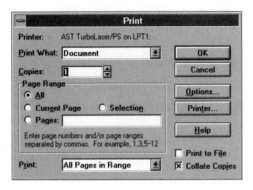

12. Click on the **down arrow** to the right of the Print What list box to display the Print options. Select **Summary Info** to tell Word to print the Summary Info sheet of the current document. Click on **OK** to print this sheet.

USING THE PRINT BUTTON TO PRINT A DOCUMENT

In addition to the File, Print command, Word provides a Print button that you can use to print a single copy of an entire document. To do this, click on the Print button (the fourth from the left in the toolbar; it shows a printer).

Let's end this chapter's activities by using the Print button to print your entire document. (If you do not have a printer, please skip this activity.)

1. Click on the **Print** button (the one showing a printer) to print a single copy of your entire document.

2. Save the disk file and close the document.

SUMMARY

In this chapter, you learned the basics of page formatting. You now know how to create, edit, and view headers and footers; how to use Print Preview to preview a printed document; how to set margins; how to use page breaks to paginate a document; how to work in Page Layout view, how to hyphenate text; and how to control the printing of your documents.

Congratulations on completing your foundation of Word formatting techniques! You now know how to format your documents at the character, paragraph, and page levels. These skills will allow you to create highly professional-looking documents.

Here's a quick reference guide to the Word features introduced in this chapter:

Desired Result	**How to Do It**
Create a header or footer	Choose **View, Header and Footer**; type your desired header text, or click on **Switch Between Header and Footer** and type your desired footer text; click on **Close** to accept the header or footer and to close the Header or Footer area.
Delete a header or footer	Follow the previous procedure to open the Header or Footer area; choose **Edit, Select All** to select the entire contents of the area; press **Del** to delete these contents; click on **Close** to close the Header or Footer area.
Use Print Preview to preview a printed document	Choose **File, Print Preview** to open the Print Preview window.
Set margins in Print Preview	Drag the desired margin boundary to your desired margin position; repeat the previous step until all margin boundary lines are set as desired.
Set margins by using the Page Setup dialog box	Choose **File, Page Setup** to open the Page Setup dialog box; enter the new margin settings in the appropriate margin text boxes; click on **OK** (or press **Enter**).

Desired Result	How to Do It
Insert a manual page break	Place the insertion point immediately to the left of the first character that you want on the new page; choose **Insert, Break**; verify that **Page Break** is selected; click on **OK**; or place the insertion point and press **Ctrl+Enter**.
Delete a manual page break	Move the mouse pointer into the selection bar; select the page break; press **Del**.
Enter Page Layout view	Choose **View, Page Layout**.
Return to Normal view	Choose **View, Normal**.
Hyphenate text manually	Place the insertion point between the desired letters of the word you wish to hyphenate; insert your desired hyphen (regular, optional, or hard).
Hyphenate a document automatically	Move the insertion point to the top of the document; choose **Tools, Hyphenation**; check the **Automatically Hyphenate Document** option; and click on **OK**.
Use the Print dialog box to control document printing	If you wish to print selected text, select the text; choose **File, Print** to open the Print dialog box; choose your desired Print options; click on **OK** (or press **Enter**).
Use the Print button to print a single copy of an entire document	Click on the toolbar **Print** button.

In the next chapter, we'll explore ways in which Word can help you improve your writing. You'll learn how to check your documents' spelling, how to use the thesaurus to find alternative words, and how to check the grammar, style, and readability of your documents.

IF YOU'RE STOPPING HERE

If you need to break off here, please exit Word. If you want to proceed to the next chapter, please do so now.

CHAPTER 7: PROOFING YOUR DOCUMENTS

Checking the Spelling of Your Documents

Using the Thesaurus to Find Alternative Words

Checking the Grammar and Style of Your Documents

Misspellings and grammatical mistakes can severely undermine the credibility of your documents. In this chapter, we'll introduce you to tools that allow you to *proof* (check) your documents for potential spelling, grammar, and style errors. Wording is also a critical factor in determining the effectiveness of a document; using inappropriate words may alienate or confuse your readers. We'll explore Word's electronic thesaurus and see how easy it is to find vocabulary alternatives for your documents.

When you're done working through this chapter, you will know

- How to check the spelling of your documents

- How to use the thesaurus to find alternative words

- How to check the grammar, style, and readability of your documents

CHECKING THE SPELLING OF YOUR DOCUMENTS

Word provides a spelling checker that you can use to proof the spelling of your documents. The *spelling checker* checks each word in a document against the words in its own internal dictionary and highlights the words it does not recognize. The spelling checker also checks for such common typing mistakes as repeated words (such as *the the*) and irregular capitalization (such as *tHe*).

Here are Word's options for spell-checking documents:

- To spell-check a portion of a document, select the text that you wish to check; to check a single word, select that word.

- Choose *Tools, Spelling* or click on the *Spelling* button (the sixth from the left in the *Standard* toolbar) to open the Spelling dialog box and begin the spelling check. Figure 7.1 illustrates the Spelling dialog box.

- Follow the dialog box prompts to spell-check the document or selected text.

When the spelling checker finds a potential spelling error (a word not included in the checker's internal dictionary), this word appears in the Not in Dictionary text box (see Figure 7.1), and a list of suggested spelling corrections appears in the Suggestions list box. The first of these suggested spellings is placed in the Change To text box. At this point, you can choose from the following options:

Option	Action Required
Leave the word unchanged	If you want to leave the word as it is and continue the spelling check, click on *Ignore*. To ignore all further occurrences of the word, click on *Ignore All*.

Figure 7.1   **The Spelling dialog box**

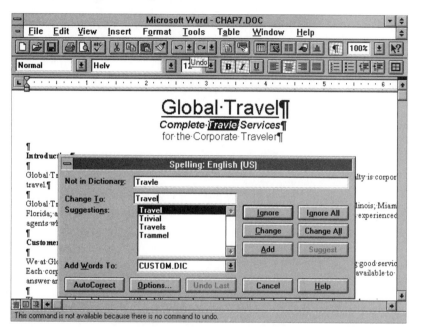

Option	Action Required
Correct the spelling	If the correction that you want is in the Change To text box, click on *Change*. If the correction that you want is in the Suggestions list box, click on that correction and then click on *Change*. (Or, as a shortcut, simply double-click on the desired correction.) If the correction that you want is not suggested, type the correction in the Change To text box and then click on *Change*. To change all the occurrences of the word throughout the document, click on *Change All*.
Add the word to a dictionary	Word allows you to build a custom dictionary that contains words not found in the spelling checker's dictionary. This is particularly useful for proper names (such as *Alexa*), abbreviations (such as *ACCTDEPT*), and acronyms (such as *UNICEF*) that you use frequently in your documents. If you want to add the word to a custom dictionary, click on *Add*.

Option	Action Required
Delete the word	If you want to delete the highlighted word from the document, delete the word in the Change To text box and then click on the *Delete* button (this button appears in place of the Change button when you delete the contents of the Change To text box). To delete all further occurrences of the word, delete the word in the Change To text box and then click on *Delete All* (this button appears in place of the Change All button when you delete the contents of the Change To text box).
Undo the last correction	If you want to undo the last correction, click on *Undo Last*. Word allows you to undo your most recent corrections, one by one.
Stop the spelling check	If you want to cancel the spelling check procedure at any point, click on *Cancel* (or *Close*). All changes made up to that point will be preserved. If you used the Change All or Delete All options, instances of these words that appear after the point where you cancel will not be changed or deleted.

If the error is repeated words (such as *the the*), you can

- Click on *Delete* to delete the second instance of the word.

- Click on *Ignore* to ignore the repeated words and continue the spelling check.

If you are not running Word, please start it now. Let's begin by opening a document and spell-checking a selected portion of it:

1. Open **chap7.doc** from your WRKFILES directory.

2. Select the heading of the document (the first three lines).

3. Choose **Tools, Spelling** to open the Spelling dialog box (see Figure 7.1). Note the dialog box title, *Spelling: English (US)*. By default, United States English is the language against which the words in your document are checked. Word allows you to specify a different language (for example, UK English, French, German, Italian, and so on) by using the *Tools, Language* command.

4. Observe the dialog box. In the Not in Dictionary text box, Word displays the first word it found that was not in its internal dictionary (*Travle*, which appears in the second line of the heading). In the Suggestions list box, Word displays a list of suggested spelling corrections (*Travel, Trivial,* and so on). The first of these suggestions (*Travel*) is also placed in the Change To box.

5. Click on **Change** to change *Travle* to *Travel* and to search for the next potential spelling error in your text selection. In this case, no further errors are found. Word prompts

> Word finished checking the selection. Do you want to continue checking the remainder of the document?

6. Click on **No** to end the spelling check and return to the document. Note that *Travle* has been corrected to *Travel* (see Figure 7.2).

Figure 7.2   **A corrected spelling error**

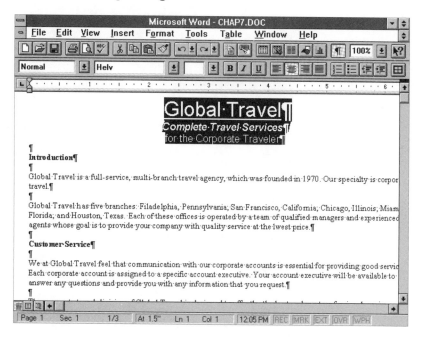

Now let's check the spelling of the entire document:

1. Press **Ctrl+Home** to deselect and move the insertion point to the top of the document.

2. Click on the Standard toolbar **Spelling** button (the one with the check below the letters *ABC*) to open the Spelling dialog box and initiate the spelling check. Word displays the first word it finds that is not in its dictionary (*multi-*).

3. Click on **Change** to replace *Filadelphia* with *Philadelphia* (the entry in the Change To box) and to search for the next potential spelling error. Word displays *lwest*. Note that *lowest* is listed in the Change To text box.

4. Select (click on) **lowest** to place it in the Change To text box. Click on **Change** to change *lwest* to *lowest* and to search for the next potential spelling error. Word displays *the* in the uppermost text box, which is now titled *Repeated Word*, instead of *Not in Dictionary* (see Figure 7.3). Although *the* is not misspelled, it appears twice in a row (*the the*) in your document.

Figure 7.3   **Correcting a repeated word**

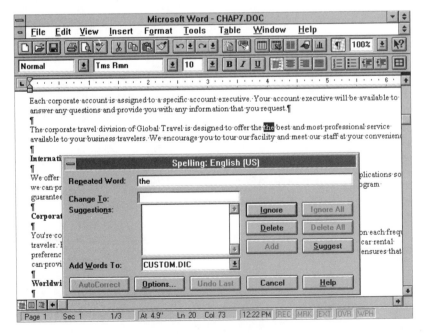

5. Click on **Delete** to delete the second *the*. Word prompts

`The spelling check is complete.`

6. Click on **OK** (or press **Enter**) to close the message box.

7. Save the disk file as **mychap7**.

USING THE THESAURUS TO FIND ALTERNATIVE WORDS

You can use Word's internal thesaurus to look up vocabulary alternatives in your documents. The thesaurus provides both *synonyms* (words with similar meanings) and *antonyms* (words with opposite meanings). Having a powerful and lightning-fast electronic thesaurus at your fingertips can greatly enhance the quality of the writing in your documents.

To use the thesaurus to find alternative words:

- Select the desired word in your document, or simply place the insertion point anywhere within the word.

- Choose *Tools, Thesaurus* (or press *Shift+F7*) to open the Thesaurus dialog box; a list of synonyms appears.
  Note: If antonyms are available, an Antonyms option appears in the Meanings list box. If you click on *Antonyms*, a list of antonyms will replace the list of synonyms.

- To replace the selected word, select the desired synonym or antonym and click on *Replace*.

Let's practice using the thesaurus to find synonyms:

1. Select the word **specialty** (located in the first line of the paragraph beginning with *Global Travel is a full-service*).

2. Choose **Tools, Thesaurus** to open the Thesaurus dialog box and display a list of synonyms for *specialty* (see Figure 7.4). Note the dialog box title, *Thesaurus: English (US)*. As with the spelling checker, you can use the Tools, Language command to change your thesaurus language.

3. Under Replace with Synonym, select **forte** from the list of synonyms. The word *forte* now appears in the Replace with Synonym text box.

4. Click on **Replace** to replace *specialty* with *forte*.

Figure 7.4   **The Thesaurus dialog box**

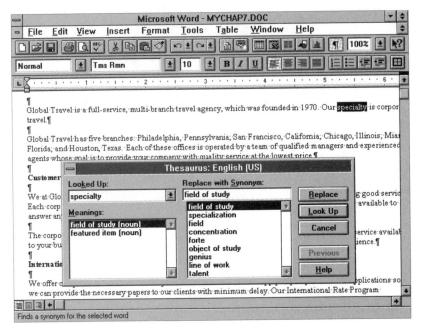

Now let's use the thesaurus to find antonyms:

1. Place the insertion point anywhere in the word *qualified* (located in the paragraph beginning with *Global Travel has five branches*).

2. Press **Shift+F7** to use the shortcut keyboard method for opening the Thesaurus dialog box.

3. In the Meanings list box, select **Antonyms** to display a list of antonyms (opposites) for *qualified*. Notice that what was the *Replace with Synonym* text box is now titled *Replace with Antonym*, and the list of antonyms is displayed below it (see Figure 7.5).

Let's say that you found none of these antonyms appealing and decided to cancel the thesaurus look-up procedure.

4. Click on **Cancel** to close the Thesaurus dialog box and return to your document.

Figure 7.5 **Displaying a list of antonyms**

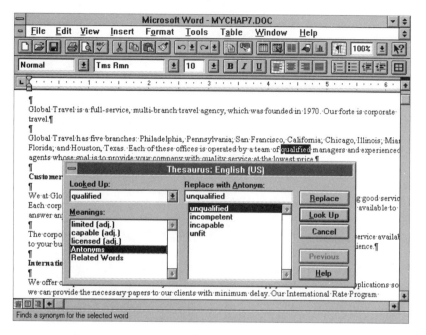

CHECKING THE GRAMMAR AND STYLE OF YOUR DOCUMENTS

You can use Word's grammar checker to identify and correct sentences in your document that contain grammatical errors and weak writing style.

Here's the general procedure for checking the grammar and style of a document:

- To check an entire document, press *Ctrl+Home* to move the insertion point to the top of the document; to check a portion of a document, select the text that you wish to check.

- Choose *Tools, Grammar* to open the Grammar dialog box and begin the grammar check (see Figure 7.6).

Figure 7.6 **The Grammar dialog box**

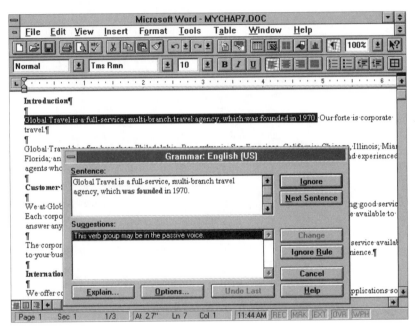

When a potential grammar or style error is found, the dialog box displays the questionable sentence in the Sentence box, with words that are related to the potential error displayed in bold letters. The dialog box might also provide one or more suggested corrections in the Suggestions list box. At this point, you can choose from the following options:

Option	Action Required
Accept a suggested correction	Select the desired correction in the Suggestions list box and click on *Change*; or, as a shortcut, simply double-click on the desired suggestion.
Leave the sentence as it is and continue the grammar check	Click on *Next Sentence*.

Option	Action Required
Leave the sentence as it is and ignore similar potential grammar or style errors	Click on *Ignore Rule.*
Undo recent corrections	Click on *Undo Last.*
Get more information about the potential error	Click on *Explain.*
Get help on using the grammar checker	Click on *Help.*
Ignore a suggested correction	Click on *Ignore.*
Stop the grammar check	Click on *Cancel* (or *Close*); all corrections made up to that point will be preserved.

CUSTOMIZING THE GRAMMAR CHECKER

You may disagree with certain rules that the grammar checker uses in assessing the correctness of a sentence. For example, you may find it perfectly acceptable to use the passive voice—a practice that the grammar checker considers to be a potential error. In recognition of the varying grammatical and style preferences of its users, Word allows you to customize the grammar checker to fit your needs. To do this:

- Click on *Options* in the Grammar dialog box.

- Click on *Customize Settings* in the Grammar tab of the Options dialog box.

- Set (check or uncheck) your desired grammar and style rules.

- Click on *OK* (or press *Enter*) to return to the Options dialog box, then click on *OK* (or press *Enter*) to accept your customized settings and return to the Grammar dialog box.

The changes you made to Word's grammar and style rules will apply to all your grammar checks from this point on.

SPELL-CHECKING WITH THE GRAMMAR CHECKER

By default, Word checks your document for spelling when you run a grammar check. When it finds a spelling error, it opens the Spelling dialog box, allows you to make any necessary changes, and then continues checking for grammar and spelling. For this reason, if you intend to perform both a spelling and grammar check for a document, simply choose Tools, Grammar.

READABILITY STATISTICS

When you complete a grammar check, Word provides character, word, paragraph, and sentence counts for your document. It also provides *readability statistics*—the average number of sentences per paragraph, words per sentence, and characters per word. These readability statistics are calculated into standard *readability indexes;* for example, the Flesch Reading Ease and Coleman-Liau Grade Level indexes. (You'll learn how to display these indexes in the following activity.)

Let's use the grammar checker to check the grammar and writing style of MYCHAP7.DOC:

1. Press **Ctrl+Home** to move the insertion point to the top of the document.

2. Choose **Tools, Grammar** to open the Grammar dialog box and search for the first potential grammar or style error (see Figure 7.6). Word finds *was founded* and informs you that this verb group may be in the passive voice. (By default, Word considers passive voice verbs to be potential errors.) Let's say we disagree and find passive verbs to be appropriate in this document's context.

3. Click on **Ignore** to leave the sentence unchanged and search for the next potential grammar or style error. Word finds *is operated*, another passive voice verb. It's clear that Word is going to call our attention to every passive verb group that it finds. Let's stop it from doing this for the remainder of the proofing session.

4. Click on **Ignore Rule** to leave all passive voice verb groups unchanged (throughout the document) and search for the next potential error. Word finds *You're* and suggests changing it to *Your.* In this case, we'll agree.

5. Click on **Change** to accept the suggested correction (to change *You're* to *Your*) and search for the next potential error. Word finds *ensures*, and suggests that the word might be confused with *assures* and *insures*. Let's leave the word as it is.

6. Click on **Ignore** to let *ensures* stand. The next occurrence of ensure is found, and Word provides the same suggestion as in step 5.

7. Click on **Ignore** to let *ensures* stand. The first sentence of the paragraph below *Hotel Accommodations* is selected. Word suggests that this is a run-on sentence; however, we know that it is not.

8. Click on **Ignore** to let the sentence stand. Word finds *provide* and suggests the alternative, *provides*.

9. Click on **Change** to accept the suggested correction and search for the next potential error. Word finds *client* and suggests the alternative *clients*.

10. Click on **Change** to accept the suggested correction and search for the next potential error. Word finds *personal*, and suggests that the word might be confused with *personnel*.

11. Click on **Ignore Rule**. The "word confusion" rule is now no longer in effect. Word finds *travel* and suggests that you change it to *travels*. In this case, we'll disagree; *travel* is what we want.

12. Click on **Ignore** to leave *travel* unchanged and search for the next potential error. A *Readability Statistics* box appears, summarizing the grammar checker's findings for your document (see Figure 7.7), and indicating that the grammar check is complete.

13. Press **F1** to display Word Help on readability statistics. You can read through this topic to learn more about what each of these statistics means.

14. Close the Help window. Take a moment to reexamine the Readability Statistics box in light of your new knowledge. When you are finished, click on **OK** (or press **Enter**) to close the box.

15. Save the disk file and close the document.

Figure 7.7   **The Readability Statistics box**

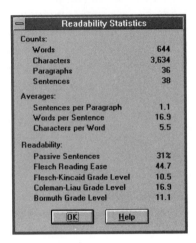

SUMMARY

In this chapter, you learned how to proof your documents and improve their quality. Now you know how to check the spelling of your documents, how to use the thesaurus to find alternative words, and how to check the grammar, style, and readability of your documents.

Here's a quick reference guide to the Word features introduced in this chapter:

Desired Result	How to Do It
Spell-check a document	Press **Ctrl+Home** to move the insertion point to the top (to spell-check an entire document) or select the desired text (to spell-check part of a document); choose **Tools, Spelling** or click on the Standard toolbar **Spelling** button; follow the Spelling dialog box prompts.
Use the thesaurus to find alternative words	Select the desired word or place the insertion point anywhere within the word; choose **Tools, Thesaurus** or press **Shift+F7**; follow the Thesaurus dialog box prompts.

Desired Result	How to Do It
Check the grammar and style of a document	Press **Ctrl+Home** to move the insertion point to the top (to check an entire document) or select the desired text (to check part of a document); choose **Tools, Grammar**; follow the Grammar dialog box prompts.
Customize the grammar checker	Click on **Options** in the Grammar dialog box; click on **Customize Settings** in the Grammar tab of the Options dialog box; set (check or uncheck) your desired grammar and style rules; click on **OK** (or press **Enter**) to return to the Options dialog box; click on **OK** (or press **Enter**) to accept your customized rule settings and return to the Grammar dialog box.

In the next chapter, you will build on the basic formatting and editing skills that you have already acquired. You'll learn advanced techniques for moving and copying text, and we'll show you how to copy font formats using the mouse. You'll also learn how to add numbers and bullets to selected text and how to replace and revise font formats.

IF YOU'RE STOPPING HERE

If you need to break off here, please exit Word. If you want to proceed directly to the next chapter, please do so now.

CHAPTER 8: ADVANCED FORMATTING AND EDITING TECHNIQUES

In Chapters 3 and 4, you learned basic techniques for editing and changing font formats of text. In this chapter, you will build on this information by learning more advanced methods of editing and formatting text. For example, you will learn how to copy text from one document to another and how to enhance the readability and visual appeal of your documents by turning selected text into a numbered or bulleted list.

When you're done working through this chapter, you will know

- How to move and copy text using the mouse and the toolbar
- How to copy text from one document to another
- How to add bullets and numbers to selected paragraphs
- How to copy font formats
- How to replace font formats using the Edit, Replace command

DISABLING THE SUMMARY INFO DIALOG BOX

When you start Word, certain defaults are already set. Summary Info, introduced in Chapter 1, is one such default. However, there are ways to customize the program so that it can best suit your specific needs. In this section, you'll learn how to *disable*, or turn off, the Summary Info dialog box.

You can modify defaults using the Tools, Options command. From the Options dialog box, shown in Figure 8.1, you can, for instance:

- Change printing options
- Change various spell-checker options
- Modify settings for saving disk files so that you can save them in fewer steps

To disable the Summary Info dialog box, which is displayed when you first save a disk file:

- Choose *Tools, Options*.
- Display the Save tab.
- Under Save Options, uncheck *Prompt for Summary Info*.
- Click on *OK*.

Now let's open the Options dialog box and disable the Summary Info dialog box:

1. Open a new document window. Then choose **Tools, Options** to open the Options dialog box.

2. Display (click on) the **Save** tab to display the save options.

Figure 8.1   **Setting save options in the Options dialog box**

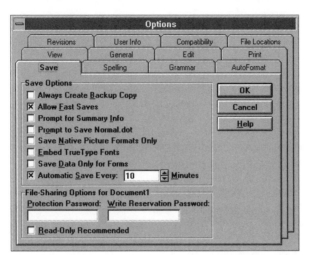

3. Under Save Options, uncheck **Prompt for Summary Info** to disable the Summary Info dialog box so that it does not display when you save a disk file for the first time. Compare your screen to Figure 8.1. Note: If this option is already unchecked, simply proceed to the next step.

4. Click on **OK**. The Summary Info dialog box is now disabled.

ALTERNATIVES FOR COPYING AND MOVING TEXT

In Chapter 3, you learned how to copy and move text by using the Edit menu. You can also copy text by using the Copy and Paste buttons on the Standard toolbar. In addition to using the Edit menu to move text, you can also use either the mouse, or the Cut and Paste buttons on the Standard toolbar.

To copy text (within the same document) using the Standard toolbar:

- Select the text you wish to copy.

- Click on the *Copy* button.

- Move the insertion point to where you want to place the text.

- Click on the *Paste* button.

To move text (within the same document) using the Standard toolbar:

- Select the text you wish to move.

- Click on the *Cut* button.

- Move the insertion point to where you want to place the text.

- Click on the *Paste* button.

To move text (within the same document) using the mouse:

- Select the text you wish to move.

- Point to the selected text.

- Press and hold the mouse button (a small dotted box and dotted insertion point appear attached to the mouse pointer).

- Drag the dotted insertion point to where you want to place the text.

- Release the mouse button.

Let's use the Standard toolbar to copy text, and then use the mouse to move text:

1. Open **chap8a.doc**.

2. Select the two lines of the *Global Travel* heading and the blank line below them.

3. Click on the **Copy** button (the eighth button from the left in the Standard toolbar). A copy of the selected text is now placed on the Clipboard.

4. Go to the top of page 2.

5. Click on the **Paste** button (the one showing a clipboard). The contents of the Clipboard are now placed at the insertion point.

6. Go to the top of page 3.

7. Click on the **Paste** button to paste the contents of the Clipboard at the insertion point (see Figure 8.2). Remember, the contents of the Clipboard will remain there until another selection is cut or copied.

8. Move the insertion point to the top of the document.

9. Scroll to view the Introduction section of the document.

Figure 8.2   **Heading copied using the Copy and Paste buttons**

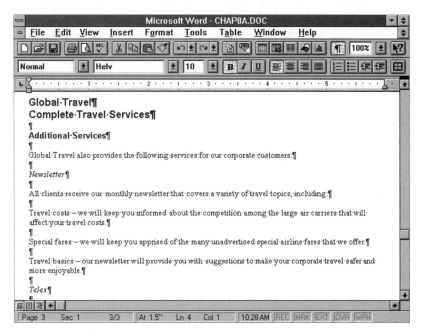

10. Drag to select the entire section, from the *Introduction* heading through the blank line above the *International Travel* heading (see Figure 8.3).

11. Point to the selected text. The mouse pointer becomes an arrow.

12. Press and hold the mouse button. A small, dotted box and a dotted insertion point appear.

13. Drag the dotted insertion point to the left of the *C* in *Customer Service* (toward the top of page 1) to place the Introduction section above the Customer Service section. Notice that the document scrolls up when you reach the top of the document window.

14. Release the mouse button. The selected text is now displayed in its new location.

15. Save the disk file as **mychap8a** and compare your screen to Figure 8.4.

Figure 8.3   **Selected text to be moved**

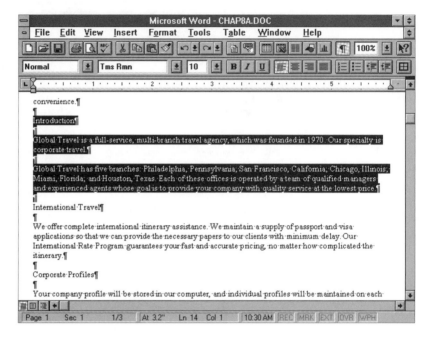

Figure 8.4   **The moved text**

COPYING TEXT FROM ANOTHER DOCUMENT

The first document you open appears in the document window. If you create or open a second document without closing the first one, Word will open the second document on top of the first document, so that both documents are open at the same time. The second document then becomes the active document. You can open several (how many depends on your computer's available memory) documents at one time, but only one document can be active.

The names of the documents appear in the title bars and under the Window menu. To make a document active, either click on the document window, if it is visible, or select the document name from the Window menu.

Tiling is the arrangement of open windows in an equally spaced layout on the screen. To view more than one document window at a time, you can tile the open windows by choosing Window, Arrange All. However, the more windows you have open, the smaller each window will be when it is tiled. You also can use the document Maximize/Restore button to enlarge or reduce the size of each window.

Once you have placed text on the Clipboard, you can move or copy the text from one document to another, in the same way that you would within a document.

Let's open a second document window, and then copy and paste between the two documents:

1. Place the I-beam to the left of the *H* in *Hotel Accommodations*, near the bottom of page 2.

2. Open **chap8b.doc**. The document consists of a single paragraph, followed by a blank line.

3. Select the paragraph and the blank line below it.

4. Click on the **Copy** button to place a copy of the selected text on the Clipboard.

5. Choose **Window, 2 MYCHAP8A.DOC** (see Figure 8.5) to move to the MYCHAP8A.DOC document window.

6. Click on the **Paste** button. The paragraph and blank line are now displayed below the *Auto Rentals* heading.

Figure 8.5   **Switching between documents**

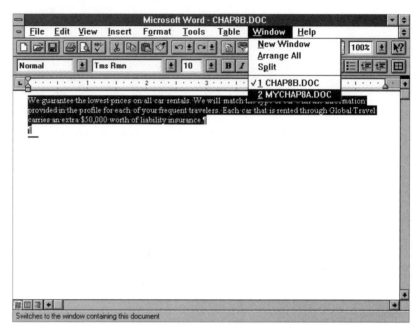

7. Click on the **Save** button (the third button from the left in the toolbar) to update the disk file. This is the same as choosing File, Save from the menu.

8. Choose **Window, 1 CHAP8B.DOC** to move to the CHAP8B-.DOC document window.

9. Choose **File, Close** to close CHAP8B.DOC.

ADDING AND REMOVING NUMBERS AND BULLETS

The longer your document, the more important it is for you to clearly define its major sections and subsections. To achieve this, you can use headings, which you can format differently from the surrounding text. In fact, you've already seen several examples of headings in exercises throughout the course of this book. Furthermore, when your document contains lists of items that you would like to call attention to, such items can be numbered or bulleted. This section focuses on using numbers and bullets to improve your document's organization and appearance.

ADDING NUMBERS AND BULLETS

To add numbers to specific paragraphs, select the desired paragraphs and click on the Numbering button. To add bullets to specific paragraphs, select the desired paragraphs and click on the Bullets button. When you add bullets or numbers to paragraphs, Word automatically formats the paragraphs with hanging indents. (See "Setting Hanging Indents" in Chapter 5 for details on this feature.)

If you apply numbers to a series of paragraphs and then want to change them to bullets, or vice versa:

* Select the desired paragraphs.

* Click on the *Bullets* or *Numbering* button.

You can also create a numbered or bulleted list before you add the text to the list. To do so:

* Position the insertion point where you wish to place the list.

* Click on the *Numbering* or *Bullets* button.

* Create as many paragraphs as you like.

* Click on the *Numbering* or *Bullets* button again to turn off the feature.

Let's select a list of items, and then add numbers and bullets to the list:

1. Scroll to place the *Newsletter* heading, on page 3, at the top of the screen.

2. Drag to select the paragraphs that begin *Travel costs...*, *Special fares...*, and *Travel basics....*

3. Click on the **Numbering** button (the fifth button from the right in the Formatting toolbar). Numbers appear to the left of the selected paragraphs.

4. Deselect the text to view the numbers. Compare your screen to Figure 8.6.

5. Drag to select the numbered list. Be sure to select all the paragraph marks.

6. Click on the **Bullets** button, immediately to the right of the Numbering button. Bullets now appear to the left of the selected paragraphs.

7. Deselect the text and compare your screen to Figure 8.7.

Figure 8.6   **The numbered list**

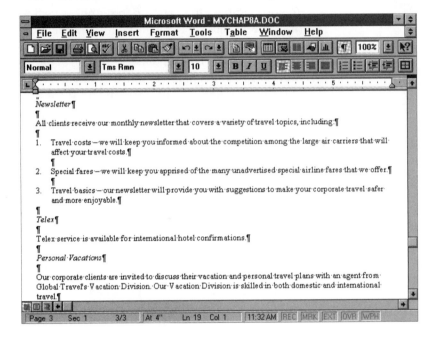

Figure 8.7   **The bulleted list**

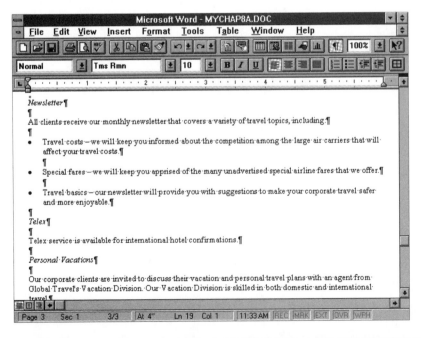

REMOVING NUMBERS AND BULLETS

You can remove bullets or numbers from a series of paragraphs. To do so:

- Select the numbered or bulleted list.
- Choose *Format, Bullets and Numbering*.
- Click on *Remove* in the Bullets and Numbering dialog box.

Note: Though the Bullets and Numbering dialog box contains separate Bulleted and Numbered tabs, you do not have to select a particular tab to remove numbers or bullets—just click on Remove. You can also use the Undo command to remove bullets or numbers.

In the Bullets and Numbering dialog box, you can set various options for the type of bullet or number character you want to use, as well as its size (accessible through the Modify option), and you can even remove the hanging indent. There is also a tab for creating multilevel lists.

Let's remove the bullets from our list:

1. Drag to select the bulleted list. Be sure to select all the paragraphs.
2. Choose **Format, Bullets and Numbering** to open the Bullets and Numbering dialog box (see Figure 8.8).
3. Click on **Remove** to remove the bullets from the selected text.

Figure 8.8   **The Bullets and Numbering dialog box**

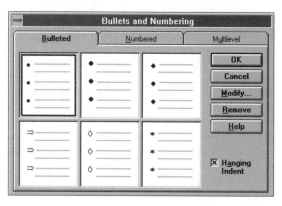

PRACTICE YOUR SKILLS

Make the paragraphs beginning with *Travel costs...*, *Special fares...*, and *Travel basics...* paragraphs with numbers.

USING THE MOUSE TO COPY FONT FORMATS

In Chapter 4, you learned how to apply multiple character, or font, styles using the Format menu. In the same chapter you also learned that you could use the F4 (Repeat) key or choose Edit, Repeat Formatting to repeat the formatting on other text. Remember, however, that when you use either of these methods, only the *last* format applied will be repeated. For example, if you select text and apply first the bold and then the italic formats from the Formatting toolbar, then select different text and press F4, only the italic formatting will be applied.

To copy all of the font formatting from one block of text to another:

- Select or place the insertion point in the text whose formatting you want to copy.

- Click on the *Format Painter* button (which shows a paintbrush) on the Standard Toolbar.

- Select the text to which you wish to copy the formatting.

Let's apply and copy some font formats:

1. Select the **Introduction** heading, near the top of the document.

2. Open the **Font** drop-down list box (in the Formatting toolbar) and select **Helvetica**.

3. Click on the **Bold, Italic,** and **Underline** buttons to apply those font styles to the selected text.

4. Select the **Customer Service** heading, below the Introduction section.

5. Open the Edit menu. Notice the second menu choice, *Repeat Underline*. If you were to choose this option (or press F4), only the underlining would be applied to the selected text.

6. Place the insertion point anywhere within the *Introduction* heading to point to the font formats that you will copy.

7. Click on the **Format Painter** button (immediately to the right of the Paste button; it shows a paintbrush), and move the mouse pointer down into the text area. Notice that it becomes a paintbrush attached to an I-beam.

8. Select the **Customer Service** heading. Notice that as you select the heading, the formatting from the Introduction heading is copied or "painted" onto it. The Format Painter button is no longer depressed, and the mouse pointer returns to normal.

9. With the *Customer Service* heading still selected, scroll down to view the *International Travel* heading.

10. Click on the **Format Painter** button, and then select the **International Travel** heading to copy the formatting from the Customer Service heading.

PRACTICE YOUR SKILLS

1. Apply bold, italic, and underline styles to the *Corporate Profiles* and *Worldwide Services* headings.

2. Deselect the text.

3. Save the disk file and compare your screen to Figure 8.9.

REPLACING FONT FORMATS

You can use the Replace dialog box to search for and replace font formats in a manner that is similar to the way you find and replace text.

To replace font formats:

- Choose *Edit, Replace*.

- Click on *Format*.

- Choose *Font* from the Format pop-up list.

- In the Find Font dialog box, click on the *Font* tab, if necessary, and then select the font formats you want to find.

- Click on *OK* to return to the Replace dialog box.

Figure 8.9   **Copied font formats**

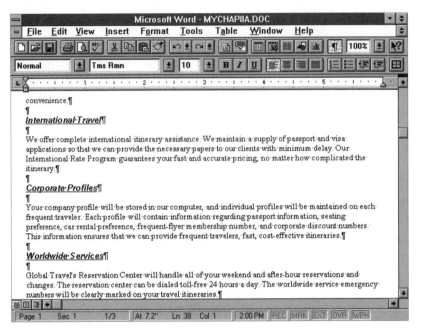

- Press *Tab* to move to the Replace With text box.

- Click on *Format*.

- Choose *Font* to open the Replace Font dialog box, and click on the *Font* tab, if necessary.

- Select the font formats that you want to change to.

- Click on *OK*.

- Click on *Find Next*.

- Click on *Replace* to replace the font formatting, or click on *Find Next* to leave the existing formatting intact.

- Click on *Close* (or *Cancel*) to close the Replace dialog box when you are finished.

In the Find Font dialog box, grayed or unchecked formats under Effects will not change. Clicking in the check box selects the format; clicking twice clears the check box, indicating that you want to remove the format.

Let's replace font formats:

1. Move to the top of the document.

2. Choose **Edit, Replace** to open the Replace dialog box. The insertion point is placed in the Find What text box.

3. Click on **Format** to open the Format pop-up list (see Figure 8.10). Then choose **Font** to open the Find Font dialog box. If necessary, display the Font tab.

Figure 8.10   **The Format pop-up list**

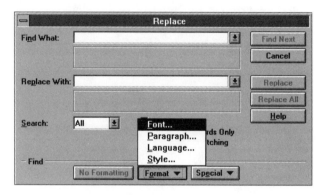

4. In the Font list box, select **Helvetica** (scroll to display it, if necessary) to search for text with the Helvetica font.

5. In the Font Style list box, select **Bold Italic** to search for text that is both bold and italic.

6. Open the **Underline** drop-down list box, and select **Single** to search for text with a single underline. Compare your screen to Figure 8.11.

7. Click on **OK** to return to the Replace dialog box.

8. Press **Tab** to move the insertion point to the Replace With text box.

9. Click on the **Format** button and choose **Font** to open the Replace Font dialog box and confirm that the Font tab is still displayed.

10. In the Font Style list box, check **Italic** to apply the italic font style to selected text. Compare your screen to Figure 8.12.

Figure 8.11   **Searching for specified font formats**

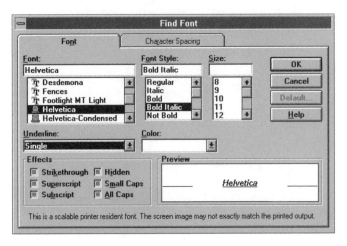

Figure 8.12   **The specified replacement font format**

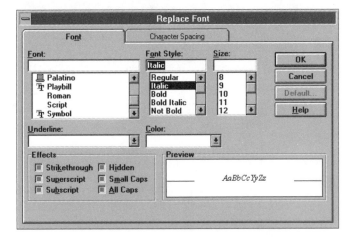

11. Click on **OK** to return to the Replace dialog box. Notice the font formats listed under the Find What and Replace With boxes, as shown in Figure 8.13.

12. Click on **Find Next** to begin the search and replace procedure. The *Introduction* heading is selected.

13. Click on **Replace** to replace the current format with the italic font style. The *Customer Service* heading is now selected.

Figure 8.13   **The specified formats listed in the Replace dialog box**

PRACTICE YOUR SKILLS

1. Continue replacing font formats until you have found and re-placed all of them.

2. Close the Replace dialog box.

3. Save the disk file.

REVISING FONT FORMATS IN THE REPLACE DIALOG BOX

When you select the font formatting you want to find and replace, the formats you choose appear below the Find What and Replace With text boxes. These formats will remain selected until you exit Word or select new formats.

Let's revise font formats in the Replace dialog box, changing the Helvetica italic text to Helvetica bold:

1. Choose **Edit, Replace** to open the Replace dialog box. The insertion point is placed in the Find What text box.

2. Observe the text below the Find What text box (see Figure 8.13); the font formats you previously specified remain selected.

3. Open the Find Font dialog box (click on **Format**, and choose **Font** from the pop-up list). You can see that all the previous selections remain selected.

4. In the Font Style list box, select **Italic** to search for italic text.

5. Open the Underline drop-down list, and select **(none)** to re-move the underline.

6. Click on **OK** to return to the Replace dialog box.

7. Press **Tab** to move the insertion point to the Replace With text box.

8. Open the Replace Font dialog box (click on **Format**, and choose **Font**).

9. In the Font Style list box, choose **Bold** to apply the bold font style to selected text.

10. Click on **OK** to return to the Replace dialog box. Compare your screen to Figure 8.14.

11. Click on **Find Next** to begin to search and replace.

Note: If you know in advance that you want to replace all oc-currences of a format, instead of clicking on Find Next, you can click on Replace All.

Figure 8.14   **The revised font formats**

PRACTICE YOUR SKILLS

1. Use the **Replace** button in the Replace dialog box to make the selected text bold.

2. Close the Replace dialog box.

3. Save the disk file.

4. Print the disk file and compare your printout to Figure 8.15.

5. Close the document.

PRACTICE YOUR SKILLS

The following instructions lead you through the steps necessary to edit the file PRAC8A.DOC to produce the document shown in Figure 8.16.

Follow these steps at your computer:

1. Open **prac8a.doc**.

2. Use the mouse to select the *International Travel* section, which is below the *Corporate Profiles* section. Be sure to select the entire section and the blank line following it.

3. Drag the selected text directly *above* the *Corporate Profiles* section.

4. Use the Standard toolbar to copy the two-line heading and the blank line below it at the top of page 1, to the top of pages 2 and 3.

5. Open **prac8b.doc**.

6. Use the Standard toolbar to copy all of PRAC8B.DOC to the Clipboard.

7. Move to the PRAC8A.DOC window.

8. Paste the contents of the Clipboard below the *Deliveries* heading. (**Hint:** Place the insertion point to the left of the *A* in *Auto Rentals* before you paste the contents of the Clipboard.)

9. In the Newsletter section, select the paragraphs that begin *Travel costs...*, *Special fares...*, and *Travel basics....*

10. Add bullets to the selected paragraphs.

11. Change the bulleted list to a numbered list.

12. Change the font formatting of the *Introduction* heading to **Helvetica**, **Bold**, and **Underline**.

13. Use the mouse to apply the font formats from the *Introduction* heading to the *Customer Service* heading.

Figure 8.15   **The completed MYCHAP8A.DOC document**

Global Travel
Complete Travel Services

Introduction

Global Travel is a full-service, multi-branch travel agency, which was founded in 1970. Our specialty is corporate travel.

Global Travel has five branches: Philadelphia, Pennsylvania; San Francisco, California; Chicago, Illinois; Miami, Florida; and Houston, Texas. Each of these offices is operated by a team of qualified managers and experienced agents whose goal is to provide your company with quality service at the lowest price.

Customer Service

We at Global Travel feel that communication with our corporate accounts is essential for providing good service. Each corporate account is assigned to a specific account executive. Your account executive will be available to answer any questions and provide you with any information that you request.

The corporate travel division of Global Travel is designed to offer the best and most professional service available to your business travelers. We encourage you to tour our facility and meet our staff at your convenience.

International Travel

We offer complete international itinerary assistance. We maintain a supply of passport and visa applications so that we can provide the necessary papers to our clients with minimum delay. Our International Rate Program guarantees you fast and accurate pricing, no matter how complicated the itinerary.

Corporate Profiles

Your company profile will be stored in our computer, and individual profiles will be maintained on each frequent traveler. Each profile will contain information regarding passport information, seating preference, car rental preference, frequent-flyer membership number, and corporate discount numbers. This information ensures that we can provide frequent travelers, fast, cost-effective itineraries.

Worldwide Services

Global Travel's Reservation Center will handle all of your weekend and after-hour reservations and changes. The reservation center can be dialed toll-free 24 hours a day. The worldwide service emergency numbers will be clearly marked on your travel itineraries.

Figure 8.15 **The completed MYCHAP8A.DOC document (Continued)**

Global Travel
Complete Travel Services

Discounts

Global Travel guarantees the lowest air fares available. Due to the volume of tickets that we issue, several of the large air carriers offer us special discounts that we can pass on to our clients.

Our quality-control specialists check each of your tickets to guarantee that you have received the lowest rate available. In addition, each ticket is checked to ensure that it includes seating assignments and boarding passes before it is delivered to you.

Deliveries

Our courier makes daily deliveries, both in the morning and afternoon, to offices within 20 miles of our local branch. All of our offices, each located across from the local airport, have drive-up windows. If you make last-minute travel plans with us you can pick up your ticket right at the drive-up window.

Auto Rentals

We guarantee the lowest prices on all car rentals. We will match the type of car with the information provided in the profile for each of your frequent travelers. Each car that is rented through Global Travel carries an extra $50,000 worth of liability insurance.

Hotel Accommodations

Our Corporate Hotel Program is the most competitive and comprehensive program in the world, offering corporate travelers cost savings and extra amenities in most business locations. Global Travel has access to more than 10,000 hotels worldwide, with a range of rooms from economy to luxury. This selection offers your corporate travelers the accommodations they want with a cost savings of 10-30% off the regular rates.

Figure 8.15   The completed MYCHAP8A.DOC document (Continued)

Global Travel
Complete Travel Services

Additional Services

Global Travel also provides the following services for our corporate customers:

Newsletter

All clients receive our monthly newsletter that covers a variety of travel topics, including:

- Travel costs – we will keep you informed about the competition among the large air carriers that will affect your travel costs.

- Special fares – we will keep you apprised of the many unadvertised special airline fares that we offer.

- Travel basics – our newsletter will provide you with suggestions to make your corporate travel safer and more enjoyable.

Telex

Telex service is available for international hotel confirmations.

Personal Vacations

Our corporate clients are invited to discuss their vacation and personal travel plans with an agent from Global Travel's Vacation Division. Our Vacation Division is skilled in both domestic and international travel.

Flight Insurance

We will supply all clients with $250,000 worth of flight insurance for every trip arranged through Global Travel.

Fax

Travel requests may be faxed to our office. Confirmed itineraries can be faxed to your office for immediate confirmation.

Figure 8.16   **The completed MYPRAC8A.DOC document**

Global Travel
Complete Travel Services

Introduction

Global Travel is a full-service, multi-branch travel agency, which was founded in 1970. Our specialty is corporate travel.

Global Travel has five branches: Philadelphia, Pennsylvania; San Francisco, California; Chicago, Illinois; Miami, Florida; and Houston, Texas. Each of these offices is operated by a team of qualified managers and experienced agents whose goal is to provide your company with quality service at the lowest price.

Customer Service

We at Global Travel feel that communication with our corporate accounts is essential for providing good service. Each corporate account is assigned to a specific account executive. Your account executive will be available to answer any questions and provide you with any information that you request.

The corporate travel division of Global Travel is designed to offer the best and most professional service available to your business travelers. We encourage you to tour our facility and meet our staff at your convenience.

International Travel

We offer complete international itinerary assistance. We maintain a supply of passport and visa applications so that we can provide the necessary papers to our clients with minimum delay. Our International Rate Program guarantees you fast and accurate pricing, no matter how complicated the itinerary.

Corporate Profiles

Your company profile will be stored in our computer, and individual profiles will be maintained on each frequent traveler. Each profile will contain information regarding passport information, seating preference, car rental preference, frequent-flyer membership number, and corporate discount numbers. This information ensures that we can provide frequent travelers, fast, cost-effective itineraries.

Worldwide Services

Global Travel's Reservation Center will handle all of your weekend and after-hour reservations and changes. The reservation center can be dialed toll-free 24 hours a day. The worldwide service emergency numbers will be clearly marked on your travel itineraries.

Figure 8.16   **The completed MYPRAC8A.DOC document (Continued)**

Global Travel
Complete Travel Services

Discounts

Global Travel guarantees the lowest air fares available. Due to the volume of tickets that we issue, several of the large air carriers offer us special discounts that we can pass on to our clients.

Our quality-control specialists check each of your tickets to guarantee that you have received the lowest rate available. In addition, each ticket is checked to ensure that it includes seating assignments and boarding passes before it is delivered to you.

Deliveries

Our courier makes daily deliveries, both in the morning and afternoon, to offices within 20 miles of our local branch. All of our offices, each located across from the local airport, have drive-up windows. If you make last-minute travel plans with us you can pick up your ticket right at the drive-up window.

Auto Rentals

We guarantee the lowest prices on all car rentals. We will match the type of car with the information provided in the profile for each of your frequent travelers. Each car that is rented through Global Travel carries an extra $50,000 worth of liability insurance.

Hotel Accommodations

Our Corporate Hotel Program is the most competitive and comprehensive program in the world, offering corporate travelers cost savings and extra amenities in most business locations. Global Travel has access to more than 10,000 hotels worldwide, with a range of rooms from economy to luxury. This selection offers your corporate travelers the accommodations they want with a cost savings of 10-30% off the regular rates.

Figure 8.16 **The completed MYPRAC8A.DOC document (Continued)**

Global Travel
Complete Travel Services

<u>**Additional Services**</u>

Global Travel also provides the following services for our corporate customers:

Newsletter

All clients receive our monthly newsletter that covers a variety of travel topics, including:

1. Travel costs – we will keep you informed about the competition among the large air carriers that will affect your travel costs.

2. Special fares – we will keep you apprised of the many unadvertised special airline fares that we offer.

3. Travel basics – our newsletter will provide you with suggestions to make your corporate travel safer and more enjoyable.

Telex

Telex service is available for international hotel confirmations.

Personal Vacations

Our corporate clients are invited to discuss their vacation and personal travel plans with an agent from Global Travel's Vacation Division. Our Vacation Division is skilled in both domestic and international travel.

Flight Insurance

We will supply all clients with $250,000 worth of flight insurance for every trip arranged through Global Travel.

Fax

Travel requests may be faxed to our office. Confirmed itineraries can be faxed to your office for immediate confirmation.

14. Apply the font formats from the Customer Service heading to the following headings:

International Travel

Corporate Profiles

Worldwide Services

Discounts

Deliveries

Auto Rentals

Hotel Accommodations

Additional Services

15. Save the disk file as **myprac8a.doc**.

16. Print the document and compare your printout to Figure 8.16.

17. Close both document windows.

In the next activity you will edit PRAC8C.DOC to produce the final document shown in Figure 8.17. You will use the Replace dialog box to replace font formats.

Follow these steps at your computer:

1. Open **prac8c.doc**.

2. Use the Replace dialog box to find text that is Helvetica, 24 point, bold, and replace these formats with **Times New Roman, 14 point, bold**.

3. Use the Replace dialog box to find text that is formatted as Tms Rmn (Times Roman), 12 point, bold and italic, and change it to **Helvetica, 10 point, bold**.

4. Use the Replace dialog box to find text that is formatted as Tms Rmn, 14 point, with a single underline. Change the formatting to **Helvetica, 10 point, bold**, and **no underline**.

5. Use the Replace dialog box to find text that is formatted as Helv (Helvetica), 14 point, italic. Replace these font formats with **Times New Roman, 10 point, italic**.

Figure 8.17   **The completed MYPRAC8C.DOC document**

Global Travel
Complete Travel Services

Introduction

Global Travel is a full-service, multi-branch travel agency, which was founded in 1970. Our specialty is corporate travel.

Global Travel has five branches: Philadelphia, Pennsylvania; San Francisco, California; Chicago, Illinois; Miami, Florida; and Houston, Texas. Each of these offices is operated by a team of qualified managers and experienced agents whose goal is to provide your company with quality service at the lowest price.

Customer Service

We at Global Travel feel that communication with our corporate accounts is essential for providing good service. Each corporate account is assigned to a specific account executive. Your account executive will be available to answer any questions and provide you with any information that you request.

The corporate travel division of Global Travel is designed to offer the best and most professional service available to your business travelers. We encourage you to tour our facility and meet our staff at your convenience.

International Travel

We offer complete international itinerary assistance. We maintain a supply of passport and visa applications so that we can provide the necessary papers to our clients with minimum delay. Our International Rate Program guarantees you fast and accurate pricing, no matter how complicated the itinerary.

Corporate Profiles

Your company profile will be stored in our computer, and individual profiles will be maintained on each frequent traveler. Each profile will contain information regarding passport information, seating preference, car rental preference, frequent-flyer membership number, and corporate discount numbers. This information ensures that we can provide frequent travelers, fast, cost-effective itineraries.

Worldwide Services

Global Travel's Reservation Center will handle all of your weekend and after-hour reservations and changes. The reservation center can be dialed toll-free 24 hours a day. The worldwide service emergency numbers will be clearly marked on your travel itineraries.

Figure 8.17   **The completed MYPRAC8C.DOC document (Continued)**

Global Travel
Complete Travel Services

Discounts

Global Travel guarantees the lowest air fares available. Due to the volume of tickets that we issue, several of the large air carriers offer us special discounts that we can pass on to our clients.

Our quality-control specialists check each of your tickets to guarantee that you have received the lowest rate available. In addition, each ticket is checked to ensure that it includes seating assignments and boarding passes before it is delivered to you.

Deliveries

Our courier makes daily deliveries, both in the morning and afternoon, to offices within 20 miles of our local branch. All of our offices, each located across from the local airport, have drive-up windows. If you make last-minute travel plans with us you can pick up your ticket right at the drive-up window.

Auto Rentals

We guarantee the lowest prices on all car rentals. We will match the type of car with the information provided in the profile for each of your frequent travelers. Each car that is rented through Global Travel carries an extra $50,000 worth of liability insurance.

Hotel Accommodations

Our Corporate Hotel Program is the most competitive and comprehensive program in the world, offering corporate travelers cost savings and extra amenities in most business locations. Global Travel has access to more than 10,000 hotels worldwide, with a range of rooms from economy to luxury. This selection offers your corporate travelers the accommodations they want with a cost savings of 10-30% off the regular rates.

Figure 8.17   **The completed MYPRAC8C.DOC document (Continued)**

Global Travel
Complete Travel Services

Additional Services

Global Travel also provides the following services for our corporate customers:

Newsletter

All clients receive our monthly newsletter that covers a variety of travel topics, including:

- Travel costs – we will keep you informed about the competition among the large air carriers that will affect your travel costs.

- Special fares – we will keep you apprised of the many unadvertised special airline fares that we offer.

- Travel basics – our newsletter will provide you with suggestions to make your corporate travel safer and more enjoyable.

Telex

Telex service is available for international hotel confirmations.

Personal Vacations

Our corporate clients are invited to discuss their vacation and personal travel plans with an agent from Global Travel's Vacation Division. Our Vacation Division is skilled in both domestic and international travel.

Flight Insurance

We will supply all clients with $250,000 worth of flight insurance for every trip arranged through Global Travel.

Fax

Travel requests may be faxed to our office. Confirmed itineraries can be faxed to your office for immediate confirmation.

6. Use the Replace dialog box to find text that is formatted as Helvetica, 12 point, with a single underline. Replace the formats with **Times New Roman, 10 point** font formats, and **no underline**.

7. Close the Replace dialog box.

8. Save the disk file as **myprac8c.doc**.

9. Print the document and compare your printout to Figure 8.17.

10. Close the document.

SUMMARY

In this chapter, you learned a number of advanced formatting and editing techniques that make use of the Standard toolbar and mouse, including copying and moving text within a single document and between documents. You learned how to create numbered lists and bulleted lists by adding numbers or bullets to a contiguous string of paragraphs. You also learned how to change a numbered list to a bulleted list, and vice versa. Finally, you learned how to copy and replace font formats.

Here is a quick reference guide to the Word features introduced in this chapter:

Desired Result	How to Do It
Disable the Summary Info dialog box	Choose **Tools, Options**; in the Save tab, uncheck **Prompt for Summary Info** under Save Options; click on **OK**.
Copy text using the Standard toolbar	Select the desired text; click on the **Copy** button; place the insertion point in the desired destination; click on the **Paste** button.
Move text using the mouse pointer	Select the desired text; point to the selected text; drag the selection to the desired destination; release the mouse button.

Desired Result	How to Do It
Copy text from one document to another	Open the second document; select the desired text; click on the **Copy** button; choose **Window** and choose the file name of the destination document; place the insertion point where you wish to place the copied text; click on the **Paste** button.
Save a document using the Standard toolbar	Click on the **Save** button (if the disk file has not been previously named, the Save As dialog box will open and you should name the disk file).
Close an inactive document window	Choose **Window** and the name of the document you wish to close; choose **File, Close**.
Add numbers or bullets to existing text	Select the desired paragraphs; click on the **Numbering** button or the **Bullets** button.
Change numbers to bullets or vice versa	Select the numbered or bulleted list; click on the **Bullets** or **Numbering** button, whichever you desire; click on **Yes**.
Remove numbers or bullets	Select the desired text; choose **Tools, Bullets and Numbering**; click on Remove.
Copy font formats	Place the insertion point anywhere within the text that has the formatting that you wish to copy; click on the **Format Painter** button in the Standard toolbar; and select the text to which you wish to copy the formats.

Desired Result	**How to Do It**
Replace font formats	Place the insertion point at the top of the document; choose **Edit, Replace**; click on **Format**, and choose **Font**; select the settings you want to find; click on **OK**. Press **Tab**; click on **Format**, and choose **Font**; select the replacement settings; click on **OK**. Click on **Find Next**; click on **Replace**; continue clicking on **Find Next**, then **Replace**, until you have finished replacing the formats.
Revise font formats	Place the insertion point at the top of the document; choose **Edit, Replace**; click on **Format**, and choose **Font**; select the settings you wish to find; click on **OK**. Press **Tab**; click on **Format**, and choose **Font**; select the new replacement settings; click on **OK**. Click on **Find Next**; click on **Replace**; and so on.

In the next chapter, you will learn how to create and use the Auto-Text feature to store frequently used text and graphics.

IF YOU'RE STOPPING HERE

If you need to break off here, please exit Word. If you want to proceed directly to the next chapter, please do so now.

CHAPTER 9: STORING FREQUENTLY USED TEXT WITH THE AUTOTEXT FEATURE

Creating AutoText Entries

Inserting AutoText Entries

Modifying AutoText Entries

Saving Global AutoText Entries

Printing AutoText Entries

Suppose you needed to send out a large number of letters with the same letterhead and closing. It would certainly save you a great deal of time to enter the letterhead and closing only once, and then simply paste them into each document, as needed. You could copy the information to the Clipboard and paste it into each letter. However, you already know that the Clipboard is only a temporary storage area; as soon as you cut or copied other text or exited Windows, the information would be lost.

Word enables you to save such information as an AutoText entry. Word's *AutoText* feature is a kind of shorthand that allows you to save text (or graphics), and then retrieve it whenever you need it. You can insert AutoText entries anywhere in your documents.

When you're done working through this chapter, you will know

- How to create AutoText entries

- How to modify and delete AutoText entries

- How to print AutoText entries

CREATING AUTOTEXT ENTRIES

AutoText entries enable you to store frequently used text and graphics so that you can insert them into your documents quickly and easily. AutoText entries are stored so that they can be used *globally,* in all templates. A *template* is a kind of "model" that determines the general format of the document it is attached to. Templates allow you to custom-tailor your documents. (You'll learn about templates in Chapter 13.) If you do not wish to use AutoText entries globally, you can store them to be used with a specific template.

To create an AutoText entry:

- Select the text or graphics you want in the AutoText entry.

- Click on the *AutoText* button (ninth from the right on the Standard toolbar), or choose *Edit, AutoText* to open the AutoText dialog box.

- In the Name text box, type a name for the AutoText entry (or accept the default one).

- Click on *Add.*

AutoText entries can contain any type of formatting. Entry names can have up to 32 characters and can contain spaces. For ease of use, you might want to keep your AutoText entry names brief.

Let's create AutoText entries for a letterhead and closing:

1. Click on the **New** button (the first Standard toolbar button on the left) to open a new document window.

2. Type **Global Travel** and press **Enter.**

3. Type **2345 Industrial Parkway** and press **Enter**.

4. Type **Chicago, Illinois 60603** and press **Enter** three times.

5. Select all of the text. Do *not* select the blank lines below the text.

6. Change the font to **Helvetica** (use the **Font** drop-down list box).

7. Apply the **Bold** character style to the selected text.

8. Center the selected text, and compare your screen to Figure 9.1.

9. Deselect the text.

10. This time, select all of the text *and* the three blank lines. The heading and blank lines will be included in the AutoText entry.

11. Choose **Edit, AutoText** (see Figure 9.2) to open the AutoText dialog box.

Figure 9.1   **The completed letterhead**

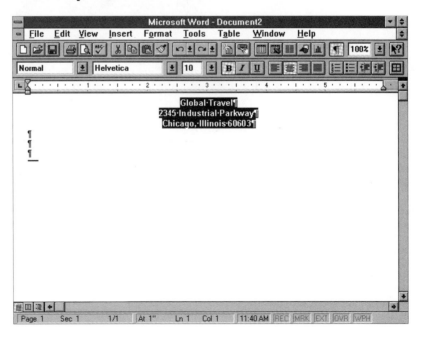

Figure 9.2   **Choosing Edit, AutoText**

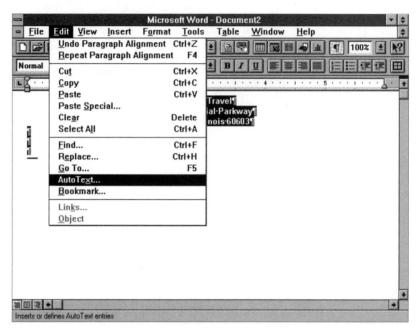

12. Observe the Selection box at the bottom of the AutoText dialog box. It allows you to verify the desired selection. Notice that a default name is provided in the Name text box; however, let's change the name.

13. In the Name text box, type **letterhead** to name the AutoText entry. Compare your screen to Figure 9.3.

14. Click on **Add** to add the AutoText entry to the list.

15. Close the document without saving it; saving is not necessary because the document's text has already been saved as an AutoText entry.

16. Click on the **New** button (the first Standard toolbar button on the left) to open a new document window.

17. Type **Cordially,** and press **Enter** four times.

18. Type your name and press **Enter**.

19. Type **Corporate Sales Coordinator** and press **Enter** twice.

Figure 9.3   **Naming the letterhead AutoText entry**

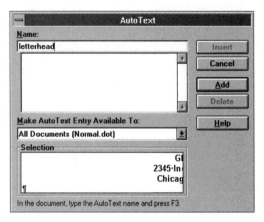

20. Type **cc:** and press **Tab** to move to the first tab stop.

21. Type **R. Allen** and press **Enter**.

22. Press **Tab**, type **G. Berg** and compare your screen to Figure 9.4.

23. Select all of the text and paragraph marks. The selected text will be included in the AutoText entry.

24. Click on the **Edit AutoText** button (ninth from the right in the Standard toolbar, directly above the Italic button) to open the AutoText dialog box again.

25. In the Name text box, type **cordially** to name the AutoText entry. Compare your screen to Figure 9.5. Notice that the letterhead entry, which you created earlier, is listed in the Name list box.

26. Click on **Add** to add the AutoText entry to the list.

27. Close the document without saving it.

INSERTING AUTOTEXT ENTRIES

To insert an AutoText entry in a document:

- Place the insertion point where you want to insert the Auto-Text entry.

- Click on the *AutoText* button (or choose *Edit, AutoText*).

Figure 9.4   Completed letter closing

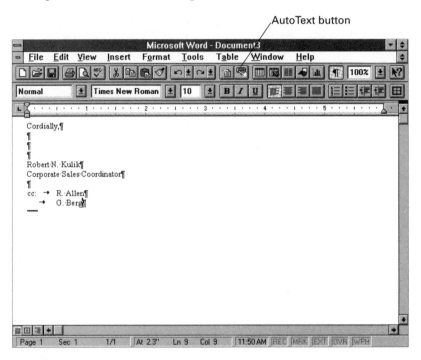

Figure 9.5   Naming the letter-closing AutoText entry

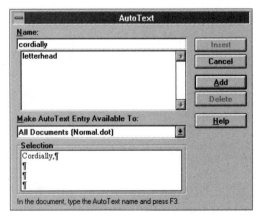

- Select the name of the AutoText entry you want to insert.
- Click on *Insert*.

Directly below the Name text box is the Insert As portion of the AutoText dialog box. Under Insert As, two choices are provided:

- *Formatted Text*, which will retain the formatting of the Auto-Text entry as it was originally created
- *Plain Text*, which tells Word to apply the formatting of the surrounding text to the AutoText entry

To insert an AutoText entry using the keyboard:

- Place the insertion point where you want to insert the Auto-Text entry.
- Type the name of the AutoText entry.
- Press *F3*.

If you want to insert the AutoText entry quickly, retaining its original formatting, we recommend using the AutoText button or the keyboard. However, if you don't remember the name of the entry, wish to insert it as plain text (without its original formatting), or simply wish to preview its contents, use the Edit, AutoText command.

Note: If you type the AutoText entry name in front of text, be sure to type a space after the AutoText name, and if you type an entry after text, make sure there is a space before the name. Otherwise, Word will beep to let you know that it can't determine which portion of the text is the AutoText name. Also remember that the AutoText name must be typed exactly the way you typed it when you named it (although the case of the name doesn't matter).

Let's insert the AutoText entries in a document:

1. Open **chap9.doc**. This letter contains no letterhead or closing.
2. Verify that the insertion point is at the top of the document.
3. Choose **Edit, AutoText** to open the AutoText dialog box.
4. In the Name list box, select **letterhead** (see Figure 9.6).
5. Click on **Insert** to insert the letterhead AutoText entry in the document. Compare your screen to Figure 9.7.
6. Move the insertion point to the end of the document.

Figure 9.6   **Inserting an AutoText entry**

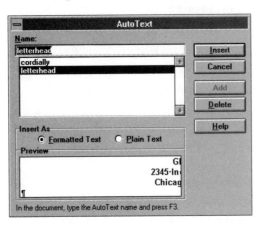

Figure 9.7   **The inserted *letterhead* AutoText entry**

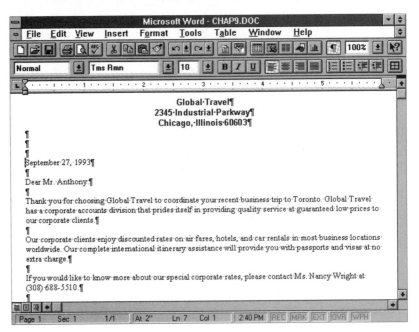

7. Click on the **AutoText** button to open the AutoText dialog box.

8. In the Name list box, select **cordially** (if necessary).

9. Click on **Insert** to insert the AutoText entry in the document. Compare your screen to Figure 9.8.

10. Save the disk file as **mychap9.doc**.

Note: The "extra" paragraph mark (¶) after the closing in Figure 9.8 was produced by inserting the AutoText entry before an existing paragraph mark.

Figure 9.8   **Inserted closing AutoText entry**

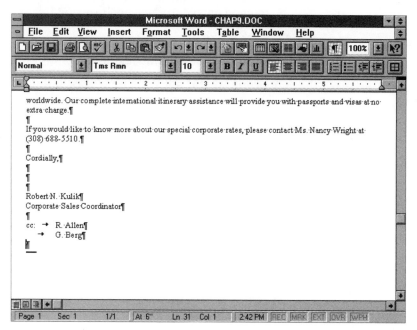

MODIFYING AUTOTEXT ENTRIES

After you have created an AutoText entry, you can go back and edit the text of the entry, in much the same way as you would a normal document.

EDITING AUTOTEXT ENTRIES

To edit an AutoText entry:

- Insert the AutoText entry that you want to edit into your document.

- Make the desired changes.

- Select the text and/or graphics you want in the AutoText entry.

- Click on the *AutoText* button, or choose *Edit, AutoText*.

- Select the original name of the AutoText entry. (If you wish to keep the original entry intact, type a new name for the entry.)

- Click on *Add*; a message box displays, asking if you want to redefine the AutoText entry. (If you used a new name for the revised entry, no message box will be displayed.)

- Click on *Yes*.

Let's edit one of our AutoText entries:

1. Verify that the insertion point is at the end of the document.

2. Press **Tab**, then type **K. Donnelly**, and press **Enter** (to add more names to the list).

3. Press **Tab**, then type **A. Hutton**, and press **Enter**.

4. Select the entire closing, from *Cordially* through *A. Hutton*. Do *not* select the last paragraph mark.

5. Click on the **AutoText** button.

6. In the Name list box, select **cordially**.

7. Click on **Add**. A message box displays, asking if you wish to redefine the AutoText entry (see Figure 9.9).

8. Click on **Yes** to redefine the *cordially* AutoText entry under the same name.

PRACTICE YOUR SKILLS

1. Delete the selected text. Do *not* move the insertion point.

2. Insert the new *cordially* AutoText entry.

Figure 9.9   **Editing an AutoText entry**

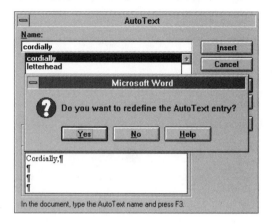

 DELETING AUTOTEXT ENTRIES

To remove an AutoText entry:

● Choose *Edit, AutoText* or click on the *AutoText* button.

● In the Name list box, select the name of the AutoText entry that you want to delete.

● Click on *Delete*.

● Click on *Close*.

Let's edit the AutoText entry, give it a new name, and then delete the old entry:

1. Select **Cordially,** and type **Sincerely,**

2. Select the entire closing, from *Sincerely* through *A. Hutton.* Do not select the last paragraph mark.

3. Click on the **AutoText** button.

4. In the Name text box, type **sincerely** to name the AutoText entry.

5. Click on **Add** to add the AutoText entry to the list.

6. Delete the selected text. Do *not* move the insertion point.

7. Type **sincerely** and press **F3** to insert the AutoText entry using the keyboard. Notice that the AutoText entry replaced the word *sincerely*.

8. Save the disk file and compare your screen to Figure 9.10.

Figure 9.10   **The new *sincerely* AutoText entry**

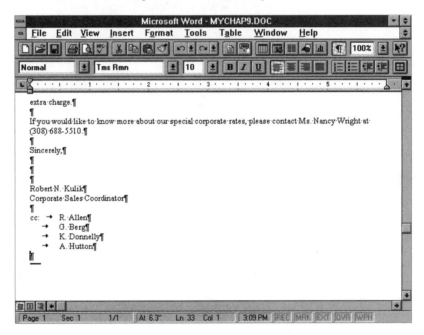

9. Open the AutoText dialog box (choose **Edit, AutoText** or click on the **AutoText** button).

10. Select **cordially** (if necessary).

11. Click on **Delete** to delete the selected AutoText entry.

12. Click on **Close** to close the AutoText dialog box.

PRACTICE YOUR SKILLS

Delete the *letterhead* AutoText entry.

PRINTING AUTOTEXT ENTRIES

You can print your AutoText entries so that you can see the contents of each entry. To print AutoText entries:

- Choose *File, Print*.

- In the Print What drop-down list box, select *AutoText Entries*.

- Click on *OK*.

All AutoText entries available to the active document are printed in alphabetical order. The formatting appears as it would if it were inserted in a document.

Let's print our AutoText entries:

1. Choose **File, Print**.

2. In the Print What drop-down list box, select **AutoText Entries** to print only AutoText entries (see Figure 9.11). Notice that under Page Range, all options are dimmed.

3. Click on **OK**.

4. Compare your printout with Figure 9.12. There is currently only one AutoText entry available (the *sincerely* entry).

5. Close the document.

Figure 9.11   **Printing AutoText entries**

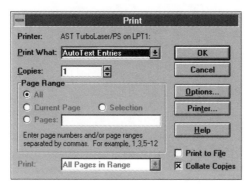

Figure 9.12   **The printed AutoText file**

AutoText entries in Global: NORMAL.DOT

     sincerely
Sincerely,

Marie C. Boyers
Corporate Sales Coordinator

cc: R. Allen
         G. Berg
         K. Donnelly
         A. Hutton

SUMMARY

In this chapter, you learned how to create AutoText entries and insert them in your documents. You also learned how to edit, delete, save, and print your AutoText entries.

Here is a quick reference guide to the Word features introduced in this chapter:

Desired Result	How to Do It
Create an AutoText entry	Select the desired text and/or graphics to be placed in the entry; choose **Edit, AutoText** or click on the **AutoText** button; name the entry in the Name text box; click on **Add**.
Insert an AutoText entry in a document using the mouse	Place the insertion point at the desired destination for the AutoText entry; choose **Edit, AutoText** or click on the **AutoText** button; select the name of the desired entry; click on **Insert**.
Insert an AutoText entry using the keyboard	Place the insertion point at the desired destination for the AutoText entry; type the name of the entry; press **F3**.
Edit an AutoText entry	Insert the AutoText entry to be edited in the document; make the desired changes; select the desired contents of the entry; choose **Edit, AutoText** or click on the **AutoText** button; select the original name of the entry; click on **Add**; click on **Yes**.
Delete an AutoText entry	Choose **Edit, AutoText** or click on the **AutoText** button; select the name of the AutoText entry to be deleted; click on **Delete**; click on **Close**.
Save an AutoText entry globally	Choose **File, Save All**.
Print all AutoText entries	Choose **File, Print**; in the Print What box, select **AutoText Entries**; click on **OK**.

In the next chapter, you will learn how to create, modify, and enhance tables.

IF YOU'RE STOPPING HERE

If you need to break off here, please exit Word. If you want to proceed directly to the next chapter, please do so now.

CHAPTER 10: WORKING WITH TABLES

Creating Tables

Modifying Tables

Enhancing Tables

Converting Tabbed
Text to a Table

If you want to arrange information in a table, you can do so by setting tabs. However, creating tabbed tables is a slow and tricky process; you must figure out exactly how the table should look, measure the width of each column, and then set tabs that correspond to each measurement. (You've already seen an example of a tabbed table in Chapter 5. See Figure 5.6 if you'd like to refer to the Hotel Accommodations tabbed table.) You can also run into problems if your text does not fit between your tabs.

Word's Table feature allows you to create rows and columns of information without having to set tabs. You can even convert tabbed text to a table. A table can be useful for enhancing the presentation of data in your document, for creating side-by-side paragraphs, and for organizing information used in form letters.

When you're done working through this chapter, you will know

- How to create a table
- How to modify a table
- How to enhance a table
- How to convert tabbed text to a table

CREATING TABLES

To insert a table into your document:

- Place the insertion point where you want to insert the table.
- Choose *Table, Insert Table*, or click on the *Insert Table* button in the Standard toolbar.

When you create tables by using the menu command, you specify the number of columns and rows in the Insert Table dialog box. You can also specify the width of the columns. When you use the Insert Table button to create tables, you drag on the Insert Table button grid to specify the number of columns and rows. This is analogous to the technique you used to print-preview multiple pages in Chapter 6. (You'll use the Insert Table button grid later in this section.)

Word creates a table that fills the area inside the margins. The width of the columns adjusts automatically according to the amount of space available between the left and right margins.

A table consists of vertical *columns* and horizontal *rows* (see Figure 10.1). The intersection of a column and a row is called a *cell*. Dotted lines called *gridlines* are displayed between the cells. You can hide the gridlines by choosing Table, Gridlines. Dotted lines called *column boundaries* are displayed between the columns. The gridlines and column boundaries are for visual reference only; they do not appear when you print the document.

If you display nonprinting characters, *end-of-cell* marks appear in each cell and *end-of-row* marks appear at the end of each row. You can use these marks to select and edit the table. Squares are displayed in the ruler above the column boundaries; these are called *column markers*. You can use these column markers to adjust the width of the columns by dragging them left or right. When you place the insertion point in a column, indent markers for that column are displayed in the ruler, enabling you to indent selected text as you desire.

Figure 10.1   **Table components**

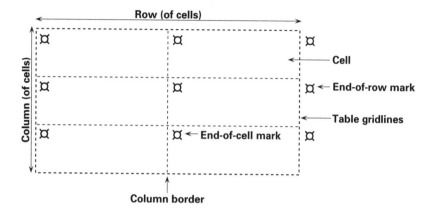

Note: When you Print Preview the table, the gridlines, end-of-cell marks, and end-of-row marks are not displayed.

Let's create and examine a table:

1. Open **chap10.doc**.

2. Go to page 2 and scroll to place the paragraph that begins *Global Travel guarantees* near the top of the document window. Place the insertion point in the blank line directly above the paragraph that begins *Our quality control.*

3. Choose **Table, Insert Table** to open the Insert Table dialog box, shown in Figure 10.2.

4. Observe the *Number of Columns* text box. You can change the number of columns by typing a number in the text box or by clicking on the increment indicators (see Figure 10.2).

5. Observe the *Number of Rows* text box. You can change the number of rows by typing a number in the text box or by clicking on the increment indicators.

6. Click on **Cancel**.

7. Click on the **Insert Table** button in the Standard toolbar (the eighth button from the right; see Figure 10.2) to display the Insert Table button grid.

8. Point to the upper-left corner of the Insert Table button grid.

Figure 10.2   **The Insert Table dialog box**

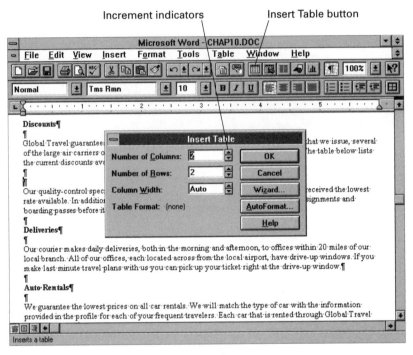

9. Press and hold the mouse button and drag down to select four rows of the grid. Then drag to the right to select two columns of the grid. The bottom of the grid displays *4x2 Table* (see Figure 10.3).

10. Release the mouse button to display the table at the insertion point.

11. Observe the *columns*, which are displayed vertically on the page (see Figure 10.1).

12. Observe the *rows*, which are displayed horizontally on the page.

13. Observe the *cells*, which are the intersections of columns and rows.

14. Observe the *gridlines*, the dotted lines between the cells.

15. Observe the *column boundaries*, the vertical dotted lines between the columns.

Figure 10.3   **Specifying table size in the Insert Table button grid**

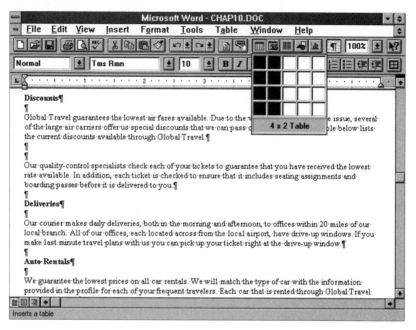

16. Observe the *end-of-cell marks*, the small circles inside the cells.

17. Observe the *end-of-row marks* at the end of each row.

18. Observe the *column markers* in the ruler (not shown in Figure 10.1); these are the square buttons placed above the column boundaries.

MOVING IN A TABLE

You can use the mouse to move to a table cell, or you can use the keyboard. To move to a specific cell using the mouse, simply place the I-beam on (or to the right of) the end-of-cell mark in the desired cell, and click. Table 10.1 lists the keystrokes used for moving within a table.

Table 10.1   **Moving in a Table Using the Keyboard**

Desired Result	How to Do It
Move one cell to the right	Press *Tab*.
Move one cell to the left	Press *Shift+Tab*.
Move up one row	Press *Up Arrow*.
Move down one row	Press *Down Arrow*.

If the insertion point is in the last cell of a row when you press Tab, the insertion point will move to the first cell in the next row. Likewise, if the insertion point is in the first cell of a row when you press Shift+Tab, it will move to the last cell in the previous row.

Note: If you use the arrow keys on the numeric keypad, Num Lock must be turned off.

Let's practice moving in the table we've created:

1. Press **Tab** to move the insertion point to the second column of the first row.

2. Press **Tab** to move the insertion point to the first column in the second row.

3. Press **Shift+Tab** to move back to the second column of the first row.

4. Press **Down Arrow** to move down one row.

5. Press **Up Arrow** to move up one row.

6. Place the I-beam in the last cell of the table on (or to the right of) the end-of-cell mark, and click the mouse button to place the insertion point in the last cell.

PRACTICE YOUR SKILLS

Place the insertion point in the first cell of the table.

SELECTING TABLE COMPONENTS

You can select a cell, a row, a column, or the entire table. Table 10.2 lists the methods used for making these selections.

Table 10.2 **Selecting in a Table**

Desired Selection	How to Do It
Cell	Click in the cell's selection bar (the area to the left of the text (if any) and the end-of-cell mark).
Row	Place the insertion point anywhere within the desired row and choose *Table, Select Row*; click in the selection bar to the left of the row; or double-click in the selection bar of any cell within the row.
Column	Place the I-beam on the top border of the desired column until it becomes a downward-pointing arrow, and click the mouse button; or place the insertion point anywhere in the column, and choose *Table, Select Column*.
Entire table	Place the insertion point anywhere within the table and choose *Table, Select Table*.

Let's try various selection techniques within our table:

1. Point to the left of the end-of-cell mark in the first cell until the mouse pointer becomes an arrow. (Make sure that the mouse pointer is still located within the cell; the mouse pointer should appear as an arrowhead.)

2. Click to select the cell. Compare your screen to Figure 10.4.

3. In the selection bar, point to the left of the first row.

4. Click the mouse button to select the entire row (see Figure 10.5).

Figure 10.4   **The selected cell**

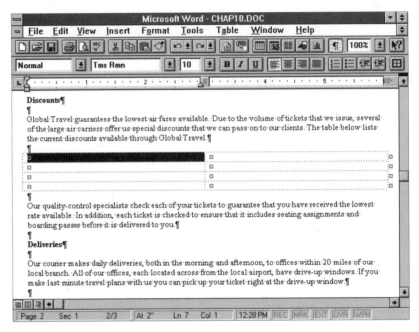

Figure 10.5   **The selected row**

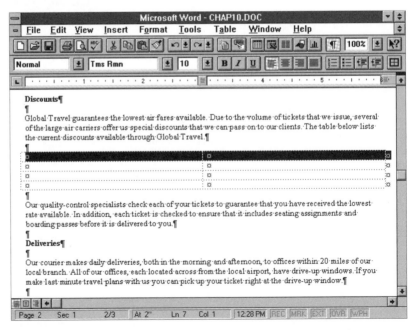

5. Point to the top border of the second column, until the mouse pointer becomes a downward-pointing arrow. Then click to select the entire column (see Figure 10.6).

Figure 10.6 **The selected column**

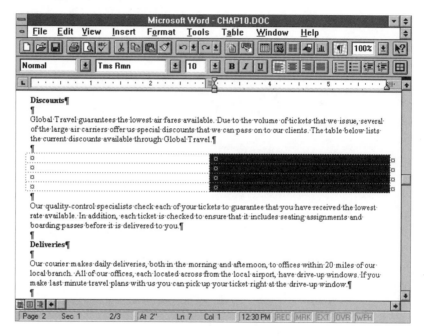

6. Choose **Table, Select Table** to select the entire table. Compare your screen to Figure 10.7.

7. Deselect the table (click above or below the table).

8. Choose **Table**. Notice that when the insertion point is not in the table, only four Table menu commands are available. Close the Table menu (click on **Table**).

ENTERING TEXT IN A TABLE

To enter text in a table, either select a cell or place the insertion point in the cell; then begin typing.

Figure 10.7   **The selected table**

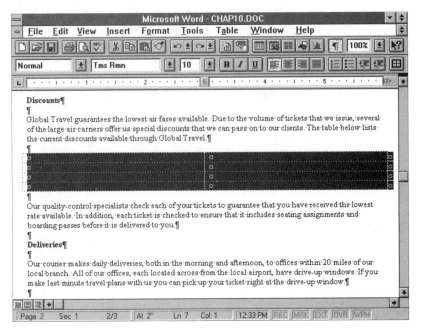

Let's enter text in our table:

1. Place the I-beam on the end-of-cell mark in the first cell and click.

2. Type **Destination**.

3. Press **Tab** to move to the next cell.

4. Type **Your Price** and press **Tab**.

PRACTICE YOUR SKILLS

1. Complete the table as shown in Figure 10.8.

2. Print Preview the table. (Don't expect much; the table is currently fairly nondescript. We'll spice up its appearance as the chapter progresses.)

3. Save the disk file as **mychap10**.

Figure 10.8   **The completed table**

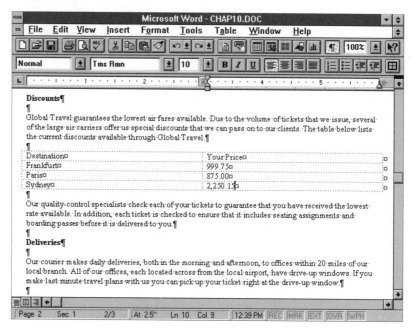

MODIFYING TABLES

After you have created your table—even after you have entered all the desired data—you can still change its structure. You can insert rows and columns within the table, add rows to the bottom or columns to the right side of the table, change the width of the columns, and delete rows and columns.

INSERTING ROWS AND COLUMNS

To insert a row at the end of a table, place the insertion point in the last cell of the table and press the Tab key. To insert a row *within* a table, select the row where you want to insert the new row (the new row will be inserted above the selected row) and choose *Table, Insert Rows*, or click on the *Insert Rows* button (the erstwhile *Insert Table* button). To insert more than one row in a table, select as many rows as you want to insert (the new rows will be inserted above the selected rows) and choose *Table, Insert Rows*, or click on the *Insert Rows* button. The number of rows that you select is the number of rows that will be inserted.

To insert a column at the end of a table, select all of the end-of-row marks (by placing the I-beam directly above the marks until it becomes a downward-pointing arrow and clicking once); then choose *Table, Insert Columns* or click on the *Insert Columns* button (you guessed it—the same button as Insert Table and Insert Rows). To insert a column within a table, select the column where you want to insert a new column (the new column will be inserted to the left of the selected column) and choose *Table, Insert Columns* or click on the *Insert Columns* button. To insert more than one column within a table, select as many columns as you want to insert (the new columns will be inserted to the left of the selected columns) and choose *Table, Insert Columns* or click on the *Insert Columns* button. The number of columns that you select is the number of columns that will be inserted.

Let's insert rows and columns in our table:

1. Verify that the insertion point is in the last cell of the table.

2. Press the **Tab** key. Voilà! A new row is inserted at the end of the table.

3. Type **Hong Kong** and press **Tab**.

4. Type **2,100.00**.

5. In the selection bar, point to the left of the second row. Press and hold the mouse button, and drag to select the second and third rows (to tell Word to insert two rows); then release the mouse button.

6. Place the mouse pointer (but do *not* click) on the Insert Table button. Notice that its name has changed to *Insert Rows*. Let's use the menu to insert our rows.

7. Choose **Table, Insert Rows** to insert two rows above the selected rows. Compare your screen to Figure 10.9.

8. Select the entire second column (click on the top border of the second column).

Figure 10.9   **The inserted rows**

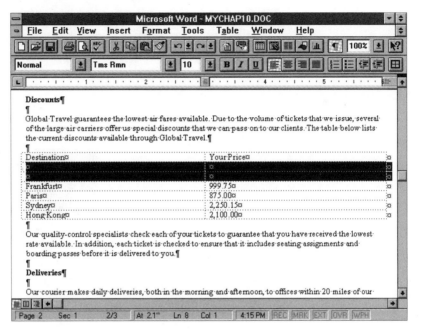

9. Open the Table menu. Notice (but do *not* choose) the first menu option: *Insert Columns.* This time, let's use the Standard toolbar. Click on **Table** to close the menu.

10. Place the mouse pointer on what was the Insert Rows button in step 6. The name *Insert Columns* is displayed.

11. Click on the **Insert Columns** button, and then compare your screen to Figure 10.10.

12. Scroll right to view the end-of-row marks.

13. Place the I-beam directly above the end-of-row mark at the end of the first row, and click once to select all the end-of-row marks.

14. Click on the **Insert Columns** button to insert a column at the end of the table.

15. Scroll right to view the entire inserted column, and compare your screen to Figure 10.11.

Figure 10.10 **The inserted column**

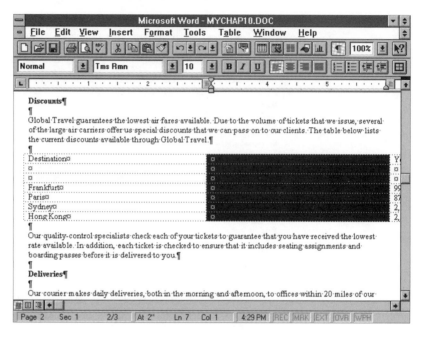

Figure 10.11 **The column added to the end of the table**

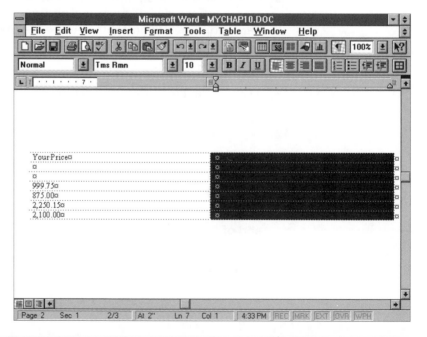

PRACTICE YOUR SKILLS

1. In the first row of the second column, enter the heading **Standard Price**.

2. Complete the second column as shown in Figure 10.12.

Figure 10.12   The data entered in the second column

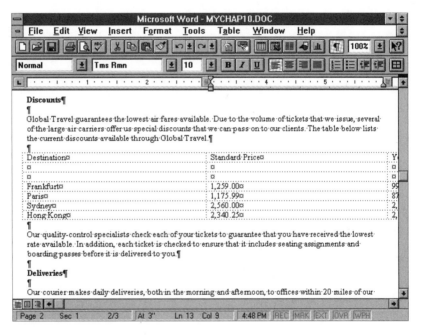

3. In the first row of the fourth column, enter the heading **Savings**.

4. Complete the fourth column as shown in Figure 10.13.

5. Save the disk file.

DELETING ROWS, COLUMNS, AND ENTIRE TABLES

To delete one or more contiguous rows in a table, select the row or rows that you want to delete; then choose *Table, Delete Rows*.

Figure 10.13   The data entered in the fourth column

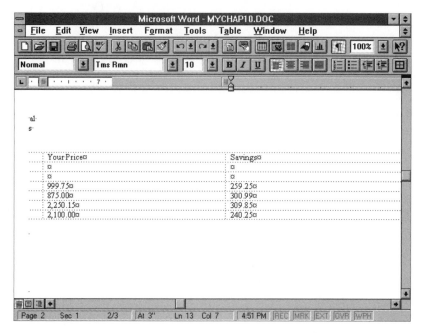

To delete one or more contiguous columns, select the column or columns that you want to delete; then choose *Table, Delete Columns*.

To delete an entire table, select the table; then choose *Table, Delete Rows*.

Let's delete a row in our table:

1. Select the second row (click in the selection bar, to the left of the second row).

2. Choose **Table, Delete Rows** to delete the selected row (see Figure 10.14).

CHANGING COLUMN WIDTH

To change column width by dragging column boundaries:

• Point to the column boundary that you want to move; the mouse pointer will become a horizontal, double-headed arrow.

Figure 10.14 **The table after deleting a row**

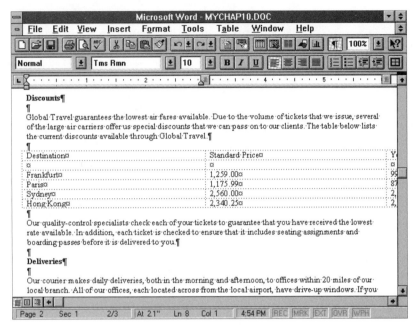

- Press and hold the mouse button.
- Drag the column boundary to the desired location.
- Release the mouse button.

To change column width by using the ruler:

- On the ruler, point to the column marker that you want to move; the mouse pointer will become a horizontal, double-headed arrow.
- Press and hold the mouse button.
- Drag the column marker to the desired location.
- Release the mouse button.

To change column width by using the menu:

- Select the desired column (or the entire table).
- Choose *Table, Cell Height and Width*.
- Click on the *Column* tab.

- Type the desired width in the Width of Column text box.

- Click on *OK*.

When you change the column width using the first two of these techniques (dragging column boundaries and column markers), all columns to the right are proportionally resized, and the width of the entire table does not change. If you change column width using the third technique (the Cell Height and Width menu command), the width of the table changes to accommodate the adjusted width of its columns. If you decrease the width of the columns, the width of the entire table decreases. If you increase the width of the columns, the width of the entire table increases.

Note: Before you print a document that contains a table, use Print Preview to make sure that the entire table fits on the page.

To automatically adjust column width so that the table fits on the page:

- Choose *Table, Cell Height and Width*.

- Click on the *Column* tab.

- Click on *AutoFit*.

Let's try using all three manual methods to change the width of columns in our table:

1. Point to the column boundary between the *Destination* and *Standard Price* headings. The mouse becomes a double-headed arrow.

2. Press and hold the mouse button, and drag the column border to the left until it is just to the right of the end-of-cell mark in the *Hong Kong* cell. This decreases the width of the first column. Release the mouse button. The second column is now considerably wider.

3. In the ruler, point to the column marker near the 5" mark. Hold down the Alt key as you drag the column marker to decrease the width of the second column to 1.66" on the ruler (holding down the Alt key displays the exact column width as you drag the column marker).

4. Select the entire table (choose **Table, Select Table**).

5. Choose **Table, Cell Height and Width** to open the Cell Height and Width dialog box, and click on the **Column** tab (if necessary).

6. In the Width of Columns 1-4 text box, click to place the insertion point, and type **1.25** to set the width of all columns in the table to 1.25" (see Figure 10.15).

Figure 10.15   Setting column width

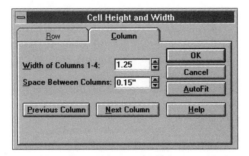

7. Click on **OK** to close the dialog box, and deselect the table. Notice that all four columns are now equal in width. Compare your screen to Figure 10.16.

ENHANCING TABLES

You already know how to enhance text in your document; doing so can improve its appearance and often its readability. Accentuating important text helps the eye to locate these reference points. The same text enhancements that are available in standard document text are also available when working in tables, including, for example, bold and italic font styles, changes in font and font size, and text alignment within a cell. In addition, you can alter the alignment of the entire table relative to the margins you're using. You can apply any font formats to text within a table. You can also enhance a table by adding a border or gridlines that will appear when the document is printed.

Figure 10.16   The table with columns of equal width

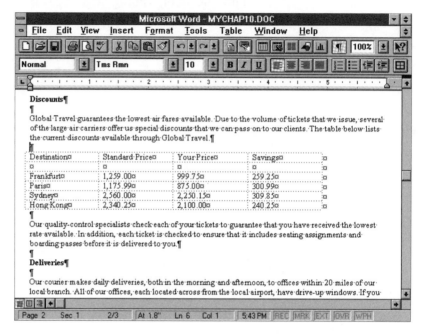

ALIGNING A TABLE

To align a table between the left and right margins:

- Select the entire table.

- Choose *Table, Cell Height and Width*.

- Click on the *Row* tab, if necessary.

- Under Alignment, select the desired alignment.

- Click on *OK*.

Let's format and align text in our table, and then center the table between the left and right margins:

1. Select the first row, which contains the column headings.

2. Make all of the text in the first row bold.

3. Select the entire second column, and then drag (within the table) to select the third and fourth columns. The second through fourth columns are now selected.

4. Right-align the selected text. All of the text in the selected columns is now right-aligned.

5. Click on the **Show/Hide** button to hide the end-of-cell marks. Now you can view the table without all the extraneous marks.

6. Click on the **Show/Hide** button to display the end-of-cell marks.

7. Print Preview page 2. The table is currently aligned along the left margin.

8. Close Print Preview.

9. Select the entire table. Then choose **Table, Cell Height and Width** to open the Cell Height and Width dialog box. Click on the **Row** tab, if necessary.

10. Under Alignment, click on **Center** to center the table between the left and right margins (see Figure 10.17).

Figure 10.17   **Centering the table**

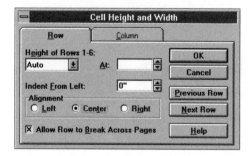

11. Click on **OK**. Then deselect the table.

12. Print Preview the document. The table is centered between the left and right margins.

13. Close Print Preview.

14. Save the disk file and compare your screen to Figure 10.18.

Figure 10.18   The centered table

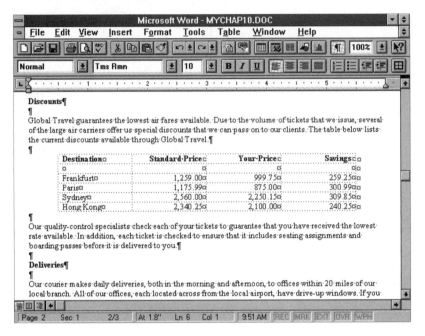

ADDING BORDERS

To add a border to a table:

- Select the table, column, row, or cell around which you want to add a border.

- Choose *Format, Borders and Shading* and click on the *Borders* tab.

- Under Presets, click on the desired border type.

- Under Line, select a line style from the Style list box.

- Click on *OK*.

Before closing the dialog box, you can observe the sample diagram in the Border portion of the dialog box to see the effect of the border and line type that you selected.

Let's add borders to our table:

1. Select the entire table.

2. Choose **Format, Borders and Shading** to open the Table Borders and Shading dialog box, and click on the **Borders** tab (if necessary).

3. Under Presets (in the top-left corner of the dialog box), click on **Box** to specify a box-type border for the table.

4. Under Line in the Style list box, select the **3/4 pt** thin double lines (approximately halfway down the list). Compare your screen to Figure 10.19.

Figure 10.19   Selecting a table border

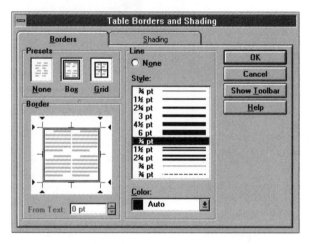

5. Observe the Border box. The double line is displayed around the sample diagram.

6. Click on **OK**. Deselect the table. Notice that the selected border is now displayed around the table.

7. Select the entire table. (Remember to click inside the table first.)

8. Choose **Format, Borders and Shading** to open the Table Borders and Shading dialog box.

9. Under Presets, click on the **Grid** option to place a grid around the cells. Unlike the dotted gridlines that currently appear in our document, this grid will display when the

document is printed. (Selecting the Grid option will also place a border around the table if it doesn't already have one.)

10. Click on **OK**. Deselect the table. Notice the change in the table. The dotted gridlines are replaced with solid ones (see Figure 10.20).

Figure 10.20   **The completed table with border and gridlines**

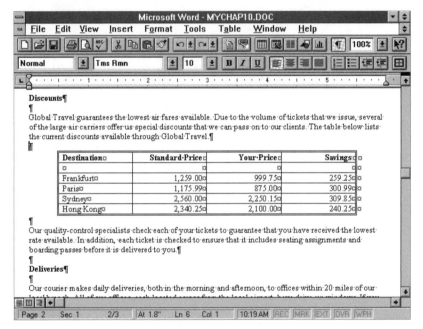

CONVERTING TABBED TEXT TO A TABLE

Word enables you to convert a tabbed table created by inserting tabs between columns of text into an actual table consisting of cells, rows, and columns. To convert tabbed text to a table:

- Select the text that you want to convert to a table.

- Choose *Table, Convert Text to Table*.

- In the Number of Columns text box, enter the desired number of columns.

- Click on *OK*.

Note: In addition to converting text separated by tabs, you can convert text that is separated by paragraph marks, commas, or other characters. To indicate the type of character you want to use to separate the text, select the character under *Separate Text At* in the *Convert Text to Table* dialog box.

You can also convert table text into ordinary text.

Let's convert tabbed text to a table:

1. Scroll to place the *Hotel Accommodations* heading, near the bottom of page 2, at the top of the screen.

2. Observe the tabbed text at the bottom of page 2.

3. Select all of the lines in the tabbed table, from *Location* to *Hong Kong*, that will be placed in the table. Notice that our tabbed table consists of three columns of information in six rows. We'll retain this structure.

4. Choose **Table, Convert Text to Table**. The Convert Text to Table dialog box is displayed. Word knows how many rows we want in our table (determined by the paragraph marks), but we need to supply the number of columns.

5. In the Number of Columns text box, type **3** to specify three columns.

6. Under Separate Text At, click on **Tabs** to tell Word that tab marks currently indicate column boundaries. Compare your screen to Figure 10.21.

7. Click on **OK**. The selected text appears in a table. Notice that the column widths need some adjustment.

8. Verify that the entire table is selected. Then choose **Table, Cell Height and Width** to open the Cell Height and Width dialog box, and display the Column tab.

9. In the Width of Columns 1-3 text box, type **1.5** to set the width of all of the columns to 1.5", and click on **OK**. The table now consists of three equally spaced columns.

PRACTICE YOUR SKILLS

1. Place a grid border around the table and between all the cells. (**Hint:** Use the **Grid** option under Presets in the Table Borders and Shading dialog box.) Accept the default line style.

Figure 10.21   **Converting tabbed text to a table**

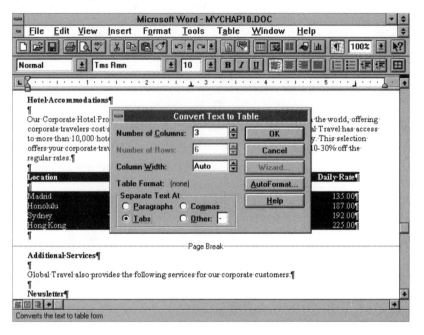

2. Center all the information in column 2.

3. Right-align all the information in column 3.

4. Center the table between the left and right margins.

5. Deselect the table.

6. Save the disk file and compare your screen to Figure 10.22.

7. Close the document.

PRACTICE YOUR SKILLS

This exercise gives you the opportunity to practice the skills you just learned. The following instructions lead you through the steps necessary to edit the disk file PRAC10A.DOC to produce the document in Figure 10.23.

Follow these steps at your computer:

1. Open **prac10a.doc** (Chapter 2).

Figure 10.22   **The converted table**

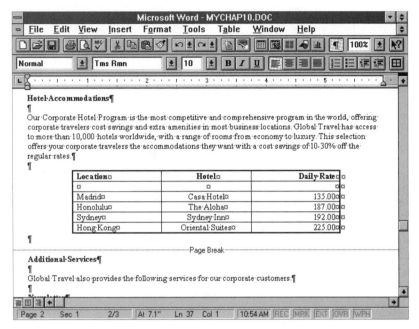

2. Type the following information into the table title *Projected Quarterly Sales Table*:

Row 3:	**Trader Tom's**	**2300**	**1.49**
Row 4:	**Aunt Emily's Market**	**4900**	**1.29**
Row 5:	**Hamlet Farms**	**6500**	**1.29**

3. Delete the row that contains information for *Price Farms*.

4. Right-align the second and third columns.

5. Change the column width for the *Boxes Sold* column to **1"**.

6. Change the column width for *Profit (per box)* to **1.25"**.

7. Center the table on the page.

8. Save the disk file as **mypr10a** (Chapter 1).

9. Print the document and compare it to Figure 10.23 (Chapter 1).

10. Close the document (Chapter 1).

Figure 10.23   The completed MYPR10A.DOC document

The Garden Patch
Product Line Announcement

Introduction

The Garden Patch is pleased to announce the unveiling of a new food line in the Garden Patch series: the Fruit Patch. The Fruit Patch product line was developed after two years of intense work through the cooperation and dedication of Dr. Faye Shad and her staff. The FDA recently approved the food and it will be released for public sale in three weeks.

The Fruit Patch includes a variety of organically grown fruit: berries (cherries, strawberries, raspberries, blackberries, and blueberries), apricots, peaches, grapes, and plums.

Projected Quarterly Sales

Our finance department has been hard at work, determining sales projections for the next quarter. The results are shown in the following table.

Projected Quarterly Sales Table

Vendors	Boxes Sold	Profit (per box)
Trader Tom's	2300	1.49
Aunt Emily's Market	4900	1.29
Hamlet Farms	6500	1.29
B and J's	10000	.79
Hout and Wallace Inc.	11500	.79

If you have finished the activity, you might like to try a more challenging one requiring similar skills. In the next activity you will edit PRAC10B.DOC to create the document shown in Figure 10.24.

Follow these steps at your computer:

1. Open **prac10b.doc** (Chapter 2).

2. Below the *Projected Quarterly Sales Table* heading, create a table that contains three columns and five rows.

3. Enter the data as shown in Figure 10.24.

4. Make the column headings in the first row bold.

5. Right-align the second and third columns.

6. Decrease the column width for the second and third columns to **1.5"**.

7. Center the table on the page.

8. Place a grid border on the table.

9. Save the disk file as **mypr10b** (Chapter 2).

10. Print the document and compare it to Figure 10.24 (Chapter 1).

11. Close the document (Chapter 1).

SUMMARY

In this chapter, you learned how to create tables using the Insert Table button in the Standard toolbar or the Table, Insert Table command from the menu. You learned how to move within a table; how to select cells, rows, columns, and the entire table; and how to enter data in a table. You also learned how to insert and delete rows and columns, how to change column width, how to change the alignment of a table between the left and right margins, and how to enhance the appearance of a table by creating various types of borders. Finally, you learned how to convert tabbed text to a table.

Figure 10.24   The completed MYPR10B.DOC document

> ### The Garden Patch
> ### Product Line Announcement
>
> **Introduction**
>
> The Garden Patch is pleased to announce the unveiling of a new food line in the Garden Patch series: the Fruit Patch. The Fruit Patch product line was developed after two years of intense work through the cooperation and dedication of Dr. Faye Shad and her staff. The FDA recently approved the food and it will be released for public sale in three weeks.
>
> The Fruit Patch includes a variety of organically grown fruit: berries (cherries, strawberries, raspberries, blackberries, and blueberries), apricots, peaches, grapes, and plums.
>
> **Projected Quarterly Sales**
>
> Our finance department has been hard at work, determining sales projections for the next quarter. The results are shown in the following table.
>
> **Projected Quarterly Sales Table**
>
> | Vendors | Boxes Sold | Total Profit |
> | --- | --- | --- |
> | | | |
> | Trader Tom's | 2,300 | 3,427.37 |
> | Aunt Emily's Market | 4,900 | 6,321.25 |
> | Hamlet Farms | 6,500 | 7,085.98 |

Here is a quick reference guide to the Word features introduced in this chapter:

Desired Result	**How to Do It**
Create a table using the menu	Choose **Table, Insert Table**; type the desired number of columns in the Number of Columns text box; type the number of rows in the Number of Rows text box; click on **OK**.
Create a table using the Standard toolbar	Click on the **Insert Table** button; drag to select the boxes of the grid corresponding to the desired number of rows and columns; release the mouse button.
Move within the table using the mouse	Place the I-beam on (or to the right of) the end-of-cell mark of the desired cell; click.
Move within the table using the keyboard:	
Move one cell to the right	Press Tab.
Move one cell to the left	Press Shift+Tab.
Move up one row	Press Up Arrow.
Move down one row	Press Down Arrow.
Select a cell	Move the mouse pointer in the cell's selection bar until it becomes an arrow; click.
Select a row	Click the mouse button in the selection bar, to the left of the row, or place the insertion point anywhere within the desired row; choose **Table, Select Row**.

Desired Result	How to Do It
Select a column	Click on the top border of the desired column; or place the insertion point in any cell within the desired column, and choose **Table, Select Column**.
Select an entire table	Place the insertion point anywhere within the table; choose **Table, Select Table**.
Add a row at the end of a table	Place the insertion point in the last cell of the table; press **Tab**.
Insert a row within a table	Select the row before which you want to insert the new row; choose **Table, Insert Rows**, or click on the **Insert Rows** button.
Insert more than one row in a table	Select as many rows as you want to insert; choose **Table, Insert Rows**, or click on the **Insert Rows** button.
Add a column to the right side of a table	Select all the end-of-row marks; choose **Table, Insert Columns** or click on the **Insert Columns** button.
Insert a column within a table	Select the column to the left of where you want to insert the new column; choose **Table, Insert Columns** or click on the **Insert Columns** button.
Insert more than one column within a table	Select as many columns as you want to insert; and choose **Table, Insert Columns** or click on the **Insert Columns** button.

Desired Result	How to Do It
Delete one or more rows	Select the row or rows that you want to delete; choose **Table, Delete Rows**.
Delete one or more columns	Select the column or columns that you want to delete; choose **Table, Delete Columns**.
Delete an entire table	Select the table; choose **Table, Delete Rows**.
Change column width by dragging column boundaries	Point to the column boundary that you want to move until the mouse pointer becomes a horizontal, double-headed arrow; drag the column boundary to the desired location; release the mouse button.
Change column width by using the ruler	On the ruler, point to the column marker that you want to move, drag the column marker to the desired location, and release the mouse button.
Change column width by using the menu	Select the desired column (or the entire table); choose **Table, Cell Height and Width**; click on the **Column** tab (if necessary); type the desired width in the Width of Column text box; and click on **OK**.
Align a table between the left and right margins	Select the entire table; choose **Table, Cell Height and Width**; click on the **Row** tab (if necessary); under Alignment, select the desired alignment; and click on **OK**.

Desired Result	How to Do It
Create a table border	Select the table, column, row, or cell around which you want to add a border; choose **Format, Borders and Shading**; click on the **Borders** tab (if necessary); under Presets, select a border type; under Line, select a line style in the Style list box; and click on **OK**.
Convert tabbed text to a table	Select the tabbed text that you want to convert to a table; choose **Table, Convert Text to Table;** enter the desired number of columns; under Separate Text At, select the desired separation character (if necessary); and click on **OK**.

In the next chapter, you will learn how to create newspaper-style columns and add graphics to your documents.

IF YOU'RE STOPPING HERE

If you need to break off here, please exit Word. If you want to proceed directly to the next chapter, please do so now.

CHAPTER 11: NEWSPAPER-STYLE COLUMNS AND GRAPHICS

Creating Multicolumn Text

Modifying Multicolumn Text Formats

Using Graphics

Word's Drawing Feature

This chapter introduces ways to format text into *newspaper-style columns* (two or more columns running side-by-side down the page). Newspaper-style columns are useful in creating documents such as newsletters, brochures, and reports. In newspaper columns, the document text "snakes," or flows, down the length of one column, then continues at the top of the next column, and so on. If all of the columns on the page become filled, any additional text continues onto the first column of the next page.

Word also provides you with powerful tools for incorporating graphic images, or *graphics,* into your documents and for creating drawings.

When you're done working through this chapter, you will know

- How to format text into newspaper-style columns
- How to insert a graphic into your document
- How to size and move a graphic
- How to create a border around a graphic
- How to draw in your document
- How to size and move a drawing
- How to superimpose text on a drawing

CREATING MULTICOLUMN TEXT

You can define your columns before typing the text, or you can reformat existing text into newspaper-style columns.

To create newspaper-style columns using the Format, Columns command:

- Place the insertion point where you want the columns to begin.
- Choose *Format, Columns* to open the Columns dialog box.
- Specify the desired number of columns in the *Number of Columns* text box, or click on one of the predefined column formats under Presets.
- In the *Apply To* drop-down list box, select *This Point Forward, Whole Document*, or *This Section* (as explained below).
- Click on *OK.*

Note: There is a limit to the number of columns you can specify, based on your document's margins and the default tab stops. Each column must be at least as wide as the distance between the default tab stops (0.5").

When you select *This Point Forward* in the Apply To drop-down list box, Word applies your specified multicolumn format from the insertion point to the end of the document. Word then inserts a *section break* directly before the insertion point; the section break is displayed as a double dotted line marked *End of Section*. Compare this to a page break, which is displayed as a single dotted line marked *Page Break*. Dividing a document into sections—each of which consists of one or more pages—allows you to apply different page-formatting options to each section. The status bar displays the section number in which the insertion point is placed.

When you select *Whole Document* in the Apply To drop-down list box, Word sets your specified multicolumn format for the entire document, regardless of where the insertion point is placed.

When you select *This Section* in the Apply To drop-down list box, Word sets your specified multicolumn format for the entire section in which the insertion point is placed. (This option will only be available if your document already contains section breaks.)

To create newspaper-style columns using the Columns button:

- Place the insertion point anywhere in the section of the document where you want to create your newspaper-style columns.

- Click on the *Columns* button in the Standard toolbar to open a miniature four-column window.

- Click on the first (leftmost) miniature column to specify a single-column format; click on the second column to specify two columns; click on the third column to specify three columns; or click on the fourth (rightmost) column to specify four columns.

Note: When you use the Columns button to create newspaper-style columns, Word automatically applies your specified number of columns (1, 2, 3, or 4) to the entire section in which the insertion point is placed.

Columns will not appear in the document window in Normal view. To display the text in columns, you must either Print Preview the document or change to Page Layout view.

Let's open a new document and create a newspaper-style column format:

1. Open **chap11.doc**.

2. Choose **File, Print Preview**. Notice that all of the text is currently in a standard, single-column format.

3. Click on the **Close** button to return to Normal view.

4. Place the insertion point to the left of the *I* in the *Introduction* heading, near the top of the page.

5. Choose **Format, Columns** to open the Columns dialog box.

6. In the Number of Columns box, click once on the **up increment indicator** to change the number to **2**. The Preview box displays a sample of the two-column format.

7. Open the **Apply To** drop-down list box. Select **This Point Forward** to format the text as two columns from the insertion point to the end of the document. Again, observe the Preview box, as shown in Figure 11.1.

Figure 11.1   **Changing to two-column format**

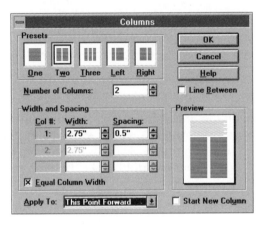

8. Click on **OK**.

9. Observe the section break, the double-dotted line marked *End of Section* above the *Introduction* heading. All of the text from the section break to the end of the document is formatted as two columns. Note that *Sec 2* appears in the status bar, because the insertion point is in the second (newly formatted) section. Note also that the side-by-side columns are not visible in Normal view.

10. Choose **View, Page Layout**. The side-by-side columns are now visible.

11. Scroll to view the document.

MODIFYING MULTICOLUMN TEXT FORMATS

When you create multiple (newspaper-style) columns, Word automatically apportions even amounts of space within each column and between columns, based on your document's margins. However, you can modify these values. For example, by default, Word places one-half inch of space between each column. Depending on the effect you desire, as well as how many columns appear on the page, you might want to increase or reduce this amount.

To change the space between columns:

- Place the insertion point in the section containing the columns.

- Choose *Format, Columns* to open the Columns dialog box.

- In the *Spacing* box, specify the desired width between columns.

- Click on *OK.*

You can also insert a vertical dividing line between adjacent columns, which can produce a visually pleasing effect and help the eye separate the columns. This is particularly true of columns that are by necessity spaced closely together.

To add a vertical line between columns:

- Place the insertion point in the section containing the columns.

- Choose *Format, Columns* to open the Columns dialog box.

- Check the *Line Between* option.

- Click on *OK.*

Let's change the space between our columns, and then add a vertical line to highlight their readability:

1. Check the status bar to verify that the insertion point is in the second section of the document.

2. Observe the space between the columns. It is large enough to be reduced slightly to make more room within the columns for text. Notice also that one or more lines of text (or blank lines) have wrapped up to the second column, above the *Worldwide Services* heading. (This may or may not be true, depending on what printer you are using.)

3. Choose **Format, Columns** to open the Columns dialog box.

4. Click twice on the Spacing **down increment indicator** to decrease the amount of space between the columns of text to 0.3" or as close to this value as your configuration will allow.

5. Click on **OK**. The text columns now appear closer together. Notice that the text that earlier wrapped to the second column has now moved to the bottom of the first column, placing the *Worldwide Services* heading near the top of the second column. (Again, this may or may not be true, depending on your printer.)

6. Delete the paragraph mark between the *End of Section* line and the *Worldwide Services* heading to move the heading to the top of the column.

7. Verify that the insertion point is still in the second section.

8. Choose **Format, Columns**.

9. Check the **Line Between** option. Compare your screen to Figure 11.2.

10. Click on **OK**.

11. Print Preview the document to see how it will look printed (see Figure 11.3).

12. Close Print Preview.

13. Save the document as **mychap11**.

Figure 11.2   **Inserting a vertical line between columns**

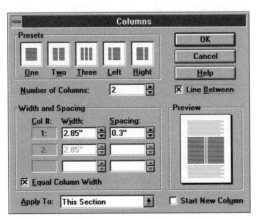

Figure 11.3   **Print Previewing the column modifications**

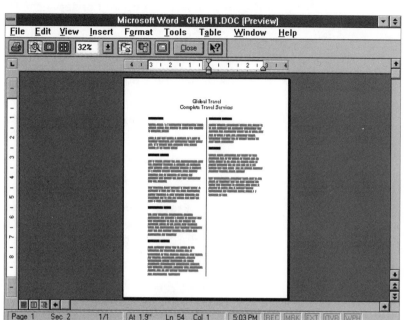

USING GRAPHICS

You can place graphics in any Word document, as well as in headers and footers. Graphics can be imported into a document from many draw or paint software programs or from *clip art* (sources of digitized images). Word also comes with a number of graphics files, which you can use in your documents and even edit.

To insert a graphic in your document:

- Switch to Page Layout view. This view is most effective for working with graphics.

- Place the insertion point where you want to insert the graphic.

- Choose *Insert, Picture* to open the Insert Picture dialog box.

- Select the drive and directory where the graphic is stored.

- Select the file name of the desired graphic.

- If you want to preview your selected graphic, check the Preview Picture option and observe the Preview box.

- Click on *OK*.

Let's insert a graphic in our document:

1. Verify that you are still in Page Layout view.

2. Place the insertion point to the left of the *W* in the *Worldwide Services* heading at the top of the second column. Doing so will place the graphic above the heading.

3. Choose **Insert, Picture** to open the Picture dialog box.

4. In the File Name list box, select **compass.wmf**.

5. Check the **Preview Picture** option, if it is not already checked. The graphic is displayed in the Preview box so that you can view it before placing it in your document (see Figure 11.4).

6. Click on **OK** to place the graphic in your document.

7. Observe the results. The compass graphic is inserted directly above the *Worldwide Services* heading. Press **Enter** twice to move *Worldwide Services* a bit further below the compass. A graphic is automatically "anchored" to the closest paragraph in the document. This is represented by an anchor symbol.

Figure 11.4   **Previewing a graphic**

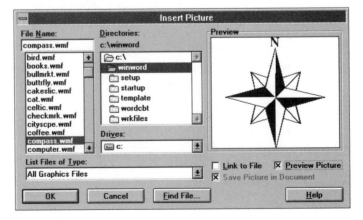

INSERTING A FRAME AROUND A GRAPHIC

If you insert a graphic in a document and the graphic is not wide enough to fill the column of text, the text will "flow" around the graphic. However, it will flow around the graphic unevenly, following the graphic's shape. You can make the text flow evenly around the graphic by placing a frame around it.

To place a frame around a graphic, you must first select the graphic by clicking on it with the mouse. When the graphic is selected, you will notice small black *selection handles* on each side and in each corner of the graphic. Once the graphic is selected, you choose the Insert, Frame command.

Let's insert a frame around our compass graphic:

1. Point to the middle of the compass and click the mouse button to select it.

2. Observe the selection handles around the compass.

3. Choose **Insert, Frame** to insert a frame around the compass.

4. Observe the results. The frame enables you to move and size the graphic; however, it will not print. Compare your screen to Figure 11.5.

 SIZING A GRAPHIC

The simplest way to size a graphic is by using the mouse to drag one of the selection handles. When you drag a handle on the side of the graphic, only the width of the graphic changes. When you drag a handle on the top or bottom of the graphic, only the height of the graphic changes. When you drag a corner handle, the width *and* height of the graphic change proportionately.

If you have sized the graphic and it appears distorted, you can restore it to its original size by choosing Format, Picture, clicking on Reset, and then clicking on OK; or you can press Ctrl and double-click on the graphic.

Let's experiment with sizing our compass graphic:

1. Place the mouse pointer on the selection handle in the middle of the right side of the graphic frame. The mouse pointer becomes a horizontal, two-headed arrow.

Figure 11.5   **Framing the graphic**

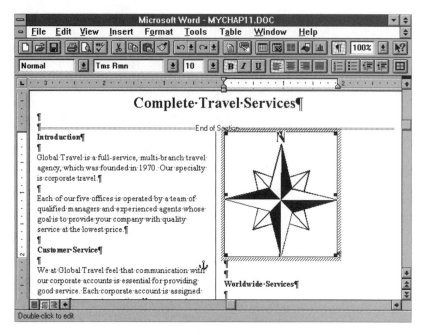

2. Press and hold the mouse button. Drag the handle rightward to the end of the *End of Section* line above it. Note that a *dotted frame* is displayed as you drag the handle.

3. Release the mouse button. The compass is now wider (not higher).

4. Place the mouse pointer on the handle in the middle of the bottom of the graphic. The pointer becomes a vertical, two-headed arrow.

5. Drag the handle down to the first line of the paragraph following the *Worldwide Services* heading. (If you need to drag below the bottom edge of the document window to reach this line, simply move the mouse pointer down into the horizontal scroll bar and wait for the screen to scroll.)

6. Release the mouse button. The compass is taller (see Figure 11.6).

7. Verify that the compass graphic is still selected (the handles are displayed on the frame).

Figure 11.6   **Enlarging the graphic**

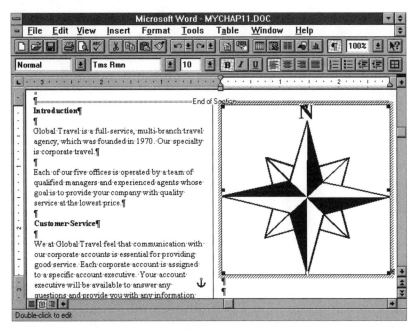

8. Choose **Format, Picture** to open the Picture dialog box.

9. Observe the *Scaling* box. The percentages of Width and Height are not equal. Once you've used the mouse to size the graphic, its width and height may no longer be proportionate.

10. Click on **Reset** to restore the compass to its original size.

11. Observe the Scaling box. The Width and Height are once again displayed as *100%*, meaning that the graphic's original size has been restored (see Figure 11.7).

12. Click on **OK**. The compass is displayed at its original size.

13. Verify that the compass graphic is still selected.

14. Scroll, if necessary, to display the compass and the *End of Section* line above it.

15. Place the mouse pointer on the handle in the bottom-right corner of the graphic. The mouse pointer becomes a diagonal, two-headed arrow.

16. Drag the handle down and to the right until the right border of the graphic is even with the end of the *End of Section* line above it.

17. Release the mouse button and compare your screen to Figure 11.8. The width and height of the compass have changed proportionately.

Figure 11.7 **Restoring the graphic to its original size**

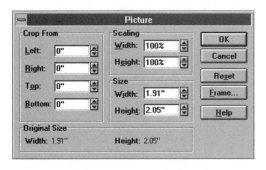

Figure 11.8 **Resizing the graphic proportionately**

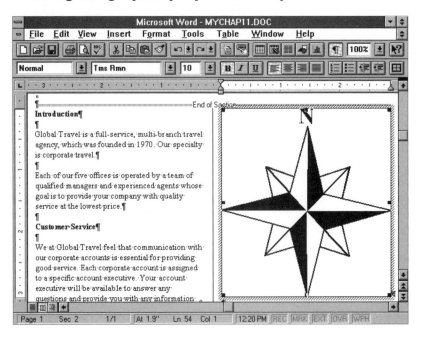

18. Choose **Format, Picture**.

19. Observe the Scaling box. The Width and Height percentages are similar (to within 1%).

20. Click on **Cancel** to close the Picture dialog box.

MOVING A GRAPHIC

Suppose that you insert a graphic, and perhaps even size it, and then decide that you don't like its placement in your document. After you have inserted a graphic in your document, you do have the option of moving it.

To move a graphic:

- Select the graphic.

- Point to the graphic and press and hold the mouse button.

- Drag the dotted frame to the desired location.

- Release the mouse button.

We have decided that our compass graphic would be more appropriate before the *Discounts* heading. Let's move it there:

1. Use the Zoom Control box in the Standard toolbar to set the magnification to **50%**, and then scroll your window until you can see the compass and the heading *Discounts* below it. When moving large graphics, you'll find it much easier to work at a lower magnification.

2. Verify that the compass graphic is selected, and point to the graphic so that the positioning pointer (a four-headed arrow) is visible.

3. Drag the compass graphic downward (taking care not to jiggle it to the left or right) until the bottom of its dotted frame slices right through the paragraph mark above *Discounts*.

4. Release the mouse button. The compass is displayed above the *Discounts* heading (see Figure 11.9).

Figure 11.9   Moving the graphic

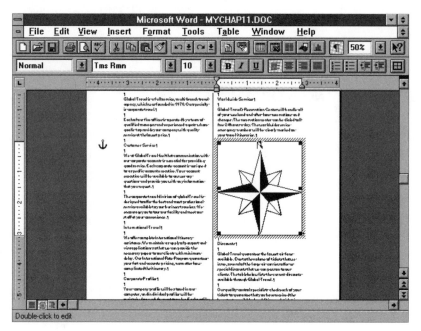

ADDING A BORDER TO A GRAPHIC

To add a border around a graphic:

- Select the graphic.

- Choose *Format, Borders and Shading* to open the Frame Borders and Shading dialog box.

- Click on the *Borders* tab, if necessary, to display the Borders settings.

- Select the desired line style from the Style list box.

- In the Presets box, click on your desired border (*None, Box,* or *Shadow*).

- Click on *OK.*

Let's add a shadow border to our compass graphic:

1. Verify that the compass graphic is selected.

2. Choose **Format, Borders and Shading** to open the Frame Borders and Shading dialog box.

3. Click on the **Borders** tab, if necessary, to display the Borders settings.

4. In the Presets box, select **Shadow** (see Figure 11.10). Observe the Border box; it shows a sample of your selected border.

Figure 11.10 **Selecting a shadow border**

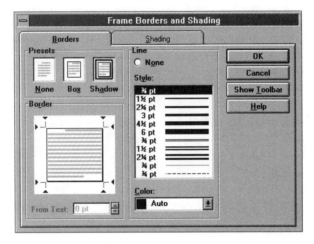

5. Verify that the *3/4 pt* line is selected under Style, and click on **OK**.

6. Deselect the graphic. A shadow (slightly thicker line) is displayed at the right and bottom borders of the compass frame. Change the magnification to **100%** to see this more clearly. Compare your screen to Figure 11.11.

MODIFYING A GRAPHIC BORDER

After you have applied a border to a graphic, you can change its thickness and style (or remove it altogether).

To modify the border:

• Select the graphic.

Figure 11.11   **Adding a shadow border**

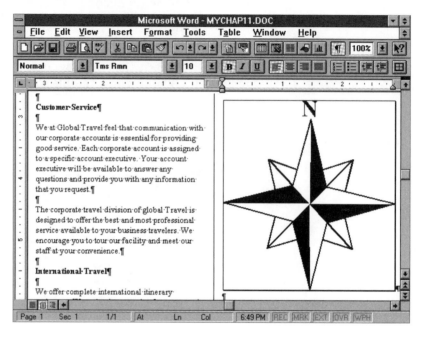

- Choose *Format, Borders and Shading* to open the Frame Borders and Shading dialog box.

- Click on the *Borders* tab, if necessary, to display the Borders settings.

- In the Border box, click on the desired border line to select it.

- In the Style box, click on the desired style.

- To apply this same style to another border line, simply click on it (in the Border box); to apply a different style, click on the border line and then click on the desired style.

- Click on *OK*.

Let's modify our compass graphic's border to increase the thickness of the shadow:

1. Select the compass graphic.

2. Choose **Format, Borders and Shading** to open the Frame Borders and Shading dialog box.

3. In the Border box, click on the right (vertical) border line to select it. Note that the border line disappears when selected.

4. In the Style box, click on the **6 pt** line to apply a thicker line to the right border. Observe the change in the Border box.

5. In the Border box, click on the bottom border line to apply the same **6 pt** thick line to the bottom border. Compare your screen to Figure 11.12.

Figure 11.12   **Modifying the shadow border**

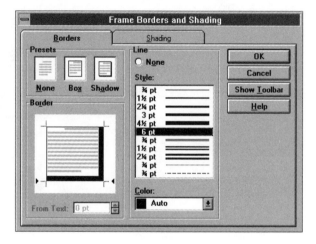

6. Click on **OK**.

7. Deselect the compass graphic and compare your screen to Figure 11.13. Observe the thicker frame shadow.

Now let's make a few final adjustments to our document, and then print it:

8. Change back to **50%** magnification.

9. If there are any blank paragraphs between the *End of Section* line and the *Worldwide Services* heading, delete them now.

10. If your compass graphic is no longer above the *Discounts* heading, move it there now.

11. Print (or Print Preview) the completed document, shown in Figure 11.14.

Figure 11.13 **The completed graphic border**

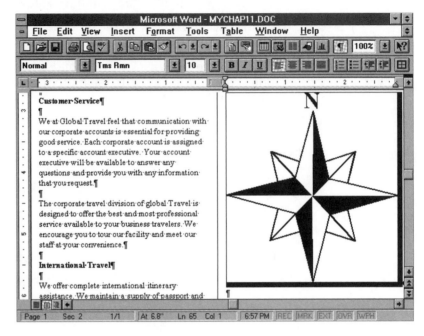

12. Close Print Preview, if necessary.

13. Save the document and then close it.

WORD'S DRAWING FEATURE

Word provides an easy-to-use drawing feature that allows you to create simple drawings in your documents. To do this,

- Place the insertion point where you want your drawing to appear.

- If the Drawing toolbar is not displayed, click on the *Drawing* button in the Standard toolbar to display it.

- Click on the *Create Picture* button in the Drawing toolbar to open a blank Picture window.

- Use the drawing tools to draw your picture within the dotted frame in the Picture window.

- When you are finished, click on *Close Picture.*

Figure 11.14   The completed MYCHAP11.DOC document

Global Travel
Complete Travel Services

Introduction

Global Travel is a full-service, multi-branch travel agency, which was founded in 1970. Our specialty is corporate travel.

Each of our five offices is operated by a team of qualified managers and experienced agents whose goal is to provide your company with quality service at the lowest price.

Customer Service

We at Global Travel feel that communication with our corporate accounts is essential for providing good service. Each corporate account is assigned to a specific account executive. Your account executive will be available to answer any questions and provide you with any information that you request.

The corporate travel division of global Travel is designed to offer the best and most professional service available to your business travelers. We encourage you to tour our facility and meet our staff at your convenience.

International Travel

We offer complete international itinerary assistance. We maintain a supply of passport and visa applications so that we can provide the necessary papers to our clients with minimum delay. Our International Rate Program guarantees you fast and accurate pricing, no matter how complicated the itinerary.

Corporate Profiles

Your company profile will be stored in our computer, and individual profiles will be maintained on each frequent traveler. Each profile will contain information regarding passport information, seating preference, car rental preference, frequent-flyer membership number, and corporate discount numbers. This information ensures that we can provide frequent travelers, fast, cost-effective itineraries.

Worldwide Services

Global Travel's Reservation Center will handle all of your weekend and after-hour reservations and changes. The reservation center can be dialed toll-free 24 hours a day. The worldwide service emergency numbers will be clearly marked on your travel itineraries.

Discounts

Global Travel guarantees the lowest air fares available. Due to the volume of tickets that we issue, several of the large air carriers offer us special discounts that we can pass on to our clients. The table below lists the current discounts available through Global Travel.

Our quality-control specialists check each of your tickets to guarantee that you have received the lowest rate available. In addition, each ticket is checked to ensure that it includes seating assignments and boarding passes before it is delivered to you.

To edit a drawing in a document:

- Double-click on the drawing to open it in the Picture window.

- Modify the drawing as desired.

- When you are finished, click on *Close Picture.*

Let's use the Drawing toolbar to draw a simple map:

1. Choose **File, New** and click on **OK** to open a new document window.

2. Type the following two lines:

   Everyone,

   Here, as promised, are the directions to our new house!

   Press **Enter** four times at the end of the second line to create some blank space between the text and the map.

3. If the Drawing toolbar is not already displayed on your screen, click on the **Drawing** button (the fifth button from the right in the Standard toolbar, it shows a triangle, circle, and square) to display it. The Drawing toolbar appears at the bottom of the screen, and the view is changed to Page Layout view (see Figure 11.15).

4. Click on the **Create Picture** button (the second button from the right in the Drawing toolbar, it shows a miniature picture with mountains and sun) to open a blank Picture window. It is within this dotted frame that you'll draw your picture. Don't worry about the size of the picture right now; later on— once we've completed it and inserted it in the document— we'll resize the picture.

5. Click on the **Line** tool (the leftmost tool in the Drawing toolbar) to select it.

6. Press and hold down the **Shift** key, and then drag (from left to right) within the dotted picture frame to draw the uppermost horizontal line shown in Figure 11.16. Holding down Shift while you drag allows you to draw straight lines easily.

7. Use the technique outlined in steps 5 and 6 to draw the remaining two straight lines shown in Figure 11.16. These are your roads.

Figure 11.15   Clicking on the Drawing button

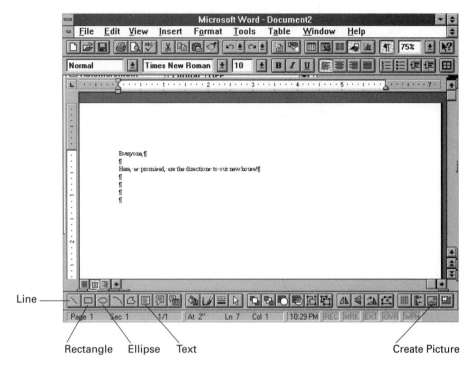

Line

Rectangle   Ellipse   Text   Create Picture

8. Click on the **Rectangle** tool (the one to the right of the Line tool) to select it.

9. Drag (from the upper-left corner to the lower-right corner) to draw the rectangle shown in Figure 11.16. This is your house.

10. Click on the **Ellipse** tool (the one to the right of the Rectangle tool) to select it.

11. Drag (again, from upper-left to lower-right) to draw the oval shown in Figure 11.16. This is a pond that marks the turnoff on the main road.

12. Click on a blank area within the dotted picture frame to de-select the oval. Your screen should now resemble that shown in Figure 11.16. (Don't worry if your drawing doesn't match ours exactly.)

13. Click on **Close Picture** (in the dialog box to the left of the dotted frame) to complete your picture and insert it in the document.

Figure 11.16   **Drawing the map**

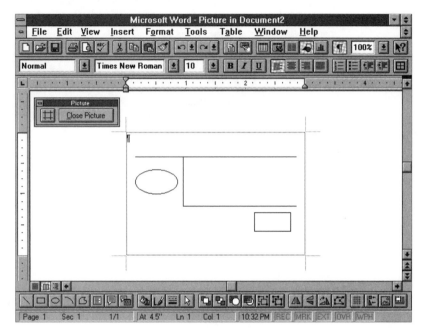

Oops...You forgot a road! Let's go back and edit the drawing:

1. Double-click on the drawing to reopen it in the Picture window.

2. Use the Line tool to add the road shown in Figure 11.17.

3. Click on **Close Picture** to complete your picture and insert it back in the document.

SIZING AND MOVING THE DRAWING

To resize and move a drawing, you proceed exactly as you would to resize and move a graphic:

- Select the drawing.

- To resize the drawing, drag one of its selection handles.

- To move the drawing, drag its dotted frame to the desired location.

Figure 11.17   **Adding a road**

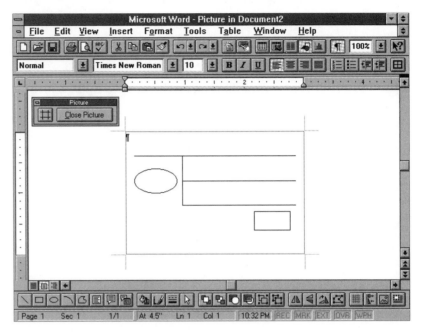

Let's enlarge our map:

1. Click on the map to select it.

2. Drag the lower-right selection handle down and to the right until the dotted right line of the picture frame is approximately even with the right margin (the 6" mark on the ruler).

3. Press **Ctrl+Home** to move the insertion point to the top of the document and deselect the map. Note how much easier it is to see the map at this size.

SUPERIMPOSING TEXT ON A DRAWING

To add text to a drawing:

• Double-click on the drawing to display it in a Picture window.

• Click on the *Text* tool to select it.

• Drag to create a text box in the dotted picture frame.

- Change the current font, font size, and/or alignment, if desired, using the Formatting toolbar.

- Type the desired text.

Let's end this chapter by superimposing text on our map to label the various roads and landmarks:

1. Double-click on the map to open it in a Picture window.

2. Change the magnification to **150%**. It will be much easier to enter text at this magnification.

3. Click on the **Text Box** tool (the sixth tool from the left in the Drawing toolbar, it shows a box with several lines of text) to select it.

4. Drag (from upper-left to lower-right) to create a text box above the uppermost road, as shown in Figure 11.18. (Don't worry if your text boxes differ slightly in size/placement from those in Figure 11.18.)

Figure 11.18   Adding text to the map

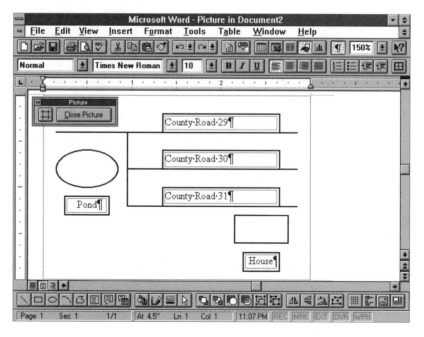

5. Change the font size to **8** points and type **County Road 29**. If the text does not fit in your text box, use your mouse to elongate the box.

6. Use the technique outlined in steps 3 through 5 to create the remaining text boxes shown in Figure 11.18. Note that *Pond* and *House* are centered within their text boxes.

7. Select all of the text boxes. To do this, press and hold **Shift** while clicking one-by-one on all the text boxes. Make sure you don't select any of the other drawn objects!

8. Choose **Format, Drawing Object** to open the Drawing Object dialog box.

9. Click on the **Line** tab to display the Line options. In the Line box (on the left), select **None** to remove the black border lines from around your text objects.

10. Click on the **Fill** tab to display the Fill options. Under Color, click on **None** to make the text boxes transparent (so that they don't obscure any of the objects in your map).

11. Click on **OK** to close the Drawing Object dialog box.

12. Click on **Close Picture** to insert your revised map into the document.

13. Click on the **Drawing** button (in the Standard toolbar) to re-move the Drawing toolbar.

14. Change the magnification to **50%**. Your screen should match that shown in Figure 11.19.

15. Save the document as **mymap** and then close it.

SUMMARY

In this chapter, you learned how to create newspaper-style columns of text, how to import a graphic image into your document, how to move and size the graphic, how to change the style of its border, how to create a drawing in a document, how to size and move the drawing, and how to superimpose text over it.

Figure 11.19 **The completed map document**

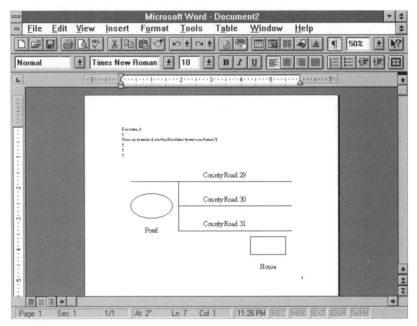

Here is a quick reference guide to the Word features introduced in this chapter:

Desired Result	How to Do It
Create newspaper-style columns	Place the insertion point where you want the columns to begin; choose **Format, Columns**; in the Number of Columns text box, specify the desired number of columns or click on the desired column format under Presets; in the Apply To drop-down list box, select the portion of the document you wish to affect; click on **OK**.
Display multicolumn text	Choose **Print, Preview** or **View, Page Layout**.

Desired Result	How to Do It
Change the space between columns	Place the insertion point in the section containing the columns to be affected; choose **Format, Columns**; in the Spacing box, type the desired value, or use the increment arrows; click on **OK**.
Insert a line between columns	Place the insertion point in the desired section; choose **Format, Columns**; check **Line Between**; click on **OK**.
Insert a graphic	Place the insertion point where you want to insert the graphic; choose Insert, Picture; select the drive and directory where the graphic is stored; select the file name of the desired graphic; click on **OK**.
Size a graphic	Select the graphic; drag the middle handle on the left or right edge of the graphic frame to affect the width; drag the middle handle on the top or bottom edge to affect the height; or drag one of the corner handles to increase or decrease the width and height proportionally.
Restore a graphic to its original size	Select the graphic; choose **Format, Picture**; click on **Reset**; click on **OK**.
Move a graphic	Select the graphic; drag it to the desired location, using the dotted rectangle as a reference; release the mouse button.
Add a graphic border	Select the graphic; choose **Format, Borders and Shading**; click on the **Borders** tab, if necessary; in the Preset box, select the desired type of border (**None, Box,** or **Shadow**); click on **OK**.

Desired Result	How to Do It
Modify a graphic border	Select the graphic; choose **Format, Borders and Shading**; click on the **Borders** tab, if necessary; in the Border box, click on the desired border line to select it; in the Style box, click on the desired style; to apply this same style to another border line, click on it; to apply a different style, click on the border line and then click on the desired style; click on **OK**.
Create a drawing in a document	Place the insertion point where you want your drawing to appear; if the Drawing toolbar is not displayed, click on the **Drawing** button; click on the **Create Picture** button in the Drawing toolbar to open a blank Picture window; use the drawing tools to draw your picture within the dotted frame; when you are finished, click on **Close Picture**.
Edit a drawing in a document	Double-click on the drawing to open it in the Picture window; modify the drawing as desired; when you are finished, click on **Close Picture**.
Resize and move a drawing	Proceed exactly as you would to resize and move a graphic.
Add text to a drawing	Double-click on the drawing to display it in a Picture window; select the **Text** tool in the Drawing toolbar; drag to create a text box; change the current font and font size, if desired; type the desired text.

In the next chapter, you will learn how to create form letters.

IF YOU'RE STOPPING HERE

If you need to break off here, please exit Word. If you want to proceed directly to the next chapter, please do so now.

CHAPTER 12: CREATING FORM LETTERS

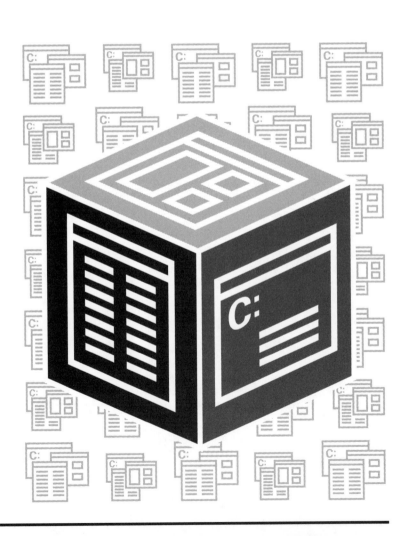

In word processing, *merging* or *mail-merge* is the process of transferring selected information from one document to another document. For example, you can write a form letter and instantly merge it with your mailing list to produce a customized letter for everyone on the mailing list. Other common mail-merge documents include mailing labels, interoffice memos, and reports.

Word's Tools, Mail Merge command enables you to take information from two documents—for example, a form letter and a list of names and addresses—and combine them into a single document. Of equal importance, perhaps, is the ability to sort the information in the mailing list, say, in alphabetical order by last name.

When you're done working through this chapter, you will know

- How to create and attach the components of form letters
- How to generate form letters
- How to sort data

COMPONENTS OF A FORM LETTER

Before using Word's Mail Merge feature, you should be familiar with three important terms that correspond to the three main components of the merge process: the main document, the data file, and the merged document.

THE MAIN DOCUMENT

The *main document* contains normal text plus *field names,* which contain the instructions for carrying out the merge. The basic information in the main document remains the same. For example, suppose a form letter of invitation were to serve as the main document. The main document would contain the invitation text and various field names that would cause Word to retrieve names and addresses from a data file (discussed after the next section). Word would then insert the names and addresses in specific places in the merged document. Before you can instruct Word to merge documents, you must have inserted field names in your main document.

FIELD NAMES

In the main document, field names are used to indicate where variable information is to be inserted. In the data file (discussed next), field names indicate the category of information in each column. The field names inserted in the main document must match the field names in the data file. You can insert field names in your main document before the data file is attached; however, then you would have to enter field names twice. Thus, it is easier to insert the field names *after* the two files have been attached (you'll learn how to attach files later in this chapter).

THE DATA FILE

The *data file* stores information to be brought into the main document. You can think of the data file as a name-and-address list from which the program gets what you want to include in the main document. However, not only can you store names and addresses in the data file, you can also use it to store sentences, whole paragraphs, as well as any text or data you expect to use repeatedly. You can set up your data file as ordinary paragraphs or as a table. In this chapter, we use a table to compile data file information. In Chapter 10, you saw how compiling data in a table is an efficient way to keep the data organized. For this reason, when you create a data file using the Mail Merge Helper dialog box, Word automatically sets up the data as a table.

The *data-file table* contains a column for each category of information, or *data field*, in the data file. The *header row* is the first row of the table; it contains field names, which indicate the type of information in each column. Except for the header row, each additional row of the table contains a set of related information, known as a *data record*. Each record includes all of the information for one person in the name-and-address list. The various types of information in each record are known as *fields*, which are the equivalent of cells in a standard table.

There are several important guidelines for naming fields in data files:

- Each field name must be unique.
- It must begin with a letter.
- It can contain up to 40 characters.
- It can contain letters, numbers, and underscore characters; however, it cannot contain spaces.

Let's open a data file with missing records and then complete it:

1. Open **ch12data.doc**.
2. Observe the header row, the top row of the table.
3. Observe the data records, located in the rows below the header row.
4. Place the insertion point in the first field of the last row.
5. Type **Dudley** and press **Tab**.

6. Type **Long** and press **Tab**.

7. Type **Unique Rugs** and press **Tab**.

8. Type **125 North Road** and press **Enter**. Then type **Suite 3904**. Notice that you can press Enter to force information to a separate line in the record. The second line of information remains within the same record, and the insertion point remains in the same field.

PRACTICE YOUR SKILLS

1. Complete the table with the following information:

   Yuma AZ   85365   Beijing

2. Save the disk file as **mydata** and compare your screen to Figure 12.1.

3. Close the document.

Figure 12.1   **The completed MYDATA.DOC document**

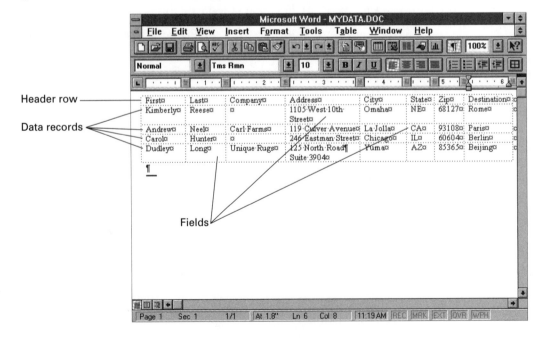

ATTACHING THE DATA FILE TO THE MAIN DOCUMENT

Attaching the data file to the main document identifies the data file as the one to be used for the variable information when the two documents are merged. Make sure that the main document is open when you attach the data file.

To attach a data file to a main document:

- Make the main document the active window.

- Choose *Tools, Mail Merge* to open the Mail Merge Helper dialog box.

- Click on *Create*, and choose the desired type of main document; for example, Form Letters.

- Click on *Active Window*.

- Click on the *Get Data* button.

- Click on *Open Data Source*.

- Specify the location and the name of the data file.

- Click on *OK*.

- Click on *Close* to close the Mail Merge Helper dialog box.

When you attach the data file, the *Mail Merge* toolbar is displayed above the ruler (see the exercise below). The Mail Merge toolbar enables you to quickly and accurately insert the field names and perform the merge.

To insert field names in the main document by using the Mail Merge toolbar:

- Place the insertion point where you want to add a field name.

- Click on the *Insert Merge Field* button.

- From the Insert Merge Field drop-down list, choose the desired field name.

Once the field name is inserted in the main document, it is enclosed by chevrons—for example, *<<First>>*, which represents the first-name field.

To enter a field name in the main document without using the Mail Merge toolbar, press Ctrl+F9 and type the field name between the braces ({ }) that appear. Be sure to use the identical field names used in the data file. If you are unsure of the field names, you can click on the Edit Data Source button in the Mail Merge toolbar to display the data file.

Let's view the main document, attach the data file, and then complete the main document:

1. Open **ch12main.doc**. You can see that this document is a form letter.

2. Observe the field names in the document.

3. Choose **Tools, Mail Merge** to open the Mail Merge Helper dialog box, shown in Figure 12.2. Notice that the dialog box conveniently places the three steps of the mail-merge process in a numbered list. As you can see, only the Create button is not dimmed. This tells us that we first need to create the main document. However, in this case, we want the current document to serve as our main document, so we must first instruct Word to use CH12MAIN.DOC as the main document.

4. Click on **Create**. Notice the various choices for a main document available in the drop-down list box (see Figure 12.3).

Figure 12.2   **The Mail Merge Helper dialog box**

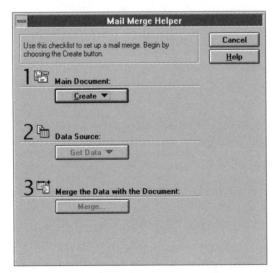

Figure 12.3   **The Create options in the Mail Merge Helper dialog box**

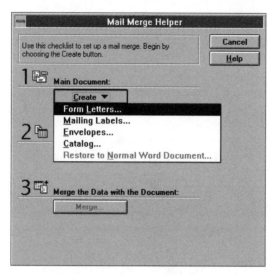

5. Choose **Form Letters**. A message box is displayed telling you that you can use CH12MAIN.DOC in the active window as the main document or select another main document.

6. Click on the **Active Window** button to select CH12MAIN.DOC as the main document and return to the Mail Merge Helper dialog box. Notice that under the Create button, the selected type of merge is displayed, as well as the name and location of the main document (see Figure 12.4). Next to the Create button, an Edit button has appeared, allowing you to edit data in the main document.

7. Click on the **Get Data** button, and choose **Open Data Source** from the drop-down list (see Figure 12.5). The Open Data Source dialog box is displayed.

8. In the File Name list box, select **mydata.doc**, the data file you saved earlier (see Figure 12.6).

9. Click on **OK** to attach the data file to the main document and return to the Mail Merge Helper dialog box. The selected data file is now listed below the Get Data button, and next to it is displayed another Edit button, this one for editing data in the data file.

Figure 12.4   **The main document listed in the Mail Merge Helper dialog box**

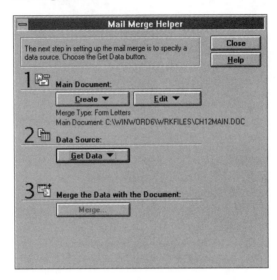

Figure 12.5   **The Get Data drop-down list**

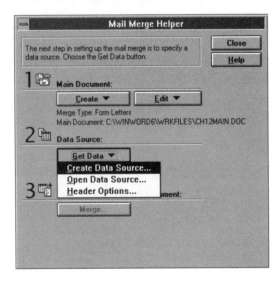

10. Click on **Close** to close the Mail Merge Helper dialog box. (Before we perform the merge, we'll insert some fields in our document.) The Mail Merge toolbar is now displayed above the ruler in the main document window (see Figure 12.7).

Figure 12.6   **The selected data file in the Open Data Source dialog box**

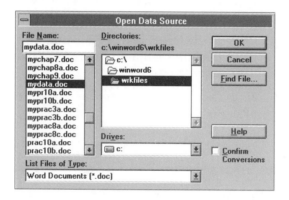

Figure 12.7   **The Mail Merge toolbar**

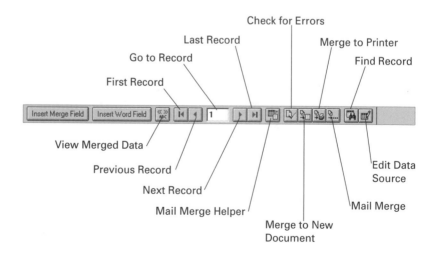

11. Place the insertion point on the first blank line below the *<<Company>>* field. Then click on the **Insert Merge Field** button. A drop-down list of fields is displayed (see Figure 12.8).

12. Choose **Address** from the list box to tell Word to place the information from the Address column of the data file in the completed form letter. The *<<Address>>* merge field is inserted in the document.

13. Press **Enter** so that three blank lines will remain between the address and the greeting.

14. Click on the **Insert Merge Field** button, and click on **City** to place the information from the City column of the data file in the completed form letter.

15. Type **,** and press the **spacebar** to place a comma and space after the city name.

Figure 12.8   **The Insert Merge Field drop-down list**

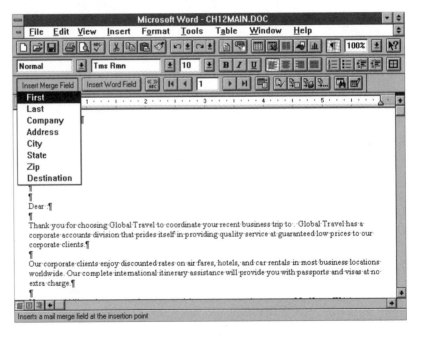

PRACTICE YOUR SKILLS

1. Complete the form letter contained in the CH12MAIN.DOC disk file, using Figure 12.9 as a guide. Be sure to include the *Destination* merge field at the end of the first sentence of the letter (before the period) and to insert any spaces where necessary.

2. Save the disk file as **mymain**.

Figure 12.9   **The form letter with inserted fields**

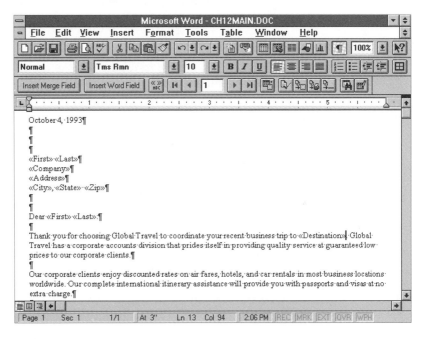

GENERATING YOUR FORM LETTERS

After you have completed and attached the data file and the main document, you can then merge the two documents. However, before you do so, you can preview your merged data in the main document window. This allows you to make any last-minute changes before committing the merge to a separate document or printing its results.

To preview the merge results, click on the View Merged Data button in the Mail Merge toolbar (see Figure 12.7). This switch is a toggle, which allows you to turn the feature on or off. With the View Merged Data feature turned on, you can

- Select specific merged records for viewing by entering a record number in the Go to Record box on the Mail Merge toolbar

- Cycle through contiguous records by using the Previous Record and Next Record buttons

- View the first or last record by clicking on the First Record or Last Record button, respectively

There are three ways to merge the documents in Word using the Mail Merge toolbar:

- Click on the *Merge to New Document* button to save the merged files in a single, new file.

- Click on the *Merge to Printer* button to print the resulting merged documents.

- Click on the *Mail Merge* button to specify a range of data records to be merged or to choose other options in the Merge dialog box.

When you click on the Merge to New Document button to merge documents, a new document is created with the name Form Letters1 (if the type of merge you've selected is Form Letters). If you merge another document before you exit Word, the new document's name will be Form Letters2, and so on. A form letter is created for each record in the data file. You can print all the form letters by clicking on the Merge to Printer button, or you can print individual form letters by merging the documents first using the Merge to New Document or Mail Merge button, and then by displaying the desired merged form letter and choosing File, Print from the menu.

Note: By default, Word deletes any blank lines in the merged document that are created by empty fields in the data file. For this reason, records should not be left blank.

Let's merge the main document and the data file to create our form letters:

1. Observe the name of the current document, *MYMAIN.DOC.*

2. Click on the **View Merged Data** button in the Mail Merge tool-bar (see Figure 12.7). The merged data are displayed for the first record listed in the data file, that of Kimberly Reese (see Figure 12.10). Notice how the various fields have been "filled-in" with their corresponding information.

3. Click on the **Next Record** button in the Mail Merge toolbar to advance to the next record of information. Kimberly Reese's information is replaced with that of Andrew Neel.

4. This time, double-click in the **Go to Record** box to select the current record number (*2*); then type **3** and press **Enter** to advance to the third record of information contained in the data file. The data for Carol Hunter is displayed.

5. Click on the **Last Record** button in the Mail Merge toolbar to go to the last record, that of Dudley Long.

6. Click on the **First Record** button to return to Kimberly Reese's data.

Figure 12.10   **Viewing the merged data**

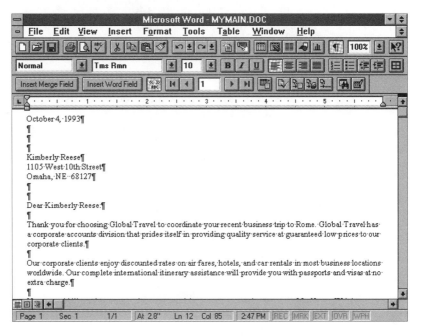

7. Click on the **View Merged Data** button to turn off the feature. Notice that the button is no longer depressed. The field codes are once again displayed in the document instead of actual merged data.

8. Click on the **Merge to New Document** button in the Mail Merge toolbar. MYDATA.DOC and MYMAIN.DOC are now merged. Notice that the new document is named *Form Letters1*. Each letter is placed in a separate section within the document.

9. Scroll through the document to view the three remaining form letters. Notice the section breaks inserted between them. A letter has been created for every data record in the MYDATA.DOC file. Notice that the first and third letters do not have a company name, and the fourth letter has a two-line address.

10. Close all of the documents *without* saving them as disk files.

SORTING THE INFORMATION IN A DATA FILE

There will probably come a time when you will need to arrange a list of data, such as an address list, in alphabetical or numerical order. For example, you might want your data file records to appear in ascending alphabetical order by last name, or in descending numerical order by zip code.

You can use the Table, Sort command to sort columns of text in tables alphabetically, numerically, or by date. If you want to sort by a column other than the first one, you need to specify the column number. Columns are numbered from left to right. (For more information about tables, see Chapter 10.)

To sort data in a table:

• Select all of the text in the column that you want to sort; do not select headings or blank lines.

• Choose *Table, Sort.*

• Under Sort By, select the desired column number from the drop-down list box.

• In the Type drop-down list box, select the type of sort: *Text, Number,* or *Date.*

- Select a sort order: *Ascending* or *Descending*.

- Click on *OK*.

Note: You can select the header row of a table before performing a sort. However, if you do so, be sure to click on the Header Row option under *My List Has* in the Sort dialog box. If you do not select the Header Row before sorting, or if your table truly has no header row and you'd like the *entire* table sorted, the No Header Row option should be selected.

Let's experiment with sorting the records in a data file a couple of ways:

1. Open **ch12list.doc**.

2. Observe the second column, which contains last names. The last names are not arranged alphabetically.

3. Select all of the rows except the header record (see Figure 12.11).

Figure 12.11   Selected records to be sorted

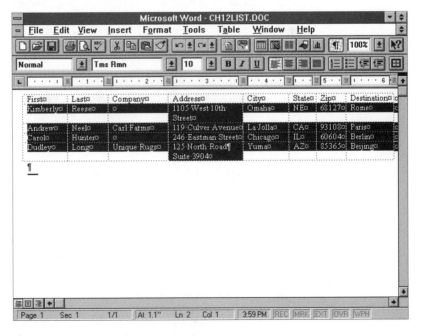

4. Choose **Table, Sort** to open the Sort dialog box.

5. Under Sort By, select **Column 2** from the column-number drop-down list box to instruct Word to sort by the second column of the table.

6. In the Type drop-down list box, verify that **Text** is selected.

7. Verify that **Ascending** order is selected, in order to sort the last names from A to Z. Compare your screen to Figure 12.12.

Figure 12.12   **The specified sort criteria**

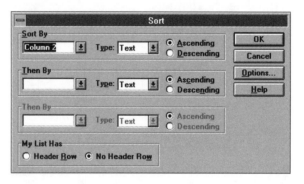

8. Click on **OK** to perform the sort.

9. Deselect the records and observe that they have been sorted, and that the last names in column 2 are listed in ascending alphabetical order (see Figure 12.13).

10. Observe that the zip-code data are not sorted in any particular order.

11. Select all of the rows of the table except for the header record.

12. Choose **Table, Sort** to open the Sort dialog box.

13. Under Sort by, select **Column 7,** and select **Descending** order, to sort the zip codes from 9 to 0. Notice that *Number* is already selected in the Type box; because we selected Column 7 for sorting, Word has detected that we want to sort by number.

14. Click on **OK** to perform the sort.

15. Deselect the data and observe that the zip-code data are sorted in descending numeric order (see Figure 12.14).

Figure 12.13   The records sorted by last name

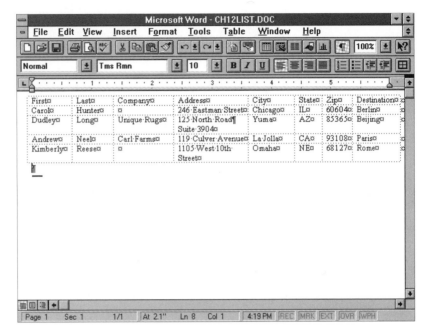

Figure 12.14   The records sorted in descending order by zip code

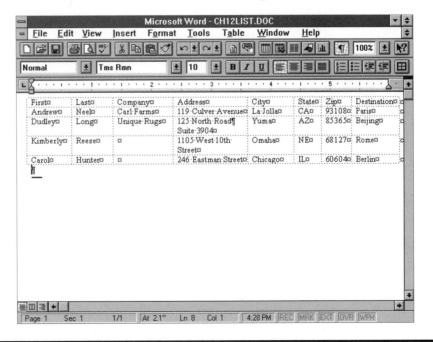

PRACTICE YOUR SKILLS

1. Sort the records by zip code in ascending order.

2. Save the disk file as **mylist**.

3. Deselect the records and compare your screen to Figure 12.15.

4. Close the document.

Figure 12.15 **The completed mylist table, sorted in ascending order by zip code**

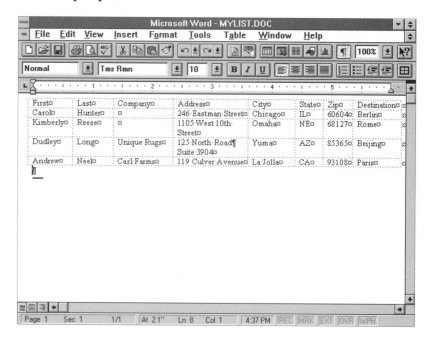

SORTING RECORDS IN THE MAIN DOCUMENT

In the previous section, you learned how to sort records in a data file. However, you can also sort the records from the main document window, even after you've already attached the data file to the main document.

To sort records in the main document:

• Activate the main document window.

• Choose *Tools, Mail Merge*.

- Under step 3—Merge the Data with the Document—click on the *Query Options* button to open the Query Options dialog box.

- Display the *Sort Records* tab.

- Under Sort By, select the field you wish to sort by from the drop-down list box.

- Select the desired sort order.

- Click on *OK*.

Let's sort the records in a main document:

1. Open **xmymain.doc** from your WRKFILES directory. This is a copy of the main document (MYMAIN.DOC) that we created earlier in this chapter. Notice that the Mail Merge toolbar is automatically displayed, since Word knows this is a main document.

2. Open the Mail Merge Helper dialog box (choose **Tools, Mail Merge**, or click on the **Mail Merge Helper** button on the Mail Merge toolbar). Notice that the name of the main document has changed to *XMYMAIN.DOC* (see Figure 12.16). The data file remains *MYDATA.DOC*. Notice the Query Options button next to the Merge button under step 3.

Figure 12.16   **The updated information in the Mail Merge Helper dialog box**

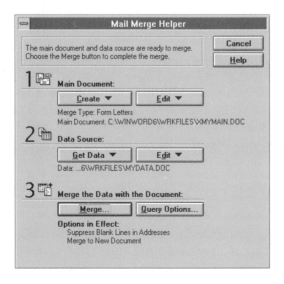

3. Click on the **Query Options** button to open the Query Options dialog box, and display the Sort Records tab.

4. Under Sort By, select **State** from the drop-down list, and retain the Ascending order. Compare your screen to Figure 12.17.

Figure 12.17   **Specifying sort criteria in the Query Options dialog box**

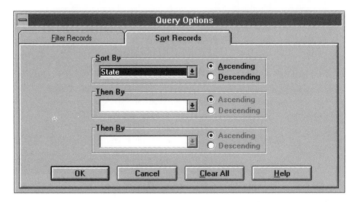

5. Click on **OK** to accept the sort criteria and return to the Mail Merge Helper dialog box. Under Options in Effect, at the bottom of the dialog box, notice the statement

       Query Options have been set

6. Close the Mail Merge Helper dialog box (click on **Close**) to return to the main document.

7. Preview the merge results (click on the **View Merged Data** button in the Mail Merge toolbar). Then view each record. Notice that the form letters are now displayed in ascending order by state. Dudley Long's data is displayed first, because his address is in Arizona (see Figure 12.18).

8. Close the file without saving your changes.

PRACTICE YOUR SKILLS

This exercise gives you the opportunity to practice the skills you just learned. The following instructions lead you through the steps necessary to complete and attach the components of a form letter.

Figure 12.18 **Previewing the results of the sort in the main document**

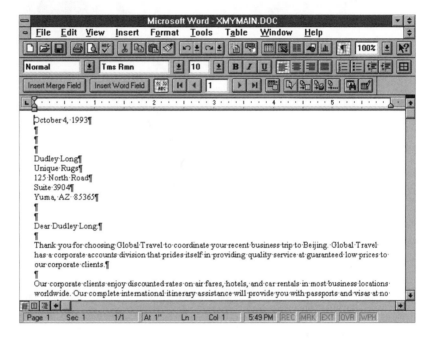

Follow these steps at your computer:

1. Open **prc12df.doc** (Chapter 2).

2. Enter the data shown in Figure 12.19 (Chapter 10, this chapter).

3. Save the disk file as **myp12dfa** (Chapter 1).

4. Open the disk file **prc12mda.doc** (Chapter 2).

5. Attach the data file **myp12dfa.doc**. (**Hint:** When the message box is displayed, click on the **Edit Main Document** button as suggested. Word displays this message only if you haven't yet inserted field names into your main document.)

6. Enter the field names shown in Figure 12.20. (**Hint:** Use the **Insert Merge Field** button on the Mail Merge toolbar.)

7. Save the disk file as **myp12mda** (Chapter 2).

8. Merge the files to create a new document.

9. Print the merged form letters and compare them to Figure 12.21.

Figure 12.19   The completed data file

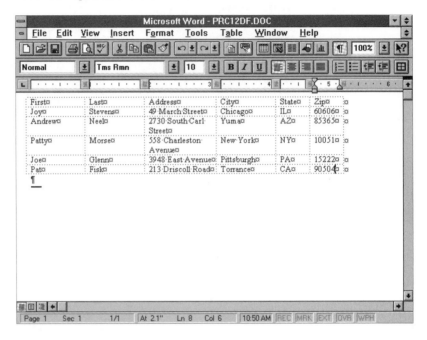

Figure 12.20   The entered fields

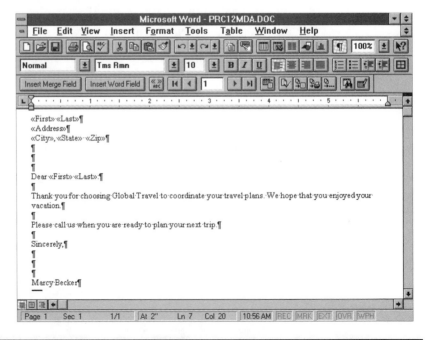

Figure 12.21   The merged form letters

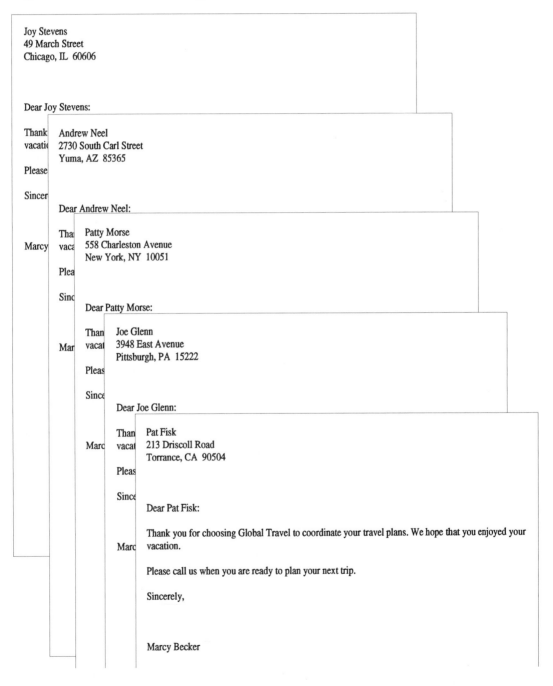

10. Close all of the documents (Chapter 1) without saving them as disk files.

If you have finished the activity, you might like to try a more challenging one requiring similar skills. In this activity, you will create a data file, complete a main document, and merge the files to create form letters.

Follow these steps at your computer:

1. Open a new document (Chapter 2).

2. Create a table with six columns and four rows (Chapter 10).

3. Enter the data shown in Figure 12.22.

4. Save the disk file as **myp12dfb** (Chapter 1).

5. Open the document **prc12mdb.doc** (Chapter 2).

6. Attach the data file **myp12dfb.doc**.

7. Enter the field names shown in Figure 12.23.

Figure 12.22   **The completed data file**

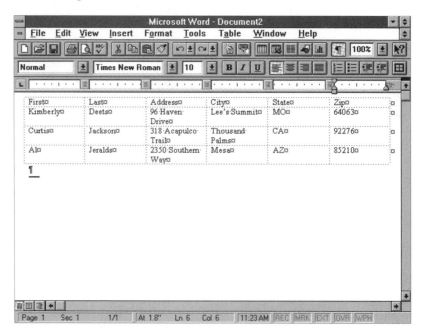

Figure 12.23 **The entered field names**

8. Save the disk file as **myp12mdb** (Chapter 2).

9. Merge the files to create a new document.

10. Print the merged form letters and compare them to Figure 12.24 (Chapter 1).

11. Close all of the documents without saving them as disk files (Chapter 1).

SUMMARY

In this chapter, you learned how to create form letters by merging the main document and the data file. You learned how to insert merge fields in a main document, and then attach the corresponding data file. You also learned how to sort a data file in alphabetical and numerical order.

Figure 12.24   The merged form letters

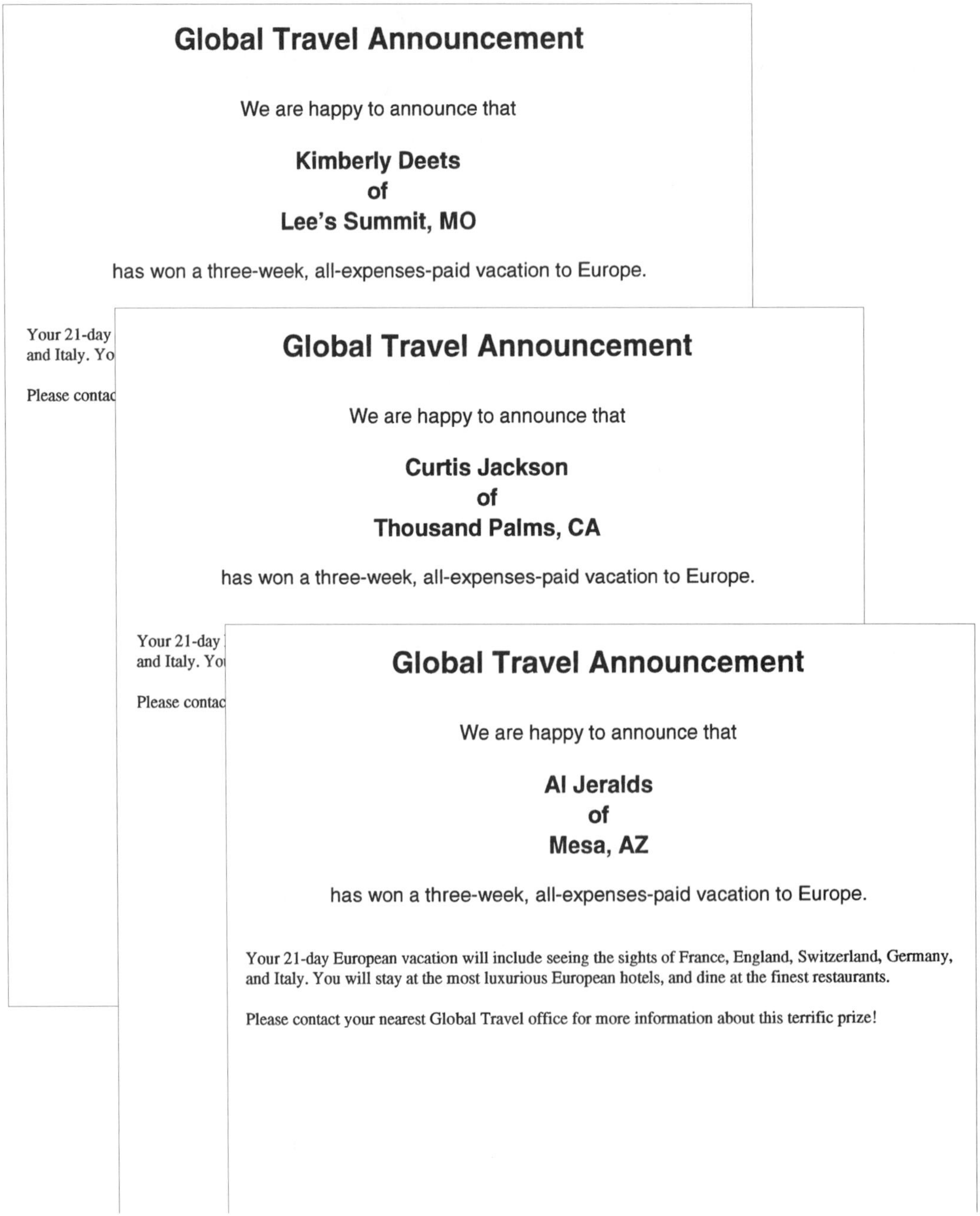

Global Travel Announcement

We are happy to announce that

**Kimberly Deets
of
Lee's Summit, MO**

has won a three-week, all-expenses-paid vacation to Europe.

Your 21-day
and Italy. Yo

Please contac

Global Travel Announcement

We are happy to announce that

**Curtis Jackson
of
Thousand Palms, CA**

has won a three-week, all-expenses-paid vacation to Europe.

Your 21-day
and Italy. Yo

Please contac

Global Travel Announcement

We are happy to announce that

**Al Jeralds
of
Mesa, AZ**

has won a three-week, all-expenses-paid vacation to Europe.

Your 21-day European vacation will include seeing the sights of France, England, Switzerland, Germany, and Italy. You will stay at the most luxurious European hotels, and dine at the finest restaurants.

Please contact your nearest Global Travel office for more information about this terrific prize!

Here is a quick reference guide to the Word features introduced in this chapter:

Desired Result	How to Do It
Attach a data file to a main document	Activate the main document window; choose **Tools, Mail Merge**; click on **Create**; click on **Active Window**; click on **Get Data**; click on **Open Data Source**; select the desired data file; click on **OK**.
Insert field names in the main document	Place the insertion point in the desired location; click on the **Insert Merge Field** button; select the desired field name.
Merge documents	Attach the data file; activate the main document window; click on the **Merge to New Document** button.
Sort data in a data file table	Select all the data to be sorted; choose **Table, Sort**; under Sort By, select the desired sort criteria; click on **OK**.
Sort records in the main document	Activate the main document window; choose **Tools, Mail Merge**; click on **Query Options**, and display the **Sort Records** tab; under Sort By, select the desired sort criteria; click on **OK**.

In Chapter 13, you will work with templates and styles.

IF YOU'RE STOPPING HERE

If you need to break off here, please exit Word. If you want to proceed directly to the next chapter, please do so now.

CHAPTER 13: USING TEMPLATES AND STYLES TO AUTOMATE YOUR WORK

Using the Normal Template

Creating a Memo with Memo Wizard

Using Styles

Each time you instruct Word to create a document, the program does so according to a template. A *template* is a stored file that contains boilerplate text and/or special formatting information. It serves as a kind of skeleton or blueprint, providing your documents with an underlying structure. Templates also include styles, which contain special character and paragraph formats. (You were introduced to character and paragraph formats in Chapters 4 and 5, respectively.) Each style is stored under a specific name—for example, *Heading 1.*

Word comes with a number of useful templates, each designed for a specific kind of document. For example, the Normal template is used to create a standard document, while the Invoice template can be used to create a business invoice. Word also comes with several *wizards*, whch are specialized templates that walk you through the steps required to create a specific type of document. For example, the Memo Wizard leads you through the process of creating a business memo.

The primary benefit of using a template or a wizard is that all, or at least some, of the document's characteristics have been defined in advance. This enables you to create documents that have similar character and paragraph formats, as well as similar page setups, without having to specify each parameter for each document.

When you're done working through this chapter, you will know

- How to create a document using the Normal template
- How to create a document using the Memo Wizard
- How to use styles
- How to create and modify styles

USING THE NORMAL TEMPLATE

Every document that you create in Word uses a template. By default, Word uses the Normal template for each new document. You can select a different template for a new document by choosing File, New to open the New dialog box and selecting a template in the Template list box.

To attach a different template to a document:

- Choose *File, Templates* to open the Templates and Add-ins dialog box.
- Click on *Attach* to open the Attach Template dialog box.
- In the File Name list box, select the desired template.
- Click on *OK* once to close the Attach Template dialog box and again to close the Templates and Ad-ins dialog box.

Let's create a memo using the Normal template:

1. Choose **File, New** to open the New dialog box, shown in Figure 13.1.

2. Observe the Template list box. The Normal template is selected by default.

3. Click on **OK**.

4. Type **Interoffice Memo** and press **Enter** twice.

5. Type **To:** and press **Tab**.

6. Type **Ruth Allen** and press **Enter**.

Figure 13.1 **The New dialog box**

7. Type **From:** and press **Tab**.

8. Type **Nancy Wright** and press **Enter**.

9. Type **Date:** and press **Tab**. We'll insert the date in the next exercise.

 ## INSERTING THE CURRENT DATE

Rather than typing the current date in every document that you create, you can have Word enter your computer's current system date.

To insert the current date:

● Place the insertion point where you want to add the date.

● Choose *Insert, Date and Time*.

● In the Available Formats list box, select the desired format.

● Click on *OK*.

Let's insert your computer's current system date:

1. Choose **Insert, Date and Time** to open the Date and Time dialog box.

2. In the Available Formats list box, select the fourth option (see Figure 13.2), which gives the full month, followed by the day, followed by the full year. (The date displayed is the current date.)

Figure 13.2   **Selecting a date format**

3. Click on **OK**. The system date is displayed in the document.

4. Press **Enter**.

5. Type **Subject:** and press **Tab**.

6. Type **Change in Additional Services** and press **Enter** twice.

INSERTING A FILE

In Chapter 8 you learned how to use the Edit, Copy and the Edit, Paste commands to copy and move selected text from one document to another document. However, the easiest way to insert the entire contents of one document in another document is to use the Insert, File command.

To insert an entire file:

• Place the insertion point where you want the document to appear.

• Choose *Insert, File*.

• Select the desired directory in the Directories list box, if necessary.

• Select the desired disk file.

• Click on *OK*.

Note: If you have more than one window open, remember to activate the window of the document receiving the inserted disk file before you choose Insert, File. The inserted file is always placed in the active window.

Let's insert the contents of the CHAP13A.DOC disk file in our memo:

1. Choose **Insert, File** to open the File dialog box.

2. Double-click on **chap13a.doc** in the WRKFILES directory to place the contents of the file in the current document.

3. Verify that the insertion point is at the end of the document.

4. Press **Enter** twice.

5. Type **cc:** and press **Tab**.

6. Type **Grace Berg, Keith Donnelly**.

7. Save the disk file as **mych13a.doc**.

8. At the top of the document, select *Interoffice Memo,* apply the bold font style, and change the point size to **12**.

9. Select the four paragraphs beginning with *To:* and ending with *Subject:.* Then set a left-aligned tab at the 1" mark.

10. Deselect the text.

11. Select *To:* (do *not* select the entire line) and apply the bold font style.

12. Apply the bold font style to *From:, Date:,* and *Subject:.*

13. Select *Additional Services,* below the *Subject* line, and apply the bold font style. Change the point size to **11**.

14. Select the *Newsletter* heading, and apply the bold font style. Then select *Telex* and repeat the character formatting. Deselect the text, and compare your screen to Figure 13.3.

PRACTICE YOUR SKILLS

1. Apply the bold font style to the *Personal Vacations, Flight Insurance,* and *Fax* headings.

2. Print Preview the document.

3. Save the disk file and close the document.

Figure 13.3   **Formatting the memo**

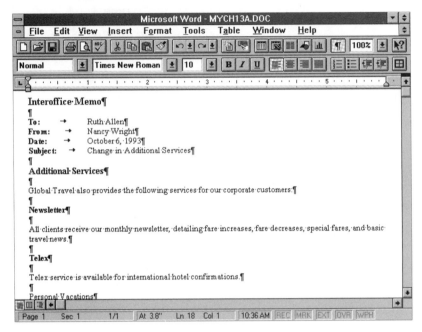

CREATING A MEMO WITH MEMO WIZARD

Word's *wizards* provide you with a fast way to create letters, memos, newsletters, resumes, calendars, faxes, and other common types of documents. For example, earlier you learned how to create a memo using the Normal template. However, you can also create a business-style memo by using Word's Memo Wizard.

To create a document using a wizard:

- Choose *File, New*.

- In the Template list box, select the desired wizard; for example, Memo Wizard.

- Click on *OK*.

- In the wizard dialog box, answer the question or prompt provided.

- Click on *Next* to move to the next prompt, and answer it.

- Repeat the previous step until the Next button is dimmed (meaning that you have responded to the last prompt).

- To change a setting, click on *Back* until that prompt is displayed; then change the setting.

- Click on *Finish*.

Note: If you do not wish to change any settings in the Memo Wizard dialog box, simply click on Finish when the first prompt (or any thereafter) is displayed.

Let's create a memo using the Memo Wizard:

1. Choose **File, New.** (Remember, clicking on the New button in the Standard toolbar does *not* open the New dialog box.)

2. In the Template list box, select **Memo Wizard** (see Figure 13.4; the files in your list box may differ from those shown). Notice the message in the Description box:

   ```
   Helps you design a customized memo
   ```

Figure 13.4   Choosing the Memo Wizard

3. Click on **OK.** After some furious hard-disk activity, the first prompt in the Memo Wizard dialog box is displayed (see Figure 13.5). In the left side of the box, a preview of the memo's current structure is displayed. Notice the first prompt:

   ```
   Do you want to include a heading?
   ```

Under the Yes option, the heading box suggests *Interoffice Memo*. The heading text will be inserted as a first-page header in the memo. Click on **Next** to accept the suggested heading. (It is possible to alter the suggested heading: Simply click in the heading box, and edit the existing heading as desired. An example of why you might choose No would be that you were going to print the memo on stationery that already contains a heading.)

Figure 13.5   **The first prompt in the Memo Wizard dialog box**

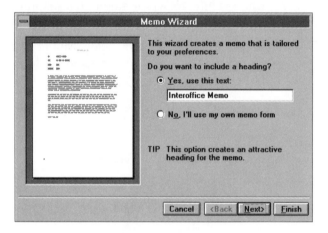

4. At the prompt

        Do you want a separate page for your
        distribution list?

   verify that *No* is selected, and click on **Next** to accept the option and display the next prompt.

5. At the prompt

        Which items do you want to include in your
        memo?

   verify that *Date, To, CC, From,* and *Subject* are checked. Then check the **A separator line** option to add a separator line between these items and the body of the memo. Compare your screen to Figure 13.6. Notice that a separator line is now visible in the preview box. Click on **Next**.

Figure 13.6   **Selecting memo items**

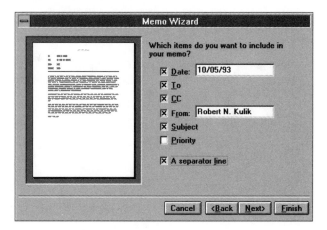

6. At the prompt

    Which of these items would you like?

verify that all the options are unchecked, and click on **Next**. Two prompts are now displayed in the dialog box.

7. Under the prompt

    Which items would you like in the header
    after the first page?

verify that *Topic* is checked and that *Interoffice Memo* is displayed in the Topic box. (This selection will actually be moot because our memo will only consist of a single page.)

8. Under the prompt

    Would you like to include a footer for all
    of the pages?

verify that *Confidential, Date,* and *Page number* are checked.

9. Click on **Next** to display the next prompt:

    Which style would you like?

10. Click on **Contemporary**, and click on **Next**. The final prompt (and quite a snazzy one it is!) is displayed (see Figure 13.7):

    Would you like to display Help after the
    memo is created?

Notice that the Next button is now dimmed.

Figure 13.7 **The final Memo Wizard prompt**

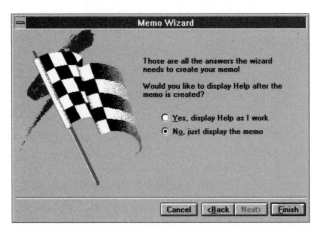

11. Verify that *No* is selected, and click on **Finish**. After another considerable bout of hard-disk activity, the memo template is inserted in a new document, and the placeholder provided for body text is selected (see Figure 13.8).

12. Choose **Insert, File** to open the File dialog box, and double-click on **chap13b.doc**. The body of the memo is inserted in the document.

13. Save the disk file as **mych13b**.

14. Move to the top of the document. Notice that the current date is displayed in the Date field, and your name is displayed in the From field. Placeholders are provided for the To, CC, and Subject fields.

15. Select the *[Names]* placeholder in the To field. (Don't forget to select the brackets.) Then type **Ruth Allen**.

16. In the CC (carbon copy) field, select the *[Names]* placeholder, and type **N. Boulanger, J. Coltrane, H. Gorecki, A. Berg**.

17. Select the *[Subject]* placeholder, and type **Change in Additional Services**. Then compare your screen to Figure 13.9.

18. Save the disk file, and display the document in Page Layout view. You can see the Header at the top of the page. Notice that it is dimmed, indicating that it can't be edited.

Figure 13.8   **The completed Memo Wizard**

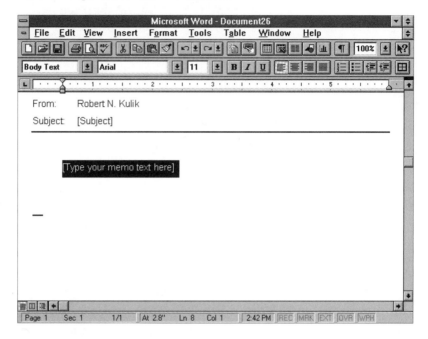

Figure 13.9   **The memo with completed fields**

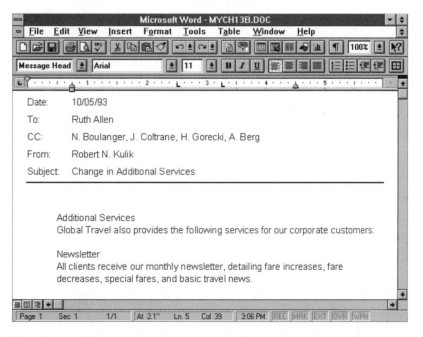

19. Scroll to view the footer; it too is dimmed. Notice that the header and footer information is exactly as you selected it in the Memo Wizard dialog box.

20. Return to Normal view.

USING STYLES

Templates contain styles, which are named sets of formatting instructions. Styles enable you to quickly and easily format the paragraphs in a document. You can use the styles included in the templates, or you can create your own.

Note: These styles differ from the ones you learned about in Chapter 4 in that here each style might contain a set of instructions, as opposed to a single instruction. For example, in Chapter 4 you saw how a word can have the bold font style applied to it. As it is used here, a style might refer to bold, 10 point, Times Roman, *and* underline. Furthermore, these styles are applied to whole paragraphs. All of the paragraphs using the same style will contain the same formatting.

The Style drop-down list box, at the left end of the Formatting toolbar, lists all of the styles included in the template of the current document.

To apply a style to one or more paragraphs:

- Select (or place the insertion point in) the appropriate paragraph, or, for more than one paragraph, select the paragraphs.

- Open the Style drop-down list box.

- Select the desired style.

Let's examine styles that have already been applied, and then apply some of our own:

1. Open the Header area (choose **View, Header and Footer**), and take a look at the first-page header, *InterOffice Memo*. Observe the Style list box (in the Formatting toolbar). The style applied to the header is named (appropriately enough) *Header*.

2. Observe the font, font size, and bold font style. The Header style applies Arial font, 9-point type size, and bold formatting to the text (see Figure 13.10).

Figure 13.10   The Header style

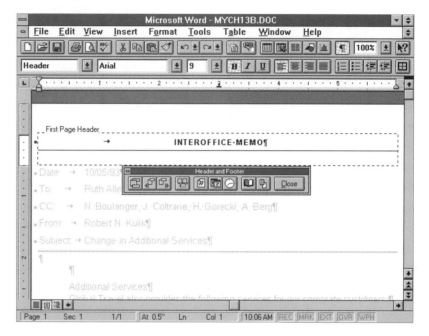

3. Close the Header area.

4. Place the insertion point anywhere in the name *Allen* (the last name of the addressee). Notice that the current style name applied to Allen is *Message Head*.

5. Observe the font style and size: The Message Head style applies Arial 11-point font to the text.

6. Place the insertion point in *Global Travel*, below *Additional Services*. Notice that the current style applied to Global Travel is *Normal*.

7. Observe the font style and size. Because we chose the Contemporary style for our memo, the Normal style applies the Arial 11-point font to the text. Had we applied, say, the Classic style to our memo, the body text would have been Times New Roman 10-point font.

8. Place the insertion point in the *Additional Services* heading.

9. Open the Style drop-down list box and select the **Heading 4** style. The Heading 4 style applies the 12-point font size and bold formatting to text, and places it at the left margin.

10. Place the insertion point in the *Newsletter* heading. Open the Style drop-down list box, and select the **Heading 6** style. This style makes text bold and places it at the left margin.

11. Place the insertion point in the *Telex* heading and apply the Heading 6 style to it (press **F4**). Do *not* use the Format Painter button; doing so will copy only the font formatting and not the heading style. Compare your screen to Figure 13.11.

Figure 13.11   **The applied heading styles**

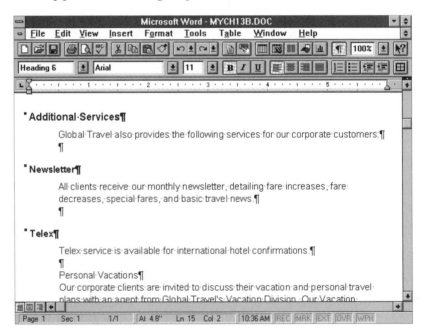

PRACTICE YOUR SKILLS

1. Apply the heading 6 style to the *Personal Vacations, Flight Insurance,* and *Fax* headings.

2. Print Preview the document.

3. Save the disk file and close the document.

CREATING STYLES

You now know how to select an existing style from the Style list box. You can also create customized styles. The first step is to apply the desired formatting to text, or place the insertion point in text that already has the desired formatting applied to it. Then, either choose Format, Style from the menu or use the Style list box in the Formatting toolbar. We recommend using the Style list box, as it is simpler and faster.

To create a style based on a formatted paragraph:

- Select the formatted paragraph.

- Select the style name in the Style list box (or press *Ctrl+Shift+S*).

- Type the new style name.

- Press *Enter*.

Style names can contain up to 253 characters, though we recommend keeping them as short as possible. They can include any combination of characters and spaces, except the backslash (\), braces ({}), and semicolon (;). Of course, style names should be as descriptive as possible, and they must be unique; you can't have two styles with the same name. However, as you saw in the previous section, styles with names such as "Heading 1," "Heading 2," and so on, are perfectly acceptable.

When you create a new style for a document, it is saved whenever you save the disk file. The styles created in a document can be used only in that document. If you create a style in a template, it can be used in any new documents that are based on that template.

Let's examine the styles in the Normal template and then create our own style:

1. Open **chap13c.doc**.

2. Select the **Introduction** heading, near the top of the document.

3. Observe the Formatting toolbar. The Normal style applies the Tms Rmn font and the 10-point size to the paragraph.

4. Apply the **Heading 1** style (or any heading style that your printer can support). The Heading 1 style applies the Arial 14-point font and bold formatting to the paragraph.

5. Apply the **Heading 2** style. This style applies the Arial 12-point font, and bold and italic formatting.

6. Apply the **Heading 3** style. This style applies the Times New Roman 12-point font, and bold formatting.

7. Apply the **Normal** style.

8. Verify that the insertion point is placed in the *Introduction* heading.

9. Use the Formatting toolbar to change the font size to **12** and make the heading bold and italic. These formats will be used in our new style.

10. Drag across the style name *Normal* in the Style box (or double-click on **Normal**) to select it.

11. Type **Subhead** to name the new style (see Figure 13.12).

12. Press **Enter**.

13. Open the Style list box and observe the list of styles. The Subhead style is included at the bottom of the list.

Figure 13.12   **Naming a style**

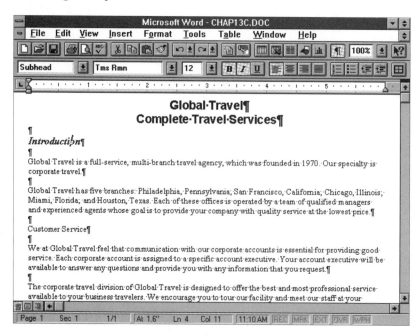

14. Close the Style list box.

15. Apply the Subhead style to the *Customer Service* heading.

PRACTICE YOUR SKILLS

Apply the Subhead style to the following headings:

International Travel

Corporate Profiles

Worldwide Services

MODIFYING STYLES

Using styles to format a document is an easy way to make formatting changes. For example, if you format the Subhead style (see the previous section) to include bold and italics, and then want to remove the italic font style and add underlining, all you have to do is redefine, or modify, the style. When you modify the style, all of the paragraphs that have the Subhead style applied to them will be updated with the new formatting.

To modify a style:

- Apply the formatting changes to a paragraph containing the desired style.

- Select or place the insertion point in the paragraph.

- Choose *Format, Style*.

- Click on *Modify*.

- To modify the style's font, click on *Format*, and choose *Font*.

- Make the desired modifications in the Font dialog box.

- Click on *OK*.

- Click on *OK*.

- Click on *Apply*.

Let's modify our Subhead style:

1. Place the insertion point in the *Introduction* heading.

2. Use the Formatting toolbar to remove the italic font style and apply the underline font style.

3. Choose **Format, Style** to open the Style dialog box (see Figure 13.13). In the Styles list box, notice that the *Subhead* style is currently selected. The Paragraph Preview box displays a sample of the text. The Description box describes the characteristics of the style. Notice that the Subhead style is defined as based on the Normal style, which we indeed used to create it.

Figure 13.13   **The Style dialog box**

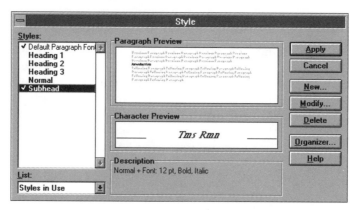

4. Click on **Modify** to open the Modify Style dialog box, and click on **Format** to open the Format drop-down menu (see Figure 13.14).

5. In the Format drop-down menu, choose **Font** to open the Font dialog box. Click on the **Font** tab, if necessary. In the Font Style list box, select **Bold** (to remove the italic formatting), and choose **Single** from the Underline drop-down list box. Then compare your screen to Figure 13.15. Notice the sample text displayed in the Preview box.

6. Click on **OK** to close the Font dialog box and return to the Modify Style dialog box.

7. Click on **OK** to return to the Style dialog box. Notice the difference in the sample text displayed in the Character Preview box. In the Description box, *Underline* replaces *Italic*.

Figure 13.14   **The Format drop-down menu in the Modify Style dialog box**

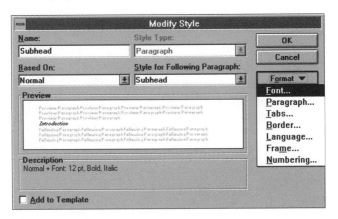

Figure 13.15   **Modifying a style in the Font dialog box**

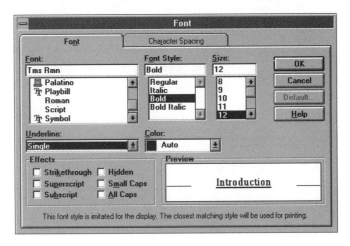

8. Click on **Apply** to close the Style dialog box. Notice that all text with the Subhead style now reflects the changes. Scroll to view all the headings. All of the headings are updated.

9. Save the disk file as **mych13c**.

10. Print the document and compare your printout to Figure 13.16.

11. Close the document.

Figure 13.16   The completed MYCH13C.DOC document

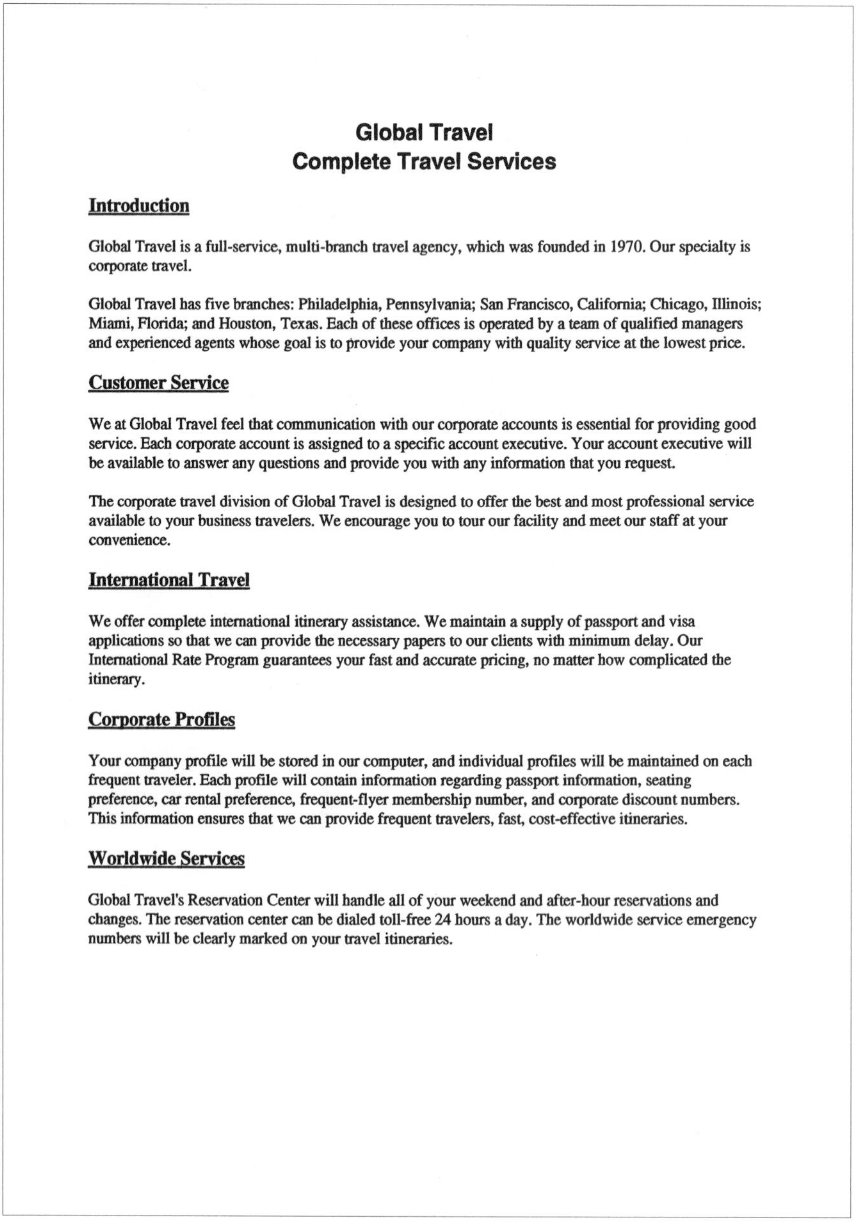

Global Travel
Complete Travel Services

Introduction

Global Travel is a full-service, multi-branch travel agency, which was founded in 1970. Our specialty is corporate travel.

Global Travel has five branches: Philadelphia, Pennsylvania; San Francisco, California; Chicago, Illinois; Miami, Florida; and Houston, Texas. Each of these offices is operated by a team of qualified managers and experienced agents whose goal is to provide your company with quality service at the lowest price.

Customer Service

We at Global Travel feel that communication with our corporate accounts is essential for providing good service. Each corporate account is assigned to a specific account executive. Your account executive will be available to answer any questions and provide you with any information that you request.

The corporate travel division of Global Travel is designed to offer the best and most professional service available to your business travelers. We encourage you to tour our facility and meet our staff at your convenience.

International Travel

We offer complete international itinerary assistance. We maintain a supply of passport and visa applications so that we can provide the necessary papers to our clients with minimum delay. Our International Rate Program guarantees your fast and accurate pricing, no matter how complicated the itinerary.

Corporate Profiles

Your company profile will be stored in our computer, and individual profiles will be maintained on each frequent traveler. Each profile will contain information regarding passport information, seating preference, car rental preference, frequent-flyer membership number, and corporate discount numbers. This information ensures that we can provide frequent travelers, fast, cost-effective itineraries.

Worldwide Services

Global Travel's Reservation Center will handle all of your weekend and after-hour reservations and changes. The reservation center can be dialed toll-free 24 hours a day. The worldwide service emergency numbers will be clearly marked on your travel itineraries.

SUMMARY

In this chapter you learned how to create documents using the templates provided with Word. You also learned how to use existing styles, as well as how to create your own styles and apply them to your documents. Finally, you learned how to modify styles.

Here is a quick reference guide to the Word features introduced in this chapter:

Desired Result	How to Do It
Attach the Normal template to a file	Choose **File, New**; click on **OK**.
Insert the current date	Position the insertion point where you want the date to appear; choose **Insert, Date and Time**; select the desired date format; click on **OK**.
Insert a file	Activate the destination document window; place the insertion point at the desired destination; choose **Insert, File**; select the name of the file to be inserted; click on **OK**.
Attach the Memo Wizard to a document	Choose **File, New**; select **Memo Wizard**; click on **OK**; answer each prompt as desired in the Memo Wizard dialog box, and then click on **Next**; after answering the last prompt, click on **Finish**.
Apply a style	Place the insertion point in the desired paragraph or select the desired paragraphs; open the Style drop-down list box and select the desired style.
Create a style	Format a paragraph as desired; select the formatted paragraph; select the style name in the Style list box; type the new style name; press **Enter**.

Desired Result	**How to Do It**
Modify a style	Apply the formatting changes to a paragraph containing the desired style; select the paragraph; choose **Format, Style**; click on **Modify**; to modify a font, click on **Format** and choose **Font**; click on the **Font** tab, if necessary; make the desired modifications; click on **OK**; click on **OK**; click on **Apply**.

Congratulations! You have now learned how to use many of Word's features. You are now prepared to take all that you've learned and apply it to your own documents. Remember, to master the skills that you've acquired, you must supply the most important ingredient—practice. Only through practice will you be able to get beyond the techniques themselves. Good luck!

APPENDIX A: INSTALLATION

Before You Begin
Installing

Installing Word on
Your Computer

Selecting a Printer
for Use with Word

This appendix contains instructions for installing Word 6.0 for Windows on your computer and for selecting a printer for use with Word.

BEFORE YOU BEGIN INSTALLING

Please read through the following two sections before beginning the installation procedure.

PROTECTING YOUR ORIGINAL INSTALLATION DISKS

Word comes with several floppy disks that you'll need to install the program on your computer. Before you begin, you should protect your original installation disks from accidental erasure. When a disk is protected, its data can be read, but not modified.

To protect a 3½-inch disk:

- Slide the plastic locking button in the corner of the disk to its uppermost position.

To protect a 5¼-inch disk:

- Place a write-protect tab over the notch on the edge of the disk.

REQUIRED HARD-DISK SPACE

You need to have at least 24MB (24,000,000 bytes) of free hard-disk space to install Word 6.0 for Windows. (While this is the amount required for complete installation, not the installation we will perform, we recommend this upper limit to be safe.) If you do not have this much free space, you will have to delete enough files from your hard disk to bring the total free space up to 24MB. For help in doing this, please refer to your DOS or Windows manual.

Note: Remember to back up (copy to a floppy disk) any files that you wish to preserve *before* deleting them from your hard disk.

INSTALLING WORD ON YOUR COMPUTER

Follow these steps to install Word 6.0 for Windows:

1. Turn on your computer and start Windows. (If you have not already installed Windows on your system, please do so now; for help, see your Windows reference manuals.)

2. Insert the installation disk labeled *Disk 1* in the appropriately sized disk drive.

3. Choose **File, Run** from the Windows Program Manager Menu (see Figure A.1).

Figure A.1   **Choosing File, Run from the Program Manager Menu**

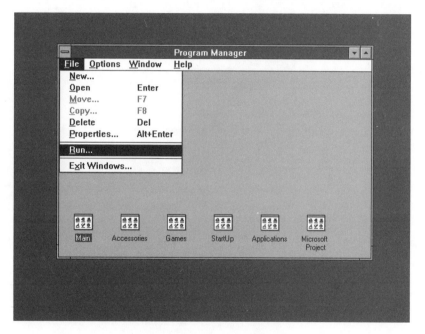

4. Type **a:setup** (for drive A) or **b:setup** (for drive B), and then compare your screen to Figure A.2.

5. Press **Enter** to start the Word installation program. The Microsoft Word 6.0 Setup dialog box is displayed (see Figure A.3).

6. Click on **OK** to continue the installation procedure.

7. When you are prompted to enter your name and organization, follow the on-screen directions to do so. Then click on **OK**.

8. The next dialog box displayed simply asks you to confirm the information that you entered in step 7. Click on **OK** to confirm. The Setup dialog box displays your program's serial number. As instructed, it's a good idea to write down the number in the back of your manual for reference.

Figure A.2 **The entered Setup command**

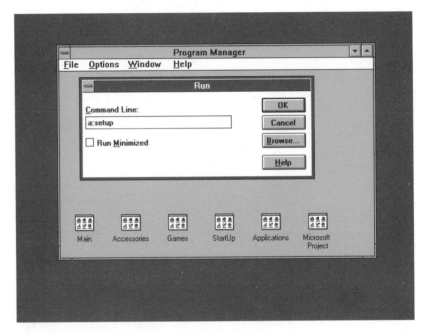

Figure A.3 **The Microsoft Word 6.0 Setup dialog box**

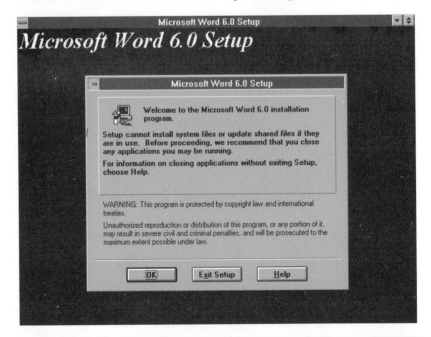

9. Click on **OK** to continue.

10. When you are prompted to specify the hard-disk directory where you want to install Word, click on **OK** to accept the default directory, C:\WINWORD. A dialog box is displayed, showing the available types of installation (see Figure A.4). To successfully complete the hands-on exercises in this book, you must select *Typical* installation; the other installations do not provide the necessary Word options.

Figure A.4   **The installation types**

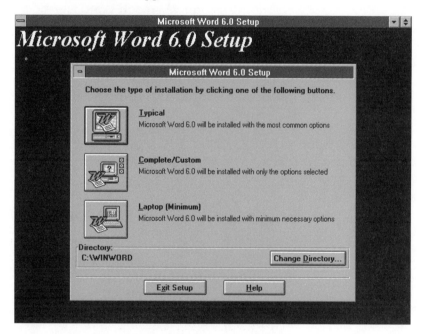

11. Click on the **Typical** button.

12. When the Choose Program Group dialog box is displayed, click on **Continue**.

13. When the Clipart dialog box is displayed, click on **Yes**.

14. When the Help for Word Users dialog box is displayed, click on **No**.

15. Momentarily, a dialog box will appear, informing you of the installation procedure's progress. (*100%* means that the installation procedure is complete.) Each time you are asked to insert a new disk, please do so.

Note: You can click on Cancel at any time to cancel the entire installation. However, if you choose to do so, bear in mind that you will have to start the entire process again from scratch.

16. When the installation procedure is complete, you are returned to Windows. To start Word, simply double-click (click the left mouse button twice in rapid succession) on the newly created **Microsoft Word icon** (located in the newly created program group *Microsoft Office*).

SELECTING A PRINTER FOR USE WITH WORD

Before you can print from Word, you must select a printer. To do so, follow these steps:

1. Start Word 6.0 for Windows.

2. Choose **File, Print** from the menu to open the Print dialog box.

3. In the Print dialog box, click on the Printer button. The Print Setup dialog box is opened (see Figure A.5), displaying a list of the printers that are currently installed on your system.

Figure A.5   **The Print Setup dialog box**

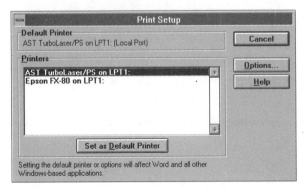

4. If your printer appears on the list (you may have to scroll), select it and click on **Set as Default Printer**. You can now use this printer with Word.

5. If your printer does not appear on the list (even after scrolling), install the printer on your system. (For instructions, refer to your Windows documentation.) Then repeat this printer-selection procedure from step 1.

6. Click on **Close** to close the Print Setup dialog box, and click on **Close** (do not click on OK) to close the Print dialog box.

Note: The printed examples shown in this book were all printed on a PostScript laser printer. Your printouts may differ somewhat, depending on which printer you are using. Printer choice also affects how text appears on your screen. If you are using a non-PostScript printer, your screen typestyles and sizes may differ from those shown in this book's figures.

APPENDIX B: KEYSTROKE REFERENCE

Insertion Pointer Movement

Text Selection

Text Entry and Formatting

Text Editing

Font Formatting

Paragraph Formatting

File and Window Management

Miscellaneous

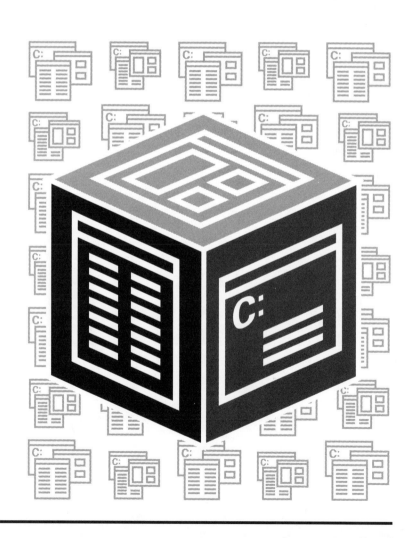

This appendix lists the keystrokes that you can use to issue Word commands.

INSERTION POINTER MOVEMENT

Move	Key/Key Combination
One character to the left	Left Arrow
One character to the right	Right Arrow
One line up	Up Arrow
One line down	Down Arrow
One word to the left	Ctrl+Left Arrow
One word to the right	Ctrl+Right Arrow
To the end of a line	End
To the start of a line	Home
Down one screen	Pg Dn
Up one screen	Pg Up
To the start of a document	Ctrl+Home
To the end of a document	Ctrl+End
To any page of a document	F5
Back to last insertion point location	Shift+F5

TEXT SELECTION

Select	Key/Key Combination
Left character	Shift+Left Arrow
Right character	Shift+Right Arrow
Previous line	Shift+Up Arrow
Next line	Shift+Down Arrow
Extend selection	F8

Select	Key/Key Combination
Shrink selection	Shift+F8
Column	Ctrl+Shift

TEXT ENTRY AND FORMATTING

Format	Key/Key Combination
Start new paragraph	Enter
Start new line	Shift+Enter
Insert hard page break	Ctrl+Enter
Insert column break	Ctrl+Shift+Enter
Insert normal hyphen	Hyphen
Insert optional hyphen	Ctrl+Hyphen
Insert hard hyphen	Ctrl+Shift+Hyphen
Insert hard space	Ctrl+Shift+Spacebar

TEXT EDITING

Edit	Key/Key Combination
Move selected text	F2
Copy selected text	Shift+F2
Delete character to the right	Del
Delete character to the left	Backspace
Delete word to the right	Ctrl+Del
Delete word to the left	Ctrl+Backspace

FONT FORMATTING

Format	Key/Key Combination
Increase point size	Ctrl+]
Decrease point size	Ctrl+[
Change point size	Ctrl+Shift+P
Change case	Shift+F3
Remove formatting	Ctrl+Spacebar
Capitalize	Ctrl+Shift+A
Capitalize (small caps)	Ctrl+Shift+K
Bold	Ctrl+B
Underline	Ctrl+U
Underline words, but not spaces	Ctrl+Shift+W
Double underline	Ctrl+Shift+D
Enlarge font	Ctrl+Shift+>
Shrink font	Ctrl+Shift+<
Change font	Ctrl+Shift+F
Hidden text	Ctrl+Shift+H
Italic	Ctrl+I
Subscript	Ctrl+Equal sign (=)
Superscript	Ctrl+Plus sign (+)

PARAGRAPH FORMATTING

Format	Key/Key Combination
Single-space lines	Ctrl+1
Double-space lines	Ctrl+2
1½-space lines	Ctrl+5
Center lines	Ctrl+E
Left-align lines	Ctrl+L
Right-align lines	Ctrl+R
Justify lines	Ctrl+J
Remove paragraph formatting	Ctrl+Q

FILE AND WINDOW MANAGEMENT

Format	Key/Key Combination
Save As	F12 or Alt+F2
Save	Ctrl+S
Open	Ctrl+O
Close document window	Ctrl+F4
Restore document window	Ctrl+F5
Maximize document window	Ctrl+F10
Close Word window	Alt+F4
Restore Word window	Alt+F5
Maximize Word window	Alt+F10
Next window	Ctrl+F6 or Alt+F6

Format	Key/Key Combination
Previous window	Ctrl+Shift+F6 or Alt+Shift+F6
Next pane	F6
Previous pane	Shift+F6

MISCELLANEOUS

Function	Key/Key Combination
Help	F1
Help pointer	Shift+F1
AutoText	F3
Repeat command	F4
Repeat Find/Go To	Shift+F4
Insert bookmark	Ctrl+Shift+F5
Spelling checker	F7
Thesaurus	Shift+F7
Menu	F10
Print	Ctrl+Shift+F12
Insert date field	Alt+Shift+D
Insert time field	Alt+Shift+T
Insert page number field	Alt+Shift+P
Update fields	F9

APPENDIX C: EXCHANGING DOCUMENTS WITH OTHER PROGRAMS

Opening Non-Word
6.0 Files

Saving Non-Word
6.0 Files

Word for Windows 6.0 is compatible with many popular word processing and spreadsheet programs. You can open a non-Word 6.0 document (disk file), edit and print it, and then save it in its original file format or as a Word 6.0 file. Or, you can open a Word 6.0 document and then save it in a file format that can be used with a non-Word 6.0 program. This appendix lists the various formats in which Word can open and save files and shows you how to make your desired file conversions.

OPENING NON-WORD 6.0 FILES

To open a non-Word 6.0 file

- Choose *File, Open* (or click on the Open button on the Standard toolbar) to display the Open dialog box.

- If necessary, select the desired drive in the Drives list box.

- If necessary, select the desired directory in the Directories list box.

- Select the desired file in the File Name list box. Or, type the desired file name (with extension) in the File Name text box.

- Click on OK (or press *Enter*). **Note:** Most of the time, Word will recognize the file format of the document you wish to convert. However, occasionally the program will not recognize a file's format, in which case the Convert File dialog box appears, listing the file formats that Word 6.0 can convert from (that is, the file types that it can open). Normally, the format of the file you specified in the previous step is highlighted; if not, select the format of the source file, and then click on OK. If the document is converted incorrectly, close it without saving it, and then try opening it again using another converter. You can do this as many times as you need to.

If the file format of your specified file does not appear in this box, but does appear in Table C.1, exit this procedure, run the Word Setup program to add the missing file-format converter, and then repeat this procedure.

Once you've opened a non-Word 6.0 file, you can edit, print, save, or close it exactly as you would any standard Word 6.0 file. If you want to save the file in Word 6.0 format, use Save (to keep the same name and location) or Save As (to change the name and/or location). If you want to save the file in its original format (for example, as a WordPerfect file), please refer to the procedure presented in the next section, "Saving Non-Word 6.0 Files."

Table C.1 lists the types of non-Word 6.0 files that can be opened.

You can also convert files from the following formats. But in order to do so you'll have to obtain the necessary file-format converters by sending in the Special Offer coupon included in your Word 6.0 for Windows package.

- Multimate versions 3.3, Advantage 3.6, and Advantage II

- Microsoft Multiplan versions 2.0, 3.0, 4.0, and 4.2

Table C.1　　　**File Types You Can Open from Word 6.0**

File Format	Type of File
BIFF	Microsoft Excel 2.x, 3.0, 4.0, and 5.0 worksheets
DCA/RFT	DisplayWrite and IBM 5520
File Templates (.DOT)	Microsoft Word for Windows
Microsoft Word for DOS	Versions 3.x and later
Rich Text Format (.RTF)	Microsoft standard file interchange
Text Only	Without line breaks
DOS Text Only	For opening plain text files created from a DOS-based product (for example, Microsoft Word for DOS or WordPerfect)
Text with Layout	Restores text to paragraph form, including indents and paragraph spacing
DOS Text with Layout	For opening plain text files created from a DOS-based product (for example, Microsoft Word for DOS or WordPerfect)
Microsoft Word for Windows	All versions
Microsoft Word for the Macintosh	Versions 4.x and 5.x
WordPerfect for DOS and Windows	Version 5.x
Lotus 1-2-3	Versions 2.x and 3.x
WordStar	Versions 3.3, 3.45, 4.0, 5.0, and 5.5
dBase	Versions II, III, and IV

Table C.1 **File Types You Can Open from Word 6.0 (Continued)**

File Format	Type of File
Microsoft Works for DOS	All versions
Microsoft Works for Windows	All versions
Microsoft Windows Write	Versions 3.0 and 3.1

SAVING NON-WORD 6.0 FILES

To save a Word 6.0 file in a non-Word 6.0 file format

- Choose *File, Save As* to display the Save As dialog box.

- If necessary, select the desired drive in the Drives list box.

- If necessary, select the desired directory in the Directories list box.

- Select the desired file format in the Save File as Type list box. (**Note:** If your desired file format does not appear in this box, but does appear in Table C.2, exit this procedure, run the Word Setup program to add the missing file-format converter, and then repeat this procedure.)

- Type the desired file name (without extension) in the File Name text box.

- Click on *OK* (or press *Enter*).

Once you've saved a file in a non-Word 6.0 file format, you can open it from the program that uses this file format (for example, WordPerfect 5.1) and then edit, print, save, or close it exactly as you would any standard file in that program.

You can save a file in the non-Word 6.0 file formats listed in Table C.2.

You can also save files in the following formats. But in order to do so you'll have to obtain the necessary file-format converters by sending in the Special Offer coupon included in your Word 6.0 for Windows package.

- Multimate versions 3.3, Advantage 3.6, and Advantage II

- Microsoft Multiplan versions 2.0, 3.0, 4.0, and 4.2

Table C.2 **File Types You Can Save from Word 6.0**

File Format	File Type
DCA/RFT	DisplayWrite and IBM 5520
File Templates (.DOT)	Microsoft Word for Windows
Microsoft Word for DOS	Versions 3.0 through 6.0
Rich Text Format (.RTF)	Microsoft standard file interchange
Text Only	Without line breaks
DOS Text Only	For saving plain text files to be opened by a DOS-based product (for example, Microsoft Word for DOS or WordPerfect)
Text with Layout	Creates a text file while maintaining columns, line spacing, tabs, text frames, paragraph spacing, indents, and tables
DOS Text with Layout	For saving plain text files to be opened by a DOS-based product (for example, Microsoft Word for DOS or WordPerfect)
Text Only with Line Breaks	Inserts a carriage return at the end of each line
DOS Text Only with Line Breaks	For saving plain text files to be opened by a DOS-based product (for example, Microsoft Word for DOS or WordPerfect)
Microsoft Word for Windows	All versions
Microsoft Word for the Macintosh	Versions 4.x and 5.x
WordPerfect for DOS and Windows	Version 5.x

Table C.2   **File Types You Can Save from Word 6.0 (Continued)**

File Format	File Type
Microsoft Windows Write	Versions 3.0 and 3.1
Lotus 1-2-3	Version 2.x
Microsoft Excel Worksheet	All versions
Microsoft Works for Windows	All versions

INDEX

Note: Page numbers in italic denote figures or illustrations.

Imagination.
Innovation. Insight.

The How It Works Series from Ziff-Davis Press

"... a magnificently seamless integration of text and graphics ..."

Larry Blasko, The Associated Press, reviewing *PC/Computing How Computers Work*

HOW COMPUTERS WORK
RON WHITE

ISBN: 094-7 Price: $22.95

No other books bring computer technology to life like the *How It Works* series from Ziff-Davis Press. Lavish, full- color illustrations and lucid text from some of the world's top computer commentators make *How It Works* books an exciting way to explore the inner workings of PC technology.

PC/Computing How Computers Work

A worldwide blockbuster that hit the general trade bestseller lists! *PC/Computing* magazine executive editor Ron White dismantles the PC and reveals what really makes it tick.

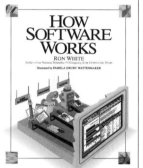

HOW SOFTWARE WORKS
RON WHITE
Illustrated by PAMELA DRURY WATTENMAKER

ISBN: 133-1 Price: $24.95

HOW NETWORKS WORK
FRANK J. DERFLER, JR. AND LES FREED
Illustrated by MICHAEL TROLLER

ISBN: 129-3 Price: $24.95

How Networks Work

Two of the most respected names in connectivity showcase the PC network, illustrating and explaining how each component does its magic and how they all fit together.

How Macs Work

A fun and fascinating voyage to the heart of the Macintosh! Two noted *MacUser* contributors cover the spectrum of Macintosh operations from startup to shutdown.

How Software Works

This dazzlingly illustrated volume from Ron White peeks inside the PC to show in full-color how software breathes life into the PC. Covers Windows™ and all major software categories.

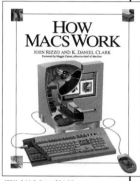

HOW MACS WORK
JOHN RIZZO AND K. DANIEL CLARK
Foreword by Maggie Canon, editor-in-chief of MacUser

ISBN: 146-3 Price: $24.95

How to Use Your Computer

Conquer computerphobia and see how this intricate machine truly makes life easier. Dozens of full-color graphics showcase the components of the PC and explain how to interact with them.

All About Computers

This one-of-a-kind visual guide for kids features numerous full-color illustrations and photos on every page, combined with dozens of interactive projects that reinforce computer basics, making this an exciting way to learn all about the world of computers.

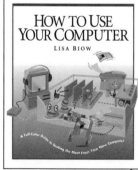

HOW TO USE YOUR COMPUTER
LISA BIOW

A Full-Color Guide to Getting the Most From Your New Computer

ISBN: 155-2 Price: $22.95

ALL ABOUT COMPUTERS
JEAN ATELSEK
Illustrated by DEBRA MUROV

DISCOVER THE WORLD OF COMPUTERS

FOR AGES 10 AND UP

ISBN: 166-8 Price: $15.95

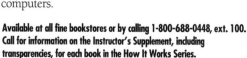

ZIFF-DAVIS
ZD
PRESS

© 1993 Ziff-Davis Press

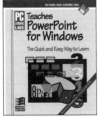

Arrrgh!

Don't you just hate it when software doesn't work the way you expect? When simple problems block your progress for hours? When your resident techie isn't around, the technical support hotline is constantly busy, on-line help is no help at all, the manual is hopeless, and the book you have tells you everything except what you really need to know?

ISBN: 099-8
Price: $29.95

ISBN: 039-4
Price: $27.95

ISBN: 151-X
Price: $29.95

ISBN: 160-9
Price: $29.95

ISBN: 014-9
Price: $27.95

Don't you just hate it?

We do too. That's why we developed ***HELP!***, a groundbreaking series of books from Ziff-Davis Press.

HELP! books mean fast access to straight answers. If you're a beginner, you'll appreciate the practical examples and skill-building exercises that will help you work confidently in no time. If you're already an experienced user, you'll love the comprehensive coverage, highly detailed indexes, and margin notes and sidebars that highlight especially helpful information.

We're launching the ***HELP!*** series with these all-new books:

HELP! WordPerfect 6.0—WordPerfect insider Stephen G. Dyson has created the most complete single source of techniques, examples, and advice that will help you clear the hurdles of WordPerfect 6.0 quickly and easily.

HELP! Microsoft Access—Best-selling author Miriam Liskin gives you fast access to the complete feature set of Microsoft's leading-edge Windows database program. Sample databases included on disk!

HELP! Paradox for Windows—Popular database and spreadsheet authority Lisa Biow provides one-stop solutions to the challenges of Borland's high-powered new database manager.

HELP! Windows NT 3.1—Windows authority Ben Ezzell has the answers to your NT questions in this highly effective quick-access format.

HELP! Lotus Notes 3.0—Learn how to harness the power of Lotus Notes with this easy-access reference guide from the ultimate Notes guru, John Helliwell.

So if you hate struggling with software as much as we do, visit your favorite bookstore and just say ***HELP!***

Ziff-Davis Press Survey of Readers

Please help us in our effort to produce the best books on personal computing.
For your assistance, we would be pleased to send you a FREE catalog
featuring the complete line of Ziff-Davis Press books.

1. How did you first learn about this book?

Recommended by a friend . . . . ☐ -1 (5)

Recommended by store personnel . . . . ☐ -2

Saw in Ziff-Davis Press catalog . . . . ☐ -3

Received advertisement in the mail . . . . ☐ -4

Saw the book on bookshelf at store . . . . ☐ -5

Read book review in: _____ ☐ -6

Saw an advertisement in: _____ ☐ -7

Other (Please specify): _____ ☐ -8

2. Which THREE of the following factors most influenced your decision to purchase this book? (Please check up to THREE.)

Front or back cover information on book . . . ☐ -1 (6)

Logo of magazine affiliated with book . . . . . ☐ -2

Special approach to the content . . . . ☐ -3

Completeness of content . . . . ☐ -4

Author's reputation. ☐ -5

Publisher's reputation . . . . ☐ -6

Book cover design or layout . . . . ☐ -7

Index or table of contents of book . . . . ☐ -8

Price of book . . . . ☐ -9

Special effects, graphics, illustrations . . . . . . ☐ -0

Other (Please specify): _____ ☐ -x

3. How many computer books have you purchased in the last six months? _____ (7-10)

4. On a scale of 1 to 5, where 5 is excellent, 4 is above average, 3 is average, 2 is below average, and 1 is poor, please rate each of the following aspects of this book below. (Please circle your answer.)

Depth/completeness of coverage	5	4	3	2	1	(11)
Organization of material	5	4	3	2	1	(12)
Ease of finding topic	5	4	3	2	1	(13)
Special features/time saving tips	5	4	3	2	1	(14)
Appropriate level of writing	5	4	3	2	1	(15)
Usefulness of table of contents	5	4	3	2	1	(16)
Usefulness of index	5	4	3	2	1	(17)
Usefulness of accompanying disk	5	4	3	2	1	(18)
Usefulness of illustrations/graphics	5	4	3	2	1	(19)
Cover design and attractiveness	5	4	3	2	1	(20)
Overall design and layout of book	5	4	3	2	1	(21)
Overall satisfaction with book	5	4	3	2	1	(22)

5. Which of the following computer publications do you read regularly; that is, 3 out of 4 issues?

Byte . . . . ☐ -1 (23)

Computer Shopper . . . . ☐ -2

Home Office Computing . . . . ☐ -3

Dr. Dobb's Journal . . . . ☐ -4

LAN Magazine . . . . ☐ -5

MacWEEK . . . . ☐ -6

MacUser . . . . ☐ -7

PC Computing . . . . ☐ -8

PC Magazine . . . . ☐ -9

PC WEEK . . . . ☐ -0

Windows Sources . . . . ☐ -x

Other (Please specify): _____ ☐ -y

Please turn page.

6. What is your level of experience with personal computers? With the subject of this book?

	With PCs	With subject of book
Beginner	☐ -1 (24)	☐ -1 (25)
Intermediate	☐ -2	☐ -2
Advanced	☐ -3	☐ -3

7. Which of the following best describes your job title?

Officer (CEO/President/VP/owner) ☐ -1 (26)
Director/head ☐ -2
Manager/supervisor ☐ -3
Administration/staff ☐ -4
Teacher/educator/trainer ☐ -5
Lawyer/doctor/medical professional ☐ -6
Engineer/technician ☐ -7
Consultant ☐ -8
Not employed/student/retired ☐ -9
Other (Please specify): _____ ☐ -0

8. What is your age?

Under 20 ☐ -1 (27)
21-29 ☐ -2
30-39 ☐ -3
40-49 ☐ -4
50-59 ☐ -5
60 or over ☐ -6

9. Are you:

Male ☐ -1 (28)
Female ☐ -2

Thank you for your assistance with this important information! Please write your address below to receive our free catalog.

Name: _____

Address: _____

City/State/Zip: _____

Fold here to mail.   1390-01-01

BUSINESS REPLY MAIL
FIRST CLASS MAIL   PERMIT NO. 1612   OAKLAND, CA

POSTAGE WILL BE PAID BY ADDRESSEE

Ziff-Davis Press
5903 Christie Avenue
Emeryville, CA 94608-1925
Attn: Marketing

NO POSTAGE
NECESSARY
IF MAILED IN
THE UNITED
STATES

■ TO RECEIVE 5¼-INCH DISK(S)

The Ziff-Davis Press software contained on the $3\frac{1}{2}$-inch disk included with this book is also available in $5\frac{1}{4}$-inch format. If you would like to receive the software in the $5\frac{1}{4}$-inch format, please return the $3\frac{1}{2}$-inch disk with your name and address to:

Disk Exchange
Ziff-Davis Press
5903 Christie Avenue
Emeryville, CA 94608